Material Cultures of Financialisation

This collection offers pathbreaking framing of the material culture of financialisation. It begins with a tight definition of financialisation in order to distinguish the phenomenon of financialisation from its effects and from the looser associations prevalent within much of the literature such as the presence of credit or even simply (more extensive) monetary relations. To locate financialisation within economic and social reproduction, of which material culture is a part, close attention is paid to the distinctive forms of financialisation arising from commodification, commodity form and commodity calculation. The differences in the extent to which, and how, these prevail are addressed through the innovative system of provision approach and its framing of material culture through use of ten distinctive attributes of such cultures, known as the 10Cs (Constructed, Construed, Conforming, Commodified, Contextual, Contradictory, Closed, Contested, Collective and Chaotic). This framing of the cultures attached to financialisation is then illustrated through case studies demonstrating the diverse ways in which shifting cultures have served to embed financialisation in our daily lives. After a discussion of the material culture of financialisation itself there are two sector examples which review financial cultures in the provision of water and housing. These are followed by considerations of financialisation in financial literacy and financial inclusion, the media and, finally, well-being.

The chapters in this book were originally published in a special issue of *New Political Economy*.

Kate Bayliss is a Research Associate at SOAS, University of London and Research Fellow at University of Leeds, UK. For over two decades she has been conducting research into the nature and impact of privatisation in the provision of infrastructure and essential services, working with UN Agencies, governments and Civil Society.

Ben Fine is Professor of Economics at SOAS, University of London, UK. His books have won both the Gunnar Myrdal Prize and the Deutscher Prize. He Chairs the International Initiative for Promoting Political Economy (iippe.org).

Mary Robertson is Head of Economic Policy for the Leader of the Labour Party. She has a MSc and PhD in Economics from SOAS, University of London, and previously worked at Leeds University Business School and the University of Greenwich, UK.

Material Cultures of Financialisation

Edited by
Kate Bayliss, Ben Fine and
Mary Robertson

Routledge
Taylor & Francis Group

LONDON AND NEW YORK

First published 2019
by Routledge
2 Park Square, Milton Park, Abingdon, Oxon, OX14 4RN, UK

and by Routledge
52 Vanderbilt Avenue, New York, NY 10017

First issued in paperback 2020

Routledge is an imprint of the Taylor & Francis Group, an informa business

British Library Cataloguing in Publication Data
A catalogue record for this book is available from the British Library

ISBN 13: 978-0-367-58652-2 (pbk)
ISBN 13: 978-1-138-54977-7 (hbk)

Typeset in Myriad Pro
by RefineCatch Limited, Bungay, Suffolk

Publisher's Note
The publisher accepts responsibility for any inconsistencies that may have
arisen during the conversion of this book from journal articles to book
chapters, namely the possible inclusion of journal terminology.

Disclaimer
Every effort has been made to contact copyright holders for their permission to
reprint material in this book. The publishers would be grateful to hear from any
copyright holder who is not here acknowledged and will undertake to rectify
any errors or omissions in future editions of this book.

Contents

Citation Information

The chapters in this book were originally published in *New Political Economy*, volume 22, issue 4 (August 2017). When citing this material, please use the original page numbering for each article, as follows:

Chapter 1
Introduction to special issue on the material cultures of financialisation
Kate Bayliss, Ben Fine and Mary Robertson
New Political Economy, volume 22, issue 4 (August 2017), pp. 355–370

Chapter 2
The material and culture of financialisation
Ben Fine
New Political Economy, volume 22, issue 4 (August 2017), pp. 371–382

Chapter 3
Material cultures of water financialisation in England and Wales
Kate Bayliss
New Political Economy, volume 22, issue 4 (August 2017), pp. 383–397

Chapter 4
(De)constructing the financialised culture of owner-occupation in the UK, with the aid of the 10Cs
Mary Robertson
New Political Economy, volume 22, issue 4 (August 2017), pp. 398–409

Chapter 5
Cultivating the self-reliant and responsible individual: the material culture of financial literacy
Ana C. Santos
New Political Economy, volume 22, issue 4 (August 2017), pp. 410–422

Chapter 6
The digital revolution in financial inclusion: international development in the fintech era
Daniela Gabor and Sally Brooks
New Political Economy, volume 22, issue 4 (August 2017), pp. 423–436

Chapter 7
Financialisation, media and social change
Catherine Happer
New Political Economy, volume 22, issue 4 (August 2017), pp. 437–449

Chapter 8
From happiness to social provisioning: addressing well-being in times of crisis
Marco Boffo, Andrew Brown and David A. Spencer
New Political Economy, volume 22, issue 4 (August 2017), pp. 450–462

For any permission-related enquiries please visit:
http://www.tandfonline.com/page/help/permissions

Notes on Contributors

Kate Bayliss is a Research Associate at the School of Oriental and African Studies at the University of London and Research Fellow at the University of Leeds, UK. She has worked for many years on privatisation and public sector reform with particular reference to water and energy, in developed and developing countries. Her research interests in this area include the impact of globalisation and financialisation on the provision of basic services.

Marco Boffo holds a PhD in Economics from SOAS, University of London, UK. He has taught development economics and the political economy of development in the Department of Development Studies at SOAS; he has worked as a Research Fellow in the Economics Division at the Leeds University Business School in the context of the FESSUD project; and he has worked as a consultant for the OECD LEED Trento Centre.

Sally Brooks is a Lecturer in International Development at the University of York, UK, and has more than 23 years' experience of research and practice within the international development sector. She holds a DPhil in Development Studies from the Institute of Development Studies (IDS) at the University of Sussex, UK (2008).

Andrew Brown is Professor of Economics and Political Economy and Divisional Director of Research at the Economics Division of Leeds University Business School, UK. His substantive research interests include theories of value, financialisation, the euro, job quality and job satisfaction, well-being, infrastructure economics and ICT.

Ben Fine is Professor of Economics at the School of Oriental and African Studies, University of London, UK, holding honorary positions at the universities of Johannesburg (Senior Research Fellow attached to the South African Research Chair in Social Change) and Rhodes University (Visiting Professor, Institute of Social and Economic Research). He is Chair of the International Initiative for Promoting Political Economy, IIPPE, and is a member of the Social Science Research Committee of the UK's Food Standards Agency.

Daniela Gabor is Associate Professor of Economics at the University of the West of England, Bristol, UK. She holds a PhD in Banking and Finance from the University of Stirling (2009).

Catherine Happer is a Lecturer in Sociology and a member of the Glasgow University Media Group, researching audience reception and social change in the context of neo-liberalism. She has given evidence at the House of Commons Select Committee on Climate, Policy and Public Understanding, presented to the Scottish Government and at national and international conferences and appeared on the BBC and Al Jazeera.

Mary Robertson is Head of Economic Policy for the Leader of the Labour Party. She previously worked as a Postdoctoral Research Fellow at the University of Leeds, and has a PhD in Economics from SOAS, University of London. Mary's research interests include housing, privatisation, neoliberalism and financialisation.

Ana C. Santos is Senior Researcher at the Centre for Social Studies, University of Coimbra, Portugal. Her research interests include methodology of economics, experimental and behavioural economics, financialisation and household finances. She has published on these topics in various journals.

David A. Spencer is Professor of Economics and Political Economy and Head of the Economics Division at Leeds University Business School, UK. His research interests lie in the areas of the political economy of work, labour economics and the sociology of work. He currently jointly coordinates the EU FP7 'Financialisation, Economy, Society and Sustainable Development' (FESSUD) project.

Acknowledgements

Research for this publication was supported by the project Financialization Economy Society and Sustainable Development (FESSUD), which is funded by the European Union under Framework Programme 7 [contract number 266800].

Introduction: material cultures of financialisation

Kate Bayliss, Ben Fine and Mary Robertson

ABSTRACT

This paper offers a wide-ranging introduction to the symposium on the material culture of financialisation. It begins by addressing the nature of financialisation itself, drawing on a tight definition in order to distinguish the phenomenon of financialisation from its effects and from the looser associations prevalent within much of the literature such as the presence of credit or even simply (more extensive) monetary relations. In order to locate financialisation within economic and social reproduction, of which material culture is a part, close attention is paid to the distinctive forms of financialisation arising from commodification, commodity form and commodity calculation. The differences in the extent to which, and how, these prevail are addressed through the system of provision approach and its framing of material culture through its use of 10 distinctive attributes of such cultures, known as the 10Cs (*Constructed*, *Construed*, *Conforming*, *Commodified*, *Contextual*, *Contradictory*, *Closed*, *Contested*, *Collective* and *Chaotic*). The analysis is then illustrated by reference to the papers that follow in this volume which demonstrate the diverse ways in which shifting cultures have served to embed financialisation in our daily lives. The first is on the material culture of financialisation itself and this is followed by a number of case studies that include the promotion of financial literacy and financial inclusion, well-being, the media and finally two sector examples are provided on housing and water.

Introduction

This paper offers a wide-ranging introduction to the symposium on the material culture of financialisation. This collection of papers provides a number of detailed examples of the diverse ways in which finance and financialisation have become absorbed into many aspects of everyday life and the way in which material cultures have adapted so that this has become increasingly normalised. Each of material culture (cultural political economy) and financialisation has now attracted extensive literatures, incorporating equally diverse sets of conceptualisations that have mixed relations to one another and to their objects of enquiry. Our approach sets out its own framings in dealing with financialisation itself and its relationships to economic and social reproduction, including material culture. These framings may appear to be arbitrary but each has its own logic relative to its subject matter and to one another, as well as in traversing the connections between financialisation and material culture. Like others, we seek to escape simple dichotomies in which finance is perceived to be either real or imagined (fictitious) by forging links in the context of finance between material practices and their associated meanings (Haiven 2014).

Our approach draws upon the system of provision (SoP) approach (Fine 2002, 2013a). It conceives the economy as dependent upon distinct but overlapping SoPs, most obviously attached but not confined to different sectors of commodity production (for consumption). These SoPs interact with the material cultures that shape norms, values, meanings and practices associated with provisioning. We characterise these material cultures in terms of a number of core features which has been termed the 10Cs – that these cultures are *Constructed, Construed, Conforming, Commodified, Contextual, Contradictory, Closed, Contested, Collective* and *Chaotic*. The 10Cs are designed to capture or to bridge both the complex nature of material cultures (the natures and contents of meanings) and the way in which they are forged through material and social processes. This general framing of material cultures attached to the economy by means of the SoP approach and the 10Cs is applied more specifically in case of financialisation in light of its being taken as a defining feature of contemporary, neoliberal capitalism and, correspondingly, a decisive factor in the restructuring and shaping of many if not all SoPs and their material cultures, as the papers in this volume testify.

However, not all provisioning takes the pure or ideal form of financialised commodity production and not all monetary relations are financialised, contingent upon how this is defined. Not only are there longstanding and increasingly complex cascades of monetary forms and practices (Jessop 2015) but these are also attached to equally diverse sets of economic practices and cultures (Dodd 2016), and theories of money (Lawson 2016).[1] Accordingly, the section 'Pinning down financialisation' begins by addressing the nature of financialisation itself, drawing on a tight definition drawn from Marxist political economy and attaching it to the accumulation of interest bearing capital. This is in order to distinguish financialisation as such from its diverse and wide-ranging effects and its looser associations within much of the literature with attachment to some sort of amorphous presence of credit or even simply (more extensive) monetary relations or ethos. These differences between financialisation and broader monetary relations within economic and social reproduction, of which material culture is a part, are addressed in the section 'Commodification, commodity form and commodity calculation – ccfcc' by drawing distinctions that prevail irrespective of financialisation as such, across the three elements of ccfcc. These three are present as forms or influences upon provisioning wherever there is commodity production even if the first alone of the three involves commodity production as such. Attributes of commodity production, however, can be present without commodity production as such, as with payment for being unemployed or retired, or nominal user charges for public services provided (commodity forms). Commodity calculation prevails when monetary valuation occurs (assessing cost or worth, for example, possibly as basis for action) without money actually passing hands. But, just as commodity production influences the material cultures of other forms of provisioning (what is the meaning of home-made if I can purchase in a shop?) so ccfcc reflect and even facilitate financialisation although they are not financialisation itself.

Nonetheless, because our experiences of financialisation are not direct, within the trading rooms of the City, ccfcc are crucial aspects in the formation of the material culture of financialisation, as these are how we tend to experience financialisation, possibly in paying a water bill, a mortgage or credit card interest.[2] Thus, our concern is not with the material culture of traders themselves, important though this is, but with the financialisation of everyday life which is experienced at a distance from the 'boiler rooms'. Our general approach to traversing this distance is laid out in the section 'From financialisation to culture', and how it is to be operationalised in the section 'The SoP approach – and the 10Cs', by framing specific economic activities through the SoP approach, which seeks to unravel the interactions across monetary forms and the activities with which they are attached or associated. This in turn leads to the framing of corresponding material cultures through use of the 10Cs as previously suggested.

Now, through our analysis, the SoP/10Cs approach can come together with the insights gained from distinguishing between financialisation as such and its consequences through ccfcc. For the material culture of financialisation is associated with pressing for commodity calculation to be more pervasive, for it to lead to commodity form, and for commodity form to lead to commodification. None of this is, however, linear or guaranteed, and it is contradictory in that commodification at one point, housing, for example, may condition or even lead to decommodification elsewhere (the hard to house). Nonetheless, commodity calculation is the most pervasive form through which financialisation is materially, and hence culturally, experienced, although not financialisation itself, since it is a pre-condition for both commodity form and commodification, and, in turn, for financialisation, although one or other or all of these can be far removed from the direct experience of everyday life and even more so in how it is interpreted/experienced.

Nor is the presence of commodity calculation unique to the era of financialisation and its material culture, as was recognised by Oscar Wilde's quip concerning the cynic knowing the price of everything and the value of nothing and, in more scholarly fashion, by Simmel's view not that every relation had become monetised in practice so much as in thought.[3] This is why, if we are to specify financialisation distinctively, it needs to be in terms of the current period of capitalism, and its attachment to neoliberalism, a leitmotif throughout our collection, with the corresponding tendency for economic and social reproduction, and its material cultures, to become incorporated into extensive and intensive forms of financialisation.

Although developed to understand the material culture of (commodity) consumption, the SoP/10Cs approach can be usefully extended to the material culture of financialisation. This is taken up in more detail in Fine (2017) which also serves to frame the other contributions, or case studies, covering financial literacy, exclusion and well-being, housing, water, and the media. The final section here deploys these case studies to illustrate and reflect back upon the approach laid out previously in the introduction – our sequentially structured concretisation of the complexities of material culture through financialisation, ccfcc, the SoP approach and the 10Cs.

Pinning down financialisation

Sporadic forays apart, over a life of little more than a decade, the notion of 'financialisation' has experienced a meteoric rise, accelerating in prominence in the wake of the global crisis. Significantly, see below, within the discipline of economics, its origins and continuing trajectory remain confined to the heavily marginalised fields of heterodox economics. Otherwise, as a scholarly 'buzzword' across the social sciences, it borders becoming a 'fuzzword' (Cornwall and Eade 2010). Specifically, it has been deployed with different meanings, methods and theories. As such, it is beginning to carry a similar burden as more longstanding concepts such as globalisation, neoliberalism and social capital, and has, significantly, overlapped with two of these.[4] For Epstein (2005: 3), 'In short, this changing landscape has been characterised by the rise of *neoliberalism, globalization* and *financialization*'.

Unsurprisingly, debates have emerged around the ambiguity over the meaning of financialisation. These have ranged over the extent, historical uniqueness, likely longevity and homogeneity of the incidence and effects of the rise of finance that financialisation is deemed to capture.[5]

In this introduction, we can hardly resolve continuing debates about whether financialisation is a useful let alone a valid concept. We can, on the basis of the articles in this special issue on the material culture of financialisation, address some of the main issues involved. And we do so with the benefits of having undertaken study of financialisation in its complex manifestation as material culture, thereby combining the abstract and general with the concrete and specific.

The first fundamental issue is how to define financialisation. Much of the literature has been casual, reflecting a lack of attention to any theory of finance and inclined to take its (expanded) presence as sufficient for working with pre-existing conceptual frameworks albeit with finance grafted on. Where finance theory is present, it does to some degree conceptually mirror the more casual, generally empiricist approaches, selectively drawing upon theories of finance as appropriate to the specific object of financialised study, whether it be the crisis or the everyday. Collectively, the result is to generate as amorphous a set of theories of financialisation as its scope in practice.[6] In our own framings, we have sought to avoid such arbitrary intellectual opportunism.

The collective theoretical chaos around financialisation is synthesised, and even celebrated, by Erturk *et al.* (eds) (2008), identifying the contemporary period as one of 'coupon pool' capitalism. Their approach involves a triangulation of four framings, each deriving from different intellectual traditions and time periods in terms of origins and influence. These are 1930s liberal collectivism, 1980s agency theory, the political economy of quantities (that is more longstanding across heterodox and Marxist schools of economics) and cultural political economy which, in its application to finance, primarily belongs to the new millennium. They are correct both to suggest that these framings are mutually incompatible *and* that each has something to offer. More questionable, though, is the assertion that these insights cannot be coherently if critically integrated, something that they seem to dismiss on the grounds of the fluid nature of finance itself, and the equally fluid and variable nature of its causes and consequences – financialisation as a veritable 'bricolage' as their favoured term.[7]

The Gordian knot around the theoretical and empirical diversities of financialisation can be cut by adopting a lean and mean definition, not least to address the closely related issue of distinguishing between financialisation and its effects and, thereby, the structures, processes, relations and agencies that yield those effects. Otherwise, by defining financialisation too broadly, it is almost inevitably found to be present and causing with whatever it is associated, just as has been found with globalisation and neoliberalism, particularly amongst those inclined towards a culture of critique of grand concepts as opposed to embracing their careless application.

In short, financialisation is in danger of becoming a conceptual fall guy for the legion of inadequacies of contemporary capitalism. In pursuit of a lean and mean alternative to this empirically rich but conceptually incoherent collective posture, our own preference is to refer to Marx's theory of interest bearing capital, that is, money capital that is advanced in anticipation of a return based on the accumulation of productive capital. Of necessity, interest bearing capital precedes financialisation but the latter can be defined, in a way that is salient for, and specific to, contemporary capitalism. Here we define financialisation, as the intensive and extensive accumulation of interest bearing capital to such an extent that there are qualitative and quantitative transformations in both economic and social reproduction. By intensive is meant what are longstanding if inventively proliferating financial markets, and by extensive is the incorporation of new domains, especially those related to social reproduction such as housing most prominently but also in privatisation, commercialisation and the varieties of financial intrusions into everyday life (Fine 2014a). Furthermore, such developments lie at the heart of neoliberalism (Fine and Saad Filho 2016).

By adopting such a narrow, and abstract, definition of financialisation, the space is opened for tracing the complex and diverse avenues through which it exerts its effects. We have adopted two strategies in this regard. First, financialisation is dependent upon, but not coterminous with monetary relations. Second, financialisation also exerts its influence through non-economic relations, most obviously in the power of finance in political and ideological arenas.

Thus understood, financialisation does not include the advance of all capital, let alone monetary relations, whether for industrial or commercial purposes, because capital might be funded from retained earnings or whatever rather than borrowing from which a return is anticipated. Only the latter case involves financialisation in that a claim on earnings is created and can be bought and sold separately in what Marx termed fictitious capital. Of course, the current period has witnessed the massive expansion of such interest bearing (and fictitious) capital in intensive form, as has been recognised in the stakeholder value literature on financialisation, although it extends much further than this in the proliferation of types and growth of financial derivatives.

Three fundamental features mark the rise of financialisation across the social sciences, pointing to and to some degree explaining its lack of conceptual tightness. One is the frequent observation of the neglect of finance in the past. Typical, for example, is Pike and Pollard (2010: 29), for whom there are, 'long-standing concerns about the relatively marginal location of finance in economic geography'. Similarly, Moran and Payne (2014: 335) observe the limited attention to (the power of) finance in political science due to its concern with the state:

In sum, with economics asserting a monopoly in the study of economic life and international political economy largely content with overarching analyses of global trends, political science was able, on the whole successfully, to assert and claim its own monopoly, so to speak, of the study of the state, and to do it, as we have seen, in its own distinctive way.

Second, possibly in reaction to such neglect, and as has already been acknowledged, is the wide variety of approaches taken to financialisation, ranging from the neoliberal subject as worker, consumer, entrepreneur or investor as in Langley (2008) to the 'state of the art' of for van der Zwan (2014), with its straddling approaches to the nature of contemporary capitalism, shareholder value and everyday life. Third, closely related but distinct, is the equally wide variety of subject matter covered by financialisation, dealing in everything from the nature of the relationship between financialisation and neoliberalism in characterising contemporary capitalism to the pervasive influence of financialisation on everyday life, let alone as a generic term for finance itself (Sawyer 2014).

No doubt, much of the way in which financialisation is approached is a consequence of the weight and diversity of finance in general, however it is understood, with an equally compelling fluidity and innovation attached to its conceptualisation (as with other 'grand' concepts). Significantly, then, as proposed by Lee *et al.* (2009: 727–8), in locating it geographically even at an early stage,

> financialisation is hardly a new phenomenon in circuits of capital. What is perhaps relatively new is the extent to which finance has found its way into most, if not all, of the nooks and crannies of social life. To illustrate, it is easily possible to identify at least 17 notions of financialisation.

The bridge(s) from our tight definition of financialisation to this array of approaches and subject matter to which the term has been attached is provided below by the trilogy of ccfcc, which both underpin financialisation and mediate social and economic reproduction.

Commodification, commodity form and commodity calculation – ccfcc

Financialisation, understood as the increased deployment of interest bearing capital, is intimately connected to, though distinct from, the monetary relations attached to commodity production. First, capitalist commodity production, and its extension through commodification (privatisation of public services for example), provides fertile ground for financialisation. In addition, financialisation can prosper where there is not necessarily commodity production but the presence of the 'commodity form' by which is meant monetary payments (most notably for mortgages for example) which generate revenue streams that can be securitised as assets and be speculatively traded as interest bearing capitals. The roll out of both commodity production proper, that is for profit, and of the commodity form, that is, payment for goods that are not necessarily produced for profit, has greatly facilitated financialisation by creating more opportunities for the securitisation of revenue streams and capture of monetary rewards by finance. By contrast, commodity calculation – the use of monetary criteria in decision making despite the relevant relations not actually being monetised – does not provide the same opportunities for financialisation due to the absence of revenue streams, but is nonetheless a ubiquitous feature of material culture in financialised economies.

Necessarily, with our definition, financialisation depends upon commodity production, by which we mean production for profit, since monetary rewards ultimately derive from such production (as finance never made any return by itself other than appropriating it from elsewhere as a result of the putative trading in risk or providing financial services).[8] Accordingly, the most prominent form in which everyday life says hello to financialisation is in the indirect form of any monetary exchange, buying and selling, creating the presumption in much of the literature that commodity production (or its creation through commodification) is part and parcel of financialisation. Yet commodity production as such may not involve finance at all as in the case of cash purchases (although financialisation may well have occurred intensively further up the chain of provision to make that cash available). But, equally, commodity production for consumption has increasingly become embroiled in credit relations, most notably with mortgages, credit cards and so on.[9]

Such is not financialisation as such by our tight definition as interest bearing capital. Mortgages have long existed, for example. What makes them financialisation is the securitisation of the potential interest payments (or the debts as such) and their bundling into derivatives for speculative purposes. Yet, as observed, one implication is that (re)commodification, even if not financialisation itself, offers fertile opportunities for financialisation, both in the productive sphere (as with privatisation and corresponding creation of financial assets representing ownership) and with its 'weaker' counterparts of commercialisation with user charges, public–private partnerships and contracting out. The associated revenues of such operations offer the scope for securitisation and, so financialisation, that may or may not (be allowed to) take place.[10]

A leading example of the commodity form is pensions, not covered in this collection but subject to future work,[11] for which this increasingly prominent element of social reproduction (of the aged) has been subject to individual responsibilisation, driven by, and as a consequence of, financialisation. This has given rise to a set of rich and contradictory cultures as a result of the clash of financialisation of pensions with a traditional ethos of collective provision for the retired, not least in the wake of the variously understood crises of pension systems (putatively assigned to a demographic time bomb). Apart from the narrowly interpreted parameters of pension systems themselves (levels of payments by whom, with what rewards), how these have been constructed on a broader perspective depends upon differential access to, participation within, and rewards from labour markets, the taxation systems and the levels of provision of social or familial welfare provision outside of the pension system, quite apart from the vagaries of financial returns when these are a proximate determinant of individual or collective pensions.[12]

The relationship between pensions and finance offers a salient example of why it is necessary to distinguish between commodification and commodity form in engaging with (the cultural) effects of financialisation. For pensions have been financialised but not, in general, in the direct experience and knowledge of pensioners themselves! Yet, commodification and commodity forms both only create the basis for financialisation, and hence condition its material culture indirectly. The same potentiality does not prevail, at least to the same degree, of what might be termed commodity calculation, in which some sorts of monetary calculations are made but in the absence of monetary exchange itself (in traditional terms, cost–benefit analysis). Brown (2015: 10) identifies commodity calculation in extreme form, exaggerating the extent to which Foucauldian reason is and can be realised in neoliberal practice, 'All conduct is economic conduct: all spheres of existence are framed and measured by economic terms and metric, even when those spheres are not directly monetized … we are only and everywhere *homo oeconomicus*'.

As with commodities and commodity form, the presence of commodity calculation is not itself financialisation, although often conceived as if so when notions, such as the neoliberalisation of this or that, are interpreted as its financialisation, not least in the university for example, and in the adoption of commercial criteria but not commerce itself in provision of public services.[13] But, unlike the other two, commodity calculation is not capable as such of providing the basis for financialisation, as we have defined it at least, as there is no monetary exchange, nor flows of income, as such, to be securitised.

The benefits of approaching financialisation through a tight, that is, narrow and precise, but abstract definition are that it allows for diversity of outcome through the troika of ccfcc, distinguishing financialisation from its effects rather than reducing or, more exactly, expanding the notion of financialisation to include the general, if multiple and diverse, presences and influences of all monetary exchange, calculation and ethos. Thus, similar to us, Jessop (2015) appropriately sees cash, credit and fictitious capital as fetishised forms of social relations.[14] But it remains necessary to specify those relations, the fetishes and the corresponding connections between them – as is our purpose in this collection.

In addition, apart from approaching the broader impact of financialisation through ccfcc, the intensive and extensive expansion of interest bearing capital points to the increasingly direct and indirect roles of financialisation in economic and social reproduction and restructuring.[15] This is, of course, a prominent theme in the political economy literature on financialisation, especially for the economic, with financialisation, from a variety of perspectives generally and understandably seen as having deleterious effects on performance whether it be through short-termism, growth, employment, distribution or stability.[16]

This, however, points to a major issue to be confronted however financialisation is defined. If understanding of it is to move beyond the acknowledgement of the greater presence and power of finance, it requires systemic understanding of the contemporary period. What are the dynamics of capitalism in the presence of financialisation and how do they differ from those that came before? In this respect, we have argued at great length that financialisation can be understood as underpinning neoliberalism which we take to be the current stage of capitalism, (Bayliss *et al.* 2015, Fine and Saad Filho 2016), and correspondingly influential over the neoliberalisation of everyday life. This is not to reduce neoliberalism to financialisation but to perceive the last thirty years as having witnessed considerable intervention on the part of the state to promote (the processes, interests and so on, associated with) financialisation. To some extent, it is precisely this systemic and dynamic significance of financialisation for contemporary capitalism that renders it, like globalisation and neoliberalism, so suitable for adoption by the social sciences in which it can sit comfortably across a variety of methods and disciplines despite, or even because of, a collective lack of coherences. The major, perverse, exception is mainstream economics, in contrast to heterodox political economy, for it is incapable of addressing the systemic and the historically dynamic.

Furthermore, though, in locating financialisation in a systemic context, there is an equal need to address its diversity, not only in its content, forms and incidence but also in its impacts. Reference to ccfcc, and attachment of these to neoliberal economic and social reproduction, is to open rather than to close analyses. In this respect, for example, the renewal of interest in Polanyian double movement is welcome.[17] However, it is also limited because the movements are not confined to finance, land and labour, and nor are we witnessing a double movement between commodity and non-commodity forms. Instead, financialisation impacts on a multidimensional and differentiated set of movements across all economic and social reproduction, with corresponding resistances and contingent outcomes in circumstances of everyday lives that those that live them do not make themselves and of which they may be only distantly conscious.

From financialisation to culture

In the previous section, we have sought to define financialisation in a particular way and to prepare the ground for examining its incidence and its effects by carefully distinguishing financialisation as such from the troika of ccfcc which can be pre-requisites but are not financialisation itself. This provides the foundation for the focus of this special issue on the transformative impact of financialisation on households and everyday life. The expanded presence of finance in social reproduction, and the ways in which households have become increasingly embroiled in financial markets, has been extensively documented elsewhere (Martin 2002; Langley 2008; Montgomerie 2009; Seabrooke 2010; Brassett *et al.* 2010; Froud *et al.* 2002; Pike and Pollard 2010, Haiven 2014). Building on this work, our interest is in how the dominance of finance has taken root and manifested at a subjective level, and how it has in turn transformed agents' subjectivities:[18]

> With the growth of what is termed 'financialisation', the widening breadth and scope of financial markets has (sic) been inherently bound up in transformations in terms of how individuals live their lives: their habits and reflexive choices, their modalities of self-discipline and their subjectivities. (Marron 2013: 787)

The multiple forms taken by households' engagement with financial markets are, therefore, explored alongside the often contradictory formation of the subjectivities that underpin these material practices (Froud *et al.* 2007). This means attending to how the needs, ideas and meanings attached to finance have facilitated finance's encroachment into everyday life, and the transformative implications for people's lives and self-understandings. In short, the contributions in this special issue collectively endeavour to study the material cultures of financialisation. The goal is to begin to grasp, on the one hand, 'the way in which financial risk, metrics and practices have become bound up with and normalised through everyday activities such as buying or improving a home; learning and obtaining skills; having children and providing for old age' (Christopherson *et al.* 2013: 354) and, on the other hand, the structures and configurations of economic, political and cultural power that underpin this normalisation.

As Christopherson *et al.* rightly note,

> An acceptance of the relationship of financial processes to changing subjectivities and understanding of the self and society contravenes conventional beliefs about the economy as a separate sphere and personhood as fixed over time in relation to changing economic roles, practices and expectations ... Instead, it emphasises a broader anthropological conception of economic activity as encompassing a 'way of life' that is mutable and socially structured. (Christopherson *et al.* 2013: 354)

Accordingly, our work is situated within the 'cultural turn' in political economy, which rejects old binaries in favour of the hybridisation of culture and economy and of use value and exchange value (Barnes 2004). This reorientation is motivated by the recognition that culture is rooted in the material world: '[c]ulture exists neither in our minds, nor does it exist independently in the world around us, but rather is an emergent property of the relationship between persons and things' (Graves-Brown 2000: 4). Furthermore, it is imperative to acknowledge in turn that economies are 'formatted by discourses' (Montgomerie 2009: 2) and hence that we need 'cultural terms such as symbol, imaginary, and rationality ... to understand crucial economic processes' (Peet 2000: 1213). Addressing culture's material foundation opens the door to comprehending the role of economic and political power in shaping financialised cultural forms, including, without being limited to, 'the extent to which elite actors can sway public opinion and assist in the framing of incentive structures' (Seabrooke 2010: 57). However, such considerations exist in conjunction with agents' capacities for reflection and resistance. These in turn focus attention on how dominant norms attain legitimacy and compliance in terms of Foucauldian ideas of governmentality: 'in principle a legitimate social system can only function through 'cumulative, individual acts of compliance or confidence' by non-elites towards those who seek to govern' (Bendix quoted in Seabrooke 2010: 57; see also Stanley 2014).

The SoP approach – and the 10Cs

The challenge for such a cultural political economy is how to pay due recognition to cultural specificity, the efficacy of cultural properties, agent reflexivity, and the co-constitution of subject and object, while 'continu[ing] to emphasize the materiality of social relations and the constraints involved in processes that also operate "behind the backs" of the relevant agents' (Jessop and Sum 2001: 94). To meet this challenge, we draw on the SoP approach, which sees the economy as constituted by overlapping, commodity-specific SoPs. These SoPs are defined in terms of the structures, agents, processes and relations that characterise the entire chain of provision underpinning particular commodities. The operation of a SoP is shaped by multiple factors – social, political, economic, geographic and historical – and in turn gives rise to distinct, commodity-specific cultures of consumption, the pattern of practices, ideas and meanings that shape patterns of consumption. For the SoP approach, then:[19]

> The material properties of a good or service fundamentally affect consumption patterns (for example water has different material attributes from housing) and goods and services are imbued (often subtly) with cultural significance. ... For the narrowly-defined physical characteristics attached to provision, and consumption, are necessarily culturally endowed in the widest sense. Such cultural content is also subject to wider considerations that range far beyond the immediate provision of the good itself (such as gender, class and nationality). Each sop needs to be addressed by reference to the material and cultural specificities that take account of the whole chain of activity, bringing together production, distribution, access, and the nature and influence of the conditions under which these occur. (Bayliss *et al.* 2013: 1)

Significantly, the SoP *approach* is consistent with different methods and conceptualisations and does not have to be applied alongside our own understanding of financialisation as laid out above. This is, though, the way in which we address the material cultures of financialisation offered here.

In particular, elsewhere (Bayliss *et al.* 2013; Bayliss 2014; Robertson 2014), we have used the SoP approach to investigate the role and impact of finance and financialisation on housing and water.[20] By locating finance within the integrated chains of provision of these two commodities, we were able to reveal how both have been restructured along the chain of provision by the expanded and transformed presence of finance. Given that our present interest is more upon the household, we focus more specifically on the point of consumption, and the desires, meanings and understandings – the cultures of consumption – to which the SoP as a whole gives rise. To do so, we adopt a further framing through which such cultures are addressed deploying what is known as the 10Cs that have become part and parcel of the SoP approach to the material culture of consumption. The purpose of the 10Cs is to provide guidance for the full comprehension of consumption cultures and how they are constituted, through the identification of 10 characteristics common to all such cultures. These are *Constructed, Construed, Conforming, Commodified, Contextual, Contradictory, Closed, Contested, Collective* and *Chaotic*. Once again, as with the SoP approach itself, use of the 10Cs is compatible with different approaches, and is applicable to a range of subject matter (and not just consumption), albeit with strong resonances to its origins within Marxist political economy.[21]

The complex characterisation of consumption cultures, across at least these ten dimensions, mitigates against any tendency to exaggerate the extent of financialisation's cultural hegemony by drawing attention to agents' capacities for reflection and resistance, as well as the multi-faceted influences on their subjectivities that derive from factors more distant than acts of financing, purchasing and consuming. The 10Cs also facilitate a deconstruction of these influences, in discursive terms and in terms of economic and political power. In short, they present a holistic understanding of the multiple channels through which the Foucauldian governance of the financialisation of everyday life is maintained, in conjunction with any dissonances in how financialisation is practised and perceived, the latter emphasised by Haiven (2014) as itself constitutive of financialisation.

As is apparent, then, not least across the case studies included in this symposium, the impact of financialisation is to strengthen and broaden the ethos of commodity calculation, through financial literacy, the media, the promotion of the homeowner and, perversely, through dichotomising it with an alter ego of financial exclusion or well-being independent of financial affairs. It is highly conducive to perceiving the economy, and ideologically promoted as such, as if a household, weighing economic and non-economic imperatives against one another but with Micawberite financial balance as the priority of both national and everyday life as opposed to provision independent of market logics (Stanley 2014). Commodity calculation does its work by occupying the space of material culture and excluding other tenants, especially those associated with the ethos of collective and non-market forms of provision, lest it be for those who are not in and cannot be in the market. In short, as with capitalist commodity production more generally, territories are laid out by financialisation on which it does or does not prevail in economic and social reproduction. What goes on outside of its narrowly confined borders of interest bearing capital is complex and varied but far from independent of what goes on inside, motivating OUR complex of analytical framings on offer.

The material culture of financialisation in practice

As illustrated by our case studies, this is where the SoP/10Cs/ccfcc approach is intended to do its work. The SoP approach provides a framework through which to explore interactions between ccfcc and financialisation within particular SoPs, while the 10Cs serve as the means to characterise the emergent material culture associated with that SoP. Our case studies deploy this approach in two different ways. There are those that look at the 'financial SoP' itself, along with how broader facets of its material culture manifest across society, including through the media, financial literacy, financial inclusion and happiness economics. Then there are those that look at how the SoPs for particular commodities – namely, housing and water – have been restructured by financialisation, and with what implications for their consumption cultures in terms of the 10Cs.

A serious and obvious challenge, not explicitly addressed here, in applying the SoP approach to the material culture of financialisation is how SoPs are to be defined and distinguished from one another. As Fine notes in the opening paper in the symposium, financial services themselves are not a commodity in any straightforward sense. While they include an array of (speculative) assets and (credit-related) services that are not readily categorised in terms of either consumption or production other than by inappropriately stretching the meanings of these terms, they are, nonetheless, subject to material practices in how they are constructed and accessed, and in how they have effects. There is, after all, a financial system that can itself be interpreted as a SoP. This is the procedure adopted by Fine in dealing with the nature of the financial system as a whole, and how it impinges on everyday lives. He goes on to examine the material culture of the financial system through the lens of the 10Cs. As well as dissecting the material culture of the financial SoP, his paper serves to elaborate further on the 10Cs, both broadening the theoretical outlook outlined in this introduction and furnishing perspective for the other papers that follow. This paves the way for the examination of the influence of financialised material culture across society, through case studies on the media, financial literacy and financial exclusion.

Significantly, other than for housing and water, none of our case studies, focusing upon the material culture of the financialisation of everyday life, bears upon financialisation directly, as the expansion of interest bearing capital. This is because, as observed through the prism of ccfcc, such activities take place behind the backs not only of 'consumers' but also even of many of the producers and commercial operatives as well, even though it is well-observed in the financialisation literature how extensive and important are the profits that derive from the financial arms of non-financial companies.

By virtue, then, of both the 'distance' of such financial operations from the nitty-gritty of everyday life and their intrinsic complexity,[22] the material culture of financialisation is far removed from direct 'knowledge' or experience of such activity and so, accordingly, is only engaged as such indirectly. But, as Fine closely argues, in light of the 10Cs and in parallel with the dysfunctional distribution and consumption of food, such (lack of) knowledge is not primarily, and certainly not purely, a consequence of such distance. Indeed, our everyday knowledge of food, and its effects given obesity at epidemic proportions, is extensive and often, if ignored, knowable and known within everyday life; however, much observed in the breach. The major difference with finance, intensified by financialisation, is that we not only are ignorant of its dynamic chaos but that, as such, it is systemically unknowable in its own way, with corresponding results filtering down to everyday lives, occasionally acutely in case of crisis just as chronically in the case of the diets of affluence.

The point, then, is not that the food, in contrast to the financial system is knowable – after all it has been subject to (unknowable) crises of its own from mad cow to horsegate – but that the nature of knowledge, and corresponding cultures, are specific to how food and finance are differentially organised (which the SoP/10Cs approach seeks to address in each case). In general, and hardly unsurprisingly, the way in which the unfillable gap in the financial knowledge of everyday life is accommodated is one that essentially turns a blind eye to its fundamental feature of systemic uncertainty, either through individual reliance upon the practices and experiences of managing individual financial affairs or through addressing these more collectively as a form of Foucauldian governance.

This syndrome is beautifully illustrated by other papers in the collection. Santos, through a study of financial literacy programmes and their promotion through national and international bodies, argues that, despite their many contradictions, such programmes perform an ideological function of inculcating calculating and individualist attitudes among individuals. Financial literacy programmes are specifically designed to insert the financial subject into a world in which the external environment is admittedly uncertain but in which the subject can get by if only gaining and applying the appropriate knowledge.

Gabor and Brooks trace the rise of financial inclusion as a model of development cooperation, focusing in particular on the growing role of digital technology in capturing data on individual consumer behaviour. What they term the fintech-philanthropy-development complex has served both to incorporate the poor into financial markets by allowing for cheaper and easier assessment of consumer behaviour and credit scores, and to shape and therefore govern financialised subjectivities. The explicit tying of financial inclusion discourses to the Foucaldian production and maintenance of the financialised subject facilitates the attribution of market failure to individual behavioural traits rather than to poor regulation of systemic dysfunctionality of financial markets and institutions, something which in turn channels policy responses to addressing individual capability rather than systemic instability.

Boffo, Brown and Spencer offer a critique of the turn towards happiness economics as a metric of well-being for its failure to take into account cultural interferences in reported happiness, with emphasis placed on the *Contextual* to be understood through political economy (of the Global Financial Crisis). Well-being, they argue, and the myriad ways in which it has been affected by financialisation can only be comprehended through the integrated study of how perceptions of needs and wants are constituted, and how their satisfaction is facilitated or constrained. Measures of well-being proceed oblivious to the views that its subjects might have over the workings of the financial system, how it reduces their aspirations, and can allow for limited shifts in reports of happiness despite devastating reductions in standards of living.

Across each of these papers, if for a different topic with correspondingly different aspects, there are common elements. One is how the individual is taken as starting point – for lessons in financial literacy, for support out of financial hardship, or for assessment of well-being, respectively. Another is how these starting points are not tied at all, or at most in the most superficial and erroneous fashion, to the systemic functioning of finance. All can be financially literate, all can be financially included, and happiness begins and ends at home irrespective of how it has been delivered there as long as it has been. In contrast, the SoP/10Cs approach directs attention to the material culture of financialisation in denying knowledge of the financial system (from the extent of government support to its iniquitous rewards through to its inability to be governed), in promoting financial exclusion as a condition of financial inclusion, and in reducing aspirations in reporting well-being.

The material cultures of financialisation do not, of course, pertain only to the financial system itself. The financialisation of everyday life has led finance to intersect more extensively with the other SoPs implicated in social reproduction, reshaping the material practices and consumption cultures associated with those SoPs. The material cultures of financialisation must therefore be approached from the perspective of both the material culture of the financial system itself, and that of the material cultures created through the financialisation of other SoPs and other activities. Happer's paper helps to bridge these two perspectives by looking at the role of the media in shaping perceptions and understandings of the financial system, and explaining this role in terms of the structures underpinning the production and dispersion of information. Complementing the SoP approach with a circuit of communication model, she finds that reduced democratic accountability, a revolving door between the political, financial and media sectors, and journalistic reliance on expert financial knowledge have all played their part in marginalising media narratives that are critical of financialisation and its effects. Moreover, precisely in the representation of finance and of the crisis in the media, in the absence of direct experience of its workings, the knowledge gap is filled by those experts and commentators who are generally heavily implicated in securing its interests, representing its views and precluding alternative forms of financial let alone economic and social organisation.

Similarly, Robertson's paper, in part, offers an illustration of the role of the media in promoting, and condoning, financialisation through close attention to the way it has, in conjunction with government discourses and material advantages, promoted owner-occupation as the most favoured form of housing tenure. Robertson draws attention away from the financial system per se to look at the financialisation of the housing sector. Taking mortgage-facilitated owner-occupation as the defining feature of financialised housing provision, Robertson investigates how a desire for owner-occupation has been inculcated and normalised in the UK. The discursive reshaping of the meanings and perceptions attached to owner-occupation emerges as a key part of the story. The paper also exposes the roots of these normalising discourses in the economic and political power imbalances that are part and product of a financialised economy such as Britain's.

Thus, the financialisation of the housing SoP is located at a distance from those taking out mortgages. On the face of it, subject to terms and conditions, buying a house through a mortgage in the UK today is no different than in the previous 100 years or more even though what was primarily a system of not-for-profit building society provision has been displaced by for-profit banking provision. But, as Robertson shows, such a shift in the forms of financial provision, even if away from the borrower as such, has contributed to a profound shift in the UK in the material culture of housing towards one unambiguously favouring individual private homeownership (as well as this being underpinned by genuine advantages to those who achieve it in the marginalised forms or quality of alternative tenures). Moreover, although common to a greater or lesser extent across many countries, this shift is not reducible simply to the greater availability of mortgage finance but this in conjunction with the conditions of housing supply, including access to land, the role of the state and planning system, and the nature of the construction industry – reinforcing the virtues of approaching the material culture of (housing) finance through the prism of the SoP/10Cs approach.

Whereas the financialisation of housing has been associated with changes in the consumption practices and perceptions of consumers, Bayliss's contribution shows how the financialisation of water has taken place behind consumers' backs. Water privatisation in England and Wales precipitated the emergence of highly leveraged corporate structures used to extract and transfer surpluses to shareholders. Household water bills are rising as a result, though consumers remain overwhelmingly unaware of why. Part of the reason for this is that the financial structures underpinning water companies remain opaque, while households have experienced no change in how they consume water – namely, from the tap, whilst their payments are tapped in entirely different ways. What has occurred is a shift away from an ethos of public provision of water towards treatment of water as a commodity, with an associated emphasis on individual responsibility for paying water bills and for the hardship that may arise from an inability to do so. Yet, the hidden nature of households' incorporation into global financial circuits has dampened contestation and resistance to water privatisation in England and Wales compared to other parts of the world, something compounded by the regulator's permissive attitude towards water companies' financial dealings.

The upshot of this attention to how other SoPs are affected by financialisation is three-fold. First, that there are multiple, competing, and contradictory pressures on material practices and cultures across commodities. Second, that, reflecting distributional and other inequalities, different agents and groups are differentially affected by financialisation. And, finally, that both of these features give rise to limitations and, potentially, resistance to the financialisation of everyday life. All of this serves as a reminder that, 'financialisation does not impose one new logic, but makes and remakes the world in complex ways' (Froud et al. 2007: 343).[23] This is precisely why the SoP and 10Cs approach offers some insight into material cultures attached to financialisation, why resistances have been so muted, and how this might become otherwise.

Notes

1. Space does not allow account of these, our own approach, nor how to accommodate new forms of money from private credit creation to electronic money.
2. Although some see households themselves as essentially financialised (Martin 2002; Bryan and Rafferty 2014).
3. See Simmel's *The Philosophy of Money*, published in 1900 (Simmel, 2004), and commentary by Dodd (1994), and also (Gronow 1997, Fine 2002).
4. Social capital has studiously avoided its most obvious application, to (international) elites, especially those attached to finance (Fine 2010b) and implicitly (Vitali et al. 2011).

5. See Michell and Toporowski (2014) but especially Christophers (2015a, 2015b) and responses in the corresponding special issue.
6. This can be seen positively, as with Aalbers (2015: 215–16):

> The literature on financialization thus is part of a larger attempt to understand the nonlinear, multidimensional, multi-scalar complexity of contemporary societies/economies … [with] potential for financialization as a concept facilitating the conversations between different (sub)disciplines that otherwise do not necessarily talk much to each other … The power of the financialization literature is not only that it connects different disciplines but also different levels of analysis, from the very micro to the very macro – and demonstrating how these are related.

7. See also Johal *et al.* (2014) for use of bricolage in the context of the power of finance.
8. For an outstanding account of how finance as productive has been rationalised, see Christophers (2013).
9. With a corresponding notion that everyone is financially exploited, Lapavitsas (2013) and Fine (2010a, 2014a) for critique, or that the household is necessarily forced into being the equivalent of a financial operative (Bryan and Rafferty 2014).
10. See Leyshon and Thrift (2007) for the early, if implicit, suggestion that financialisation be reduced to capitalisation/securitisation.
11. But see Saritas (2013) and Churchill (2014)
12. Significantly, the SoP/10Cs approach adopted here, see below, is capable of addressing how such wide-ranging systemic factors feed into the shifting cultures of what pensions are and what they mean.
13. See Engelen *et al.* (2014), Martin (2011) and Morrish and Sauntson (2013), and also Graeber (2014) and http://www.ft.com/cms/s/2/c662168a-38c5-11e6-a780-b48ed7b6126f.html
14. Less precisely, Haiven (2014: 5) refers to 'Rhizomatic manifestations throughout social and cultural life' and 'deep penetration of financial ideas, tropes, logics and processes into the fabric of everyday life' (18).
15. Other than as a general source of financial exploitation in response to the attempt to sustain standards of living in response to austerity (Lapavitsas 2013), most prominently, attention to the impact of financialisation on social (as opposed to household) reproduction, especially social policy, has been much more limited if not negligent. See emphasis by Elson (2014) in passing and Fine (2014b).
16. Varieties of post-Keynesianism and Marxism have been to the fore, see special issue of *International Journal of Political Economy*, 42 (4), 2014, and for regulationist approaches, conveniently suffering amnesia over the putatively intermediate post-fordist regime and converging with what might be termed institutional post-Keynesianism, see Aglietta and Rebérioux (2012) and Boyer (2013) for micro and macro aspects, respectively.
17. For a favourable review of Polanyi in light of financialisation that implicitly confirms our more critical stance, see Scheiring (2016).
18. And for Haiven (2014: 14), 'financialization also means a moment when the financial system, and the capitalist economy of which it is a part, is *dependent on and invested in* the ideologies, practices and fictions of daily life as never before'.
19. The SoP approach first appeared in print in Fine and Leopold (1990) in debating the putative UK Consumer Revolution of the eighteenth century. It was fully laid out in Fine and Leopold (1993) but see other references cited here, and Fine (2013a) for a retrospective account that distinguishes its origins and methods from the global value/commodity chain approach.
20. These papers were prepared as part of the EU-funded research programme *Financialisation, economy, society and sustainable development* (FESSUD) fessud.eu.
21. The 10Cs approach has been adopted as a general approach to material culture as is apparent from its application to public provision and social policy (Fine 2002, 2014b), and to topics such as identity (Fine 2009a, 2009b), the ethics of economics (Fine 2013b) and (international) legal expertise (Fine 2016).
22. Even testing the limits of academics, whose knowledge of the 'markets' often remains a black box, see Poovey (2015) and Christophers (2015b).
23. And, in addition, it is crucial to avoid the two, increasingly clichéd, logics associated with financialisation: on the one hand, especially in the context of everyday life, the unemployed or low waged household, public service deprived and over-indebted on mortgage and credit cards desperately seeking to sustain norms of consumption, see Karacimen (2014) and Santos *et al.* (2013) and Santos and Teles (2014); and, on the other hand, the fat cat financier responsible for low investment and growth, rising inequality and speculative crises. No doubt, these exist but they are in part misleading in understanding the nature, incidence, driving forces and consequences of financialisation, see Bayliss *et al.* (Deliverable).

Disclosure statement

No potential conflict of interest was reported by the authors.

Funding

Research for this paper was supported by the project Financialization Economy Society and Sustainable Development (FESSUD), which is funded by the European Union under Framework Programme 7 [contract number 266800].

References

Aalbers, M. (2015), 'The Potential for Financialization', *Dialogues in Human Geography*, 5 (2), pp. 214–19.

Aglietta, M. and Rebérioux, A. (2012), 'Financialization and the Firm', in M. Dietrich and J. Krafft (eds), *Handbook on the Economics and Theory of the Firm* (Cheltenham: Elgar), pp. 308–23.

Barnes, T. (2004), 'Culture: Economy', in P. Cloke and R. Johnston (eds), *Spaces of Geographical Thought Deconstructing Human Geography's Binaries* (London: Sage), pp. 61–80.

Bayliss, K. (2014), 'The Financialisation of Water in England and Wales', FESSUD Working Paper Series No. 52. Available from: http://fessud.eu/wp-content/uploads/2013/04/52_Case-study_The-Financialisation-of-Water-in-England-and-Wales_final_working-paper-521.pdf [accessed 16 December 2015].

Bayliss, K., Fine, B. and Robertson, M. (2013), 'From Financialisation to Consumption: The System of Provision Approach Applied to Housing and Water', FESSUD Working Paper Series, No 2. Available from: http://fessud.eu/wp-content/uploads/2013/04/FESSUD-Working-Paper-021.pdf [accessed 16 December 2015].

Bayliss, K., Fine, B., Robertson, M. and Saad-Filho, A. (2015), *A Series of Thematic Country Synthesis Papers on Relevant Themes* (Leeds, UK: FESSUD Project) (Deliverable D8.27).

Boyer, R. (2013), 'The Present Crisis: A Trump for a Renewed Political Economy', *Review of Political Economy*, 25 (1), pp. 1–38.

Brassett, J., Rethel, L. and Watson, M. (2010), 'The Political Economy of the Subprime Crisis: The Economics, Politics and Ethics of Response', *New Political Economy*, 15 (1), pp. 1–7.

Brown, W. (2015), *Undoing the Demos: Neoliberalism's Stealth Revolution* (Cambridge: MIT Press).

Bryan, D. and Rafferty, M. (2014), 'Political Economy and Housing in the Twenty First Century – From Mobile Homes to Liquid Housing', *Housing, Theory and Society*, 31 (4), pp. 404–412.

Christophers, B. (2013), *Banking across Boundaries: Placing Finance in Capitalism* (Chichester: Wiley-Blackwell).

Christophers, B. (2015a), 'The Limits to Financialization', *Dialogues in Human Geography*, 5 (2), pp. 183–200.

Christophers, B. (2015b), 'From Financialization to Finance: For "De-financialization"', *Dialogues in Human Geography*, 5 (2), pp. 229–32.

Christopherson, S., Martin, R. and Pollard, J. (2013), 'Financialisation: Roots and Repercussions', *Cambridge Journal of Regions, Economy and Society*, 6 (3), pp. 351–357.

Churchill, J. (2014), 'Towards a Framework for Understanding the Recent Evolution of Pension Systems in the European Union', FESSUD Working Paper Series, No. 12. Available from: http://fessud.eu/wp-content/uploads/2013/04/Towards-a-framework-for-understanding-the-recent-evolution-of-pension-systems-in-the-European-Union-FESSUD-working-paper-12.pdf [accessed 16 December 2015].

Cornwall, A. and Eade, D. (eds) (2010), *Deconstructing Development Discourse: Buzzwords and Fuzzwords* (Oxfam: Practical Action).

Dodd, N. (1994), *The Sociology of Money: Economics, Reason and Contemporary Society* (Cambridge: Polity Press).

Dodd, N. (2016), *The Social Life of Money* (Princeton, NJ: Princeton University Press).

Elson, D. (2014), 'Economic Crisis from the 1980s to the 2010s: A Gender Analysis', in S. Rai and G. Waylen (eds), *New Frontiers in Feminist Political Economy* (London: Routledge), pp. 189–212.

Engelen, E., Fernandez, R. and Hendrikse, R. (2014), 'How Finance Penetrates its Other: A Cautionary Tale on the Financialization of a Dutch University', *Antipode*, 46 (4), pp. 1072–1091.

Epstein, G. (2005), 'Introduction', in G. Epstein (ed) *Financialization and the World Economy* (Cheltenham: Edward Elgar), pp. 3–20.

Erturk, I., Froud, J., Johal, S., Leaver, A. and Williams, K. (eds) (2008), *Financialization at Work: Key Texts and Commentary* (London: Routledge).

Fine, B. (2002), *The World of Consumption: The Cultural and Material Revisited* (London: Routledge).

Fine, B. (2009a), 'The Economics of Identity and the Identity of Economics?', *Cambridge Journal of Economics*, 33 (2), pp. 175–91.

Fine, B. (2009b), 'Political Economy for the Rainbow Nation: Dividing the Spectrum?', Prepared for 'Making Sense of Borders: Identity, Citizenship and Power in South Africa', South African Sociological Association, Annual Conference, June/July, Johannesburg. Available from: http://eprints.soas.ac.uk/7972/1/sasa_benfine.pdf [accessed 16 December 2015].

Fine, B. (2010a), 'Locating Financialisation', *Historical Materialism*, 18 (2), pp. 97–116.

Fine, B. (2010b), *Theories of Social Capital: Researchers Behaving Badly* (London: Pluto Press).

Fine, B. (2013a), 'Consumption Matters', *Ephemera*, 13 (2), pp. 217–48. Available from: http://www.ephemerajournal.org/contribution/consumption-matters [accessed 16 December 2015].

Fine, B. (2013b), 'Economics – Unfit for Purpose: The Director's Cut', SOAS Department of Economics Working Paper Series, No. 176. Available from: http://www.soas.ac.uk/economics/research/workingpapers/file81476.pdf [accessed 16 December 2015], revised and shortened to appear as, 'Economics: Unfit for Purpose', *Review of Social Economy*, LXXI (3), 2013, pp. 373–89.

Fine, B. (2014a), 'Financialization from a Marxist Perspective', *International Journal of Political Economy*, 42 (4), pp. 47–66.

Fine, B. (2014b), 'The Continuing Enigmas of Social Policy', Prepared for the UNRISD project on Towards Universal Social Security in Emerging Economies, UNRISD Working Paper 2014-10. Available from: http://www.unrisd.org/Fine [accessed 16 December 2015].

Fine, B. (2016), 'From Performativity to the Material Culture of Legal Expertise?', *London Review of International Law*. doi:10.1093/lril/lrw009

Fine, B. (2017), 'The Material and Culture of Financialisation', *New Political Economy*. doi:10.1080/13563467.2017.1259299.

Fine, B. and Leopold, E. (1990), 'Consumerism and the Industrial Revolution', *Social History*, 15 (2), pp. 151–79.

Fine, B. and Saad Filho, A. (2016), 'Thirteen Things You Need to Know about Neoliberalism', *Critical Sociology*. doi:10.1177/0896920516655387

Froud, J., Johal, S. and Williams, K. (2002), 'Financialisation and the Coupon Pool', *Capital and Class*, 78 (9), pp. 119–51.

Froud, J., Leaver, A. and Williams, K. (2007), 'New Actors in a Financialised Economy and the Remaking of Capitalism', *New Political Economy*, 12 (3), pp. 339–347.

Graeber, D. (2014), 'Anthropology and the Rise of the Professional-Managerial Class', *Journal of Ethnographic Theory*, 4 (3), pp. 73–88.

Graves-Brown, P. (2000), 'Introduction', in P. Graves-Brown (ed.), *Matter, Materiality and Modern Culture* (London: Routledge), pp. 1–9.

Gronow, J. (1997), *The Sociology of Taste* (London: Routledge).

Haiven, M. (2014), *Cultures of Financialization: Fictitious Capital in Popular Culture and Everyday Life* (Basingstoke: Palgrave MacMillan).

Jessop, B. (2015), 'Hard Cash, Easy Credit, Fictitious Capital: Critical Reflections on Money as a Fetishised Social Relation', *Finance and Society*, 1 (1), pp. 20–37.

Johal, S., Moran, M. and Williams, K. (2014), 'Power, Politics and the City of London after the Great Financial Crisis', *Government and Opposition*, 49 (3), pp. 400–25.

Jessop, B. and Sum, N. (2001), 'Pre-disciplinary and Post-disciplinary Perspectives', *New Political Economy*, 6 (1), pp. 89–101.

Karacimen, E. (2014), 'Dynamics Behind the Rise in Household Debt in Advanced Capitalist Countries: An Overview', FESSUD Working Paper Series, No. 9. Available from: http://fessud.eu/wp-content/uploads/2013/04/Dynamics-behind-the-Rise-in-Household-Debt-FESSUD-Working-Paper-09-1.pdf [accessed 16 December 2015].

Langley, P. (2008), *The Everyday Life of Global Finance* (Oxford: Oxford University Press).

Lapavitsas, C. (2013), *Profiting without Producing: How Finance Exploits Us All* (London: Verso).

Lawson, T. (2016), 'Social Positioning and the Nature of Money', *Cambridge Journal of Economics*. doi:10.1093/cje/bew006

Lee, R., *et al.* (2009), 'The Remit of Financial Geography before and after the Crisis', *Journal of Economic Geography*, 9 (5), pp. 723–47.

Leyshon, A. and Thrift, N. (2007), 'The Capitalization of Almost Everything: The Future of Finance and Capitalism', *Theory, Culture & Society*, 24 (7–8), pp. 97–115.

Marron, D. (2013), 'Governing Poverty in a Neoliberal Age: New Labour and the Case of Financial Exclusion', *New Political Economy*, 18 (6), pp. 785–810.

Martin, R. (2002), *Financialization of Daily Life: Labor in Crisis* (Philadelphia, PA: Temple University Press).

Martin, R. (2011), *Under New Management: Universities, Administrative Labor, and the Professional Turn* (Philadelphia, PA: Temple University Press).

Michell, J. and Toporowski, J. (2014), 'Critical Observations on Financialization and the Financial Process', *International Journal of Political Economy*, 42 (4), pp. 67–82.

Montgomerie, J. (2009), 'The Pursuit of (Past) Happiness? Middleclass Indebtedness and American Financialisation', *New Political Economy*, 14 (1), pp. 1–24.

Moran, M. and Payne, A. (2014), 'Introduction: Neglecting, Rediscovering and Thinking Again about Power in Finance', *Government and Opposition*, 49 (3), pp. 331–41.

Morrish, H. and Sauntson, L. (2013), 'Business-Facing Motors for Economic Development: An Appraisal Analysis of Visions and Values in the Marketised UK University', *Critical Discourse Studies*, 10 (1), pp. 61–80.

Peet, R. (2000), 'Culture, Imagery and Rationality in Regional Economic Development', *Environment and Planning A*, 32 (7), pp. 1215–34.

Pike, A. and Pollard, J. (2010), 'Economic Geographies of Financialization', *Economic Geography*, 86 (1), pp. 29–51.

Poovey, M. (2015), 'On "the Limits to Financialization"', *Dialogues in Human Geography*, 5 (2), pp. 220–24.

Robertson, M. (2014), 'Case Study: Finance and Housing Provision in Britain', FESSUD Working Paper No. 51. Available from: http://fessud.eu/wp-content/uploads/2013/04/Case-Study_-Finance-and-Housing-Provision-in-Britain-working-paper-51.pdf [accessed 16 December 2015].

Santos, A. and Teles, N. (2014), 'Recent Trends in Household Financial Behaviour', in A. Santos and B. Fine (eds), 'Empirical Report on Cross-National Comparative Analysis of Household Financial Behaviour: Recent Trends', Leeds, UK: FESSUD project (Deliverable D5.03).

Santos, A., Teles, N., Matias, R., Brown, A. and Spencer, D. (2013), 'Empirical Report on Cross-National Comparative Analysis of Household Well-Being: Micro Analysis', Leeds, UK: FESSUD project (Deliverable D5.04).

Saritas, S. (2013), 'Review of the Pension Provisions in the European Union Countries', Fessud Working Paper Series, No 13. Available from: http://fessud.eu/wp-content/uploads/2013/04/REVIEW-OF-THE-PENSION-PROVISION-ACROSS-THE-EUROPEAN-UNION-COUNTRIES_13.pdf [accessed 16 December 2015].

Sawyer, M. (2014), 'What Is Financialization?', *International Journal of Political Economy*, 42 (4), pp. 5–18.

Scheiring, G. (2016), 'Sustaining Democracy in the Era of Dependent Financialization: Karl Polanyi's Perspectives on the Politics of Finance', *Intersections. East European Journal of Society and Politics*, 2 (2), pp. 84–103.

Seabrooke, L. (2010), 'What Do I Get? The Everyday Politics of Expectations and the Subprime Crisis', *New Political Economy*, 15 (1), pp. 51–70.

Simmel, G. (2004), *The Philosophy of Money*, 3rd ed. (London: Routledge).

Stanley, L. (2014), '"We're Reaping What We Sowed": Everyday Crisis Narratives and Acquiescence to the Age of Austerity', *New Political Economy*, 19 (6), pp. 895–917.

van der Zwan, N. (2014), 'Making Sense of Financialization', *Socio-Economic Review*, 12 (1), pp. 99–129.

Vitali, S., Glattfelder, J. and Battiston, S. (2011), 'The Network of Global Corporate Control', Available from: http://arxiv.org/pdf/1107.5728v2.pdf [accessed 16 December 2015].

The material and culture of financialisation

Ben Fine

ABSTRACT

This paper provides a framework for understanding the material cultures of financialisation. It does so through a tight definition of financialisation itself (as the spread of interest bearing capital across economic and social reproduction) but also attaches financialisation to broader influences through commodification, commodity form and commodity calculation. These in turn are used to frame the material culture(s) of financialisation through deploying the 10Cs derived from the System of Provision approach: that the material cultures of financialisation are Constructed, Construed, Conforming, Commodified, Contextual, Contradictory, Closed, Contested, Collective and Chaotic. Some emphasis is placed upon the 'distance' of financialisation as such from most everyday practices and the systemic lack of knowledge of the financial system however it is represented and experienced.

Introduction

Our introduction to the symposium in part, through reference to interest bearing capital, commodification and so on, offered what Erturk *et al.* (2008) would dub a political economy of financialisation, preparing the way in this paper to embed this within a material culture of financialisation (mcf). In our (post)postmodern world, what this means, let alone how to do it, is extremely controversial and open. The concern will be with what (often unacknowledged and unrecognised as such) financialisation means to its subjects (or objects) and how those meanings are liable to be generated. Necessarily, this involves differentiating between subjects – the futures trader as opposed to the unemployed, let alone the incidence of other individual and social characteristics – and how these subjects both interact with, and reflect upon, the various dimensions of financialisation as they experience them.

To traverse this potentially contested and, to a large extent, unchartered terrain, the system of provision (or SoP) approach will be developed to study the mcf.[1] This approach is adopted with some hesitation because, although financial services have been perceived as a consumption good (as well as a productive input), they are clearly something much more than, and different from, this. On the other hand, especially in the light of financialisation and much other literature that has both addressed and preceded it, the notion of the presence of a financial system is pervasive from many different perspectives and, of necessity, this involves the presence of material processes, structures, relations and agents (or agencies) and the systems of meanings with which they are formed and interact with one another. This is what allows the mcf to be framed within the SoP approach, drawing in particular upon the 10Cs associated with it, that the mcf is *Constructed, Construed, Conforming, Commodified, Contextual, Contradictory, Closed, Contested, Collective* and *Chaotic* (Bayliss *et al.* 2017). Given the origins of the SoP approach, some parallels will usefully be drawn between mcf and the material culture of consumption, particularly food, although not addressing the financialisation of food itself.[2] Significantly, despite the weight of financialisation of food, its impact upon food's material culture, what we consume and what it means to us, seems distant if not negligible and unknown – at least until we start to look at, for example, systemic levels of malnutrition and obesity. In this respect, as will become apparent, there are considerable resonances with the mcf. By use of the 10Cs, the diverse pathways, by which the Foucauldian governance of the financialisation of everyday life prevails, can be fully confronted.

From SoP to finance

The SoP approach to the material culture of consumption can be presented by taking Haug's (1986) notion of 'aesthetic illusion' as critical point of departure. Haug suggests that capitalist production degrades commodities as a means of cheapening them, and they can only be successfully sold by compensating for this degradation (and adulteration)[3] by endowing them with meanings (and hence enhanced use value and appeal) through advertising that, for him in particular, deploys the persuasive powers of sexuality.

This approach, however, suffers a number of deficiencies: production may become of higher not lower quality (through changes in processes, products and ingredients); advertising and sexuality are not the only, even major, determinants in bridging the putative aesthetic illusion; and, most important, how are the two sides of the aesthetic illusion (commodity as is relative to commodity as perceived) generated, reproduced and/or transformed and bridged as far as the consumer is concerned. In this respect, the aesthetic illusion can itself be seen to be illusory as it dissolves into investigating the meanings of consumption directly through its constituent determinants rather than indirectly through how it was previously and subsequently understood (and experienced) in light of change in provisioning. In other words, there is no possibility of bridging the gap spanned by the aesthetic illusion without knowing where the two sides are – which themselves shift – and how they are (re)formed. So the commodity as is and as understood might just as well be addressed directly without reference to the aesthetic illusion.

The question is how. And, here at least, the aesthetic illusion offers some guidance in having pointed in a limited way to the ensemble of factors (if illegitimately confined to product degradation and sexualised advertising) that comprise the material practices and experiences that underpin the meaning of the consumed to the consumer. Furthermore, and this is characteristic of commodity consumption,[4] those experiences and meanings are of two types – those that precede purchase (from which the consumer is essentially absented with minor, possibly exaggerated, exceptions in case of 'custom built', relevant for personal financial plans, or the more general notion of trickle effects of consumer sovereignty) and those that follow it (although there are cycles of consumption and production). Significantly, there is some case to be made for an aesthetic illusion attached to finance as, especially with mis-selling, financial products are presented as other than they are, together with varieties of powers of persuasion (if not, generally, sexuality as opposed to less risky markers of security and reward, around the home, family and life choices such as fertility and retirement, for example).

In short, it is imperative to construct an understanding of financialisation and its material culture, or cultures, in tandem and balance with one another. Even for performativity, which emphasises the role of economists in making (financial) markets rather than vice versa, and its most developed illustration, the Black-Scholes model as examined by MacKenzie (2008), it is questionable whether financialisation would have failed to progress without the, arguably more important, pressures to liberalise financial markets (Fine forthcoming). For financialisation has witnessed the geographical, or internationalised, expansion of financial markets both nationally and internationally, with such activity breaching a rather different boundary by being reinterpreted as constituting a contribution to GDP as opposed to mere transfers of income.[5] This is much more reflected than precipitated in the reconstruction of finance in the economics literature. And it is telling just how narrow has been the scope of application of the performativity thesis given the range and impact of financial markets involved.

mcf is constructed and construed

More specifically, in contrast to performativity's emphasis on how economics makes the economy (and hence financialisation), the SoP approach to the material culture (of consumption) proceeds by reference to 10 characteristics, known as the 10Cs. And these will be applied here to the financial system (and financialisation). First, the financial system is *Constructed* (and reconstructed) through its material practices.[6] By *Constructed* is understood not simply nor primarily the self-reflection upon the meanings attached to financialisation by financial subjects themselves. Rather how those meanings emerge depends upon the workings of the financial system itself as these evolve, impact and induce response in thought and deed. Such an approach is deemed essential because of the presumption (significantly, denied by performativity) that capitalism (and its associated financial system and financialisation) incorporate relations, structures and processes, within or against which agents must themselves react. This is not to suggest absence of independent agency only to situate it systemically, with different approaches to this displaying differences of emphasis, methods and theories around corresponding modes of interaction.[7]

Second, though, financial systems are *Construed*. Just as the consumer can be cynical about the sexuality deployed to promote (degraded) goods, so those engaging with the financial system do not necessarily accept the wisdoms or otherwise that it conveys deliberately or otherwise. Whatever the sources of experience and knowledge, these are reflected upon to a greater or lesser extent, and reacted to, or against, rather than simply received passively (which would also beg the question of who created the meanings that are being conveyed alongside financial dealings). Cook *et al.* (2009), for example, ask homeowners to construe mortgaging in terms of animal-types. And, for Payne (2012), the right to buy a home is seen as an attempt to induce the culture of neoliberal consumer, see also Robertson (2017).

This conditioned construal of financialisation can be taken further and, once again, comparisons with consumer (or, more exactly food) culture is telling not least by reference to Fischler's (1980, 1988) 'omnivore's paradox' as critical point of departure. He suggests that, because we can eat anything, we run the risk of poisoning contingent upon our knowledge of food. But, he argues, our knowledge, and its attachment to potential harm or distaste (think horse meat), has been increasingly undermined by detachment from food's production, a consequence of (global) commodification bringing physical as well as knowledge distance from the sources of our diets in processes of production and distribution. As argued by Fine (1993, 1998), however, by reference to what he terms the 'diet paradox', our knowledge of the food is considerably greater in many respects than of our directly producing and consuming peasant ancestors if such they were. This is because direct knowledge and experience of production (and processing, wholesaling and retailing) are not the only sources of knowledge in general and of these elements in particular. Indeed, our current common knowledge of nutritional properties of foods did not exist as such in olden times, however nostalgically viewed.

But this does not mean that we organise our eating habits around such knowledge in the sense that we have a healthy diet that we target. Such is the rationale for posing the 'diet' in place of the 'omnivore's paradox' since, whilst everyone does have a diet *ex post*, it is not necessarily determined as such by *ex ante* intentions. Nor does it make sense to understand the determinants of diet by more or less deviation from what is constructed and construed to be ideal in healthy eating advice even if this does have some, not necessarily positive, influence. Further, how our knowledge and meanings of food are generated remains to be explored (as descriptors such as fair trade, organic, natural and so on are themselves constructed and construed as much by factors other than the physical properties of the foods themselves and how they are provided).

In case of financialisation, however, we are endowed with parallel paradoxes as for food, not least concerning our knowledges of finance. Despite the limited presence of immediate physical properties as such in monetary relations (as they are performed by a paper or even electronic service in many instances), there is the presence of both omnivore's (displaced ignorance) and diet (multiple sources of knowledge) paradoxes with finance. To a large extent, other than in a token way with the minor resurgence of behavioural economics in the wake of the crisis, such absence of knowledge has been overlooked by mainstream economics (and much heterodoxy) or reduced to imperfect information or uncertainty. This follows from the presumption of the rational, optimising individual, subject only to budget and informational constraints, or otherwise deviant from rationality as exception to the norm. In this imaginary world of the efficient market hypothesis for financial markets, the omnivore's paradox simply disappears with optimal use of information subject to costs of gaining it.

However, outside the confines of orthodox economics, and in more or less explicit response to financialisation, the literature has pointed to the limits in knowledge that are attached to finance. The omnivore's paradox applies much more to finance than to food and much the same if not more is true of the diet paradox. Finlayson (2009: 402) suggests that, 'there has been a reduction of the distance between high finance and everyday life, a lowering of the barriers between global banking and household finance'. But, to the contrary, our distance in knowledge of finance, despite what may or may not be its physical proximity on a daily basis, is considerable, far more distant than our knowledge of agriculture, and so on, if such comparisons are meaningful. As Langley (2008: 3) puts it, 'the majority of mortgagors, credit card holders, and other borrowers seem unaware that claims on their future repayments, and the risks on their non-payment, are presently packaged and traded in the capital markets'.

Further, as suggested above, the diet paradox's denial of a healthy diet around which consumers organise their eating habits applies equally to finance, not least by analogy with (optimisation around) the (household) budget constraint. The budget constraint is in a sense unavoidable. But this does not imply that households organise their finances around their budget constraint, consciously or otherwise, just as consumers do not target a healthy diet (and, if they do, the evidence is that they have failed miserably given rising levels of obesity to epidemic proportions). This is not to say that a healthy budget (like a healthy diet) plays no role in financial affairs (what we eat), only that it is not the only nor necessarily the primary consideration or driving force behind behaviour and meanings. Nonetheless, of course, that the budget constraints (or dietary norms) do exist and that, as a matter of tautology, behaviour revolves around some ideal optimal financial arrangements to a greater or lesser extent can lead to the delusion that targeting such optimality is how behaviour is determined. Why this might or might not be accomplished can then be taken to be what has to be explained (and as abnormal and irrational, even deviant and pathological, if excessive). Such is the analytical take on campaigns to improve behaviour, financial or dietary, by improving knowledge as with campaigns for the promotion of financial literacy and healthy eating, respectively.[8] Moreover, such false conceptualisations of how households manage their financial affairs are compounded when they are projected to those of the nation as if household, rationalising austerity through balancing the books or 'handbag economics' in the terminology of Mellor's (2016: 136/137) critique, if falsely presuming the transparency, as opposed to the opacity, of how government can create public money free of debt, albeit to use it support private debt – 'Quantitative easing made transparent the ability of public monetary authorities to create public currency free of debt … it has replaced possibly toxic loans with good public money'.

What, however, underpins the construal of finance is not that finance is unknown but that it is unknowable. This has been most forcibly put by Engelen et al. (2012: 366). For them:[9]

> Our first claim is that finance is now technically ungovernable, so that any attempt to restore finance to some kind of equilibrium or balance is futile because instability is written into its DNA. We make this case by arguing that financial innovation takes the form of bricolage which has had four key consequences – the growth of volume, complexity, opacity and interconnectedness. With bricolage, restorative regulation ceases to be an external constraint and becomes an input for future financial improvisation by creative bricoleurs.

Further, in the context of the limitations on the knowledge to govern finance, Haldane has proved a significant, and particularly well-placed, commentator.[10] He reports that Basel I at 30 pages in 1998, went to 347 pages in Basel II in 2004, and stood at 616 pages with Basel III in 2010. For the USA, the Glass–Steagall Act in 1993 took just 37 pages compared to the 848 pages of the Dodd–Frank Act of 2010 (with 400 bits of detailed rules for regulatory agencies), with a further 8843 pages for the rulebook in covering just one-third of the rules involved. Even more striking is the (employment) burden of financial regulation with 1 UK regulator for 11,000 financial sector employees in 1980 compared to 1 for every 300 today, with less than 100 increasing to over 3000 regulatory employees involved. By the same token, in the USA, with 18,500 regulatory employees for finance, this suffices to provide 3 regulators for each US bank. On the other hand, demands on UK banks to meet reporting requirements have gone from 150 entries in regulatory returns to 7500 items of data, with new European rules possibly requiring a total of over 30,000 entries over 60 different forms. Just to meet Basel III compliance over 350 European banks is estimated to support 70,000 new jobs.

Three points emerge from these observations. One is that the knowledge displayed by Haldane is almost certainly a cause for shock, even disbelief, against the presumption that finance has been too loosely regulated and is in need of more and tighter regulation. Second, Haldane is suggesting that finance is, indeed, more or less unknowable, and regulation should be designed accordingly, unless the wood be missed for the trees.[11] Third is the sheer weight of resources being dedicated to regulation that might, alongside those used to buttress the ailing financial system as well as those lost due to its crisis, equally come as a profound shock to those supporting, let alone opposing, what is supposedly a laissez-faire source of market efficiency.

It is worth speculating what would be the reaction of households to such knowledge, if it were made available to them on a sustained basis, bearing in mind just how quickly if not completely the antipathy to finance rose and dissipated with the crisis (with its own fortunes, and rewards, following a parallel trajectory only more sharply so). It is also important to tease out why such knowledge remains distant. Here, the treatment of the crisis in the media is crucial (Happer, 2017).

The media, though, will have been informed by two other major sources of, or limitations upon, knowledge – what is received and how it is interpreted. One is scholarship within which the place of economics, including its neoliberal versions, remains prominent despite an early if uneven rush to blame the discipline for not anticipating the crisis, for not acknowledging it as a possibility, and for failing to remedy it quickly and fully. Here, neoliberal scholarship has all the bases covered: potentially blaming individuals for not making best use of knowledge should the (financial) system fail, thereby leaving unquestioned the perfect working of (financial) markets in coordinating that behaviour but for unavoidable random shocks; or highlighting the impossibility of avoiding failures of the system given imperfections in the nature of gaining and using knowledge itself; and the state can be deployed as a last resort as an impediment to the perfectly working markets from both Chicagoan and neo-Austrian perspectives.[12] Whilst neoliberal scholarship, together with its market imperfection versions, is contested, it reigns supreme within academia and through much of the media, leading to a politics of competing TINA ideologies around how to achieve deficit reduction and the like (Brassett *et al.* 2009).

From commodified to chaotic

Such relations between government/politics and knowledge limitations have profound implications for the democratic governance of finance. But, so obvious that it might be overlooked as, indeed, does often occur for commodity consumption is that the material culture of finance is *Commodified*. Of course, money and financial assets are themselves commodities, unavoidably so unlike items of consumption in general, and they have their own particular properties, or use values, as such. Here, though, the concern is with those properties from the perspective of the household as part and parcel of the (capitalist) commodity system.

How this is itself approached is contingent upon whether a universal theory of money is adopted (as favoured here) or not (with, instead, a theory of specific and differentiated monies). Precisely because money (and financial assets) are universal (although not necessarily infinitely liquid) – they have the capacity to derive from, or to be applied to, more or less any economic and social activity – although some are more or less 'sacred' from the taint of money/commerce. Indeed, financialisation draws upon the fluidity of money by incorporating ever more economic and social activity into its circuits – as (interest bearing) capital. An immediate implication is that the material culture of money (and finance) is not and cannot be useful beyond appreciation of, and response to, experience of and reflection upon its universal properties. Rather, the variegated meanings of money derive from its location in more or less fluid if structured circular flows – from kindly or grasping banker through acquisition of fashion items, to payment of rent to slum landlord. This implies the mcf derives from the cacophony of economic and social relations within which it is embroiled as universal equivalent with, 'deep penetration of financial ideas, tropes, logics and processes into the fabric of everyday life' (Haiven 2014: 18).

This involves further implications. First, it turns upside down the multiple monies approach associated with Zelizer (1994, 1996, 1998, 2000) and challenged by Fine and Lapavitsas (2000), Fine (2002) and Lapavitsas (2003). For the universality of finance endows its use with multiple meanings, not multiple meanings requiring multiple monies. Second, in particular, as there are many activities that lie outside the domain of money/commodification in principle (social as opposed to economic reproduction but not through the market), and the boundaries between these shift in practice as well as whether monetisation/commodification is viewed as appropriate, the use of money to purchase, or even to evaluate, is as varied in meaning as the uses themselves. In other words, it is economic and social activity that drives the use of money, not vice-versa. Third, then, this all reinforces the earlier argument concerning the budget constraint as a form of financial management. Individual expenditures, and earnings, are liable to incorporate a material culture and logic of their own which is rarely subject to a narrowly defined rational economic logic as opposed to one cog in a wheel of determinants. Last, there are the different aspects of the monetary across three elements/processes that have facilitated financialisation: commodification, commodity form and commodity calculation, ccfcc, as specified in Bayliss et al. (2017). As forms of finance, whether for credit in general or for profitmaking in particular, these tend to be conflated with one another, not least as the household, the (financial or non-financial) corporation, and the state are seen as similar accounting enterprises, whether it be in relation to borrowing, spending or indebtedness or the ethos surrounding these.

To some degree, these observations resonate with the received Polanyian view of the world in which a commercial (or financialised) logic is contested, in the context of labour, land and, especially, finance.[13] But they also suggest an enrichment, generalisation and even break with the Polanyian double movement, not least with the following insights to be highlighted, at least in principle, with the need:

(1) to disaggregate and widen the sphere of application of the double movement to commodities other than just land, labour and finance, with health, education and welfare, and so on, as also potentially subject to reaction against the logic of the (capitalist) market;

(2) to refine the double (or, given the complex nature of commodities as use values as opposed to exchange values, should it be multi-dimensional) movements by tracing them along the material practices attached to, and determinants of, those movements beyond their representation of use values (and access to work, home and money) – cultures are distinguished by much more than market provision or not as is provision itself;

(3) to see the 'movements' distinctively in the context of ccfcc, not just in relation to homogenised forms of in and out of the market – user charges within a free service are different from privatisation of health although both favour the 'market';

(4) to locate these movements in relation to the (evolving) material culture of household attachment to financialisation to account for contemporary outcomes.

Such considerations necessarily and appropriately locate the mcf in relation to commodification or, more accurately, to ccfcc. It follows that the mcf is *Conforming* to such commodification even if allowing for resistance in word and deed. This raises with Marx's definition of commodity fetishism: that commodities appear, as they really are, as relations between things (as opposed to the products of human labour in definite social relations). By the same token, and more specifically, financialisation carries with it the practices and logics of strengthening the presence and expanding the scope of ccfcc. This dovetails with a corresponding (neoliberal) culture of individual, or individualised, responsibility, at the expense of the collective across ever-expanding terrains of economic and social life.

The result is to give rise to a strategy in which:

> Housing policy has become a branch of social policy, justified not in terms of absolute right or simple inequality but as a contribution to the equalisation of life chances … and, beyond this, as an asset that will enable individuals to take responsibility for their own financial future. (Finlayson 2009: 407)

This is seen as 'autonomisation and responsibilisation', and is equally 'evident in education, healthcare, pensions and training'. As Beggs *et al.* (2014: 978) put it, rounding up commodification/conformity with financial literacy:

> the critical issue is not just whether individuals do or do not have capacity for financial literacy, or even whether more interventionist (paternalistic) approaches are needed. Rather it is that the agenda of financial literacy is itself a discourse of subordination to the individualism and discipline implicit in financial calculation. Moreover, this individualism is not a financial expression of democracy and of the good society, but about the facilitation of the class of capital and its new accumulation project.

Thus, commodification as an aspect of material culture does not originate with financialisation but its scope and influence is extended through ccfcc.

Nevertheless, Polanyian or otherwise, the logic of increasingly conforming to commodification is no rollercoaster with unstoppable momentum and, as already apparent, has to be put into place, or reproduced, by a transformation in material culture that has its own historical logics and traditions. Thus, the mcf is *Contextual* across time, place, financial form and even individual household itself as far as detail is concerned. Such is obvious as soon as we attend to health, education, housing and pensions, in and of themselves and in terms of how they are financed whether by free public provision, user charges, insurance, credit card or bank loan. Material culture can, in these respects, be complex, stubborn to change or rapidly turned over (especially in relation to norms of avoiding indebtedness when confronted by equally powerful norms of household provision in face of reduced real and social wages; Karacimen 2014).

Yet such stabilities and volatilities, at individual and collective levels, are indicative of the *Contradictory* nature of the mcf. By this is meant not inconsistency, but see Chaotic below, as opposed to the dependence of material culture on underlying social forces and tendencies. As Dodd (2016: 183) puts it:

> Whilst neoliberal financialization may, ultimately, be characterized by the pathological and limitless collapsing of all social values into and under the ruthless quantitative measure of economic value, it is also, contradictorily, dependent on the forms of innovation, social reproduction and subjectivity generated in the intervals.

Here, once again, an analogy with diet is compelling. As argued in case of eating disorders, the compulsions to eat and to diet are pervasive in contemporary capitalism, and each consumer has to negotiate these in thought and deed, with outcomes along a spectrum from anorexia and bulimia to obesity (Fine 1995, 1998). Remarkably, the food industries have managed to square the circle by simultaneously promoting what would otherwise appear to be mutually exclusive spheres (but bear in mind that dieting has primarily become about eating more and different over shifting cycles of behaviour).

The analogy with financialisation is striking once it is forged in terms of the imperatives both to save and to spend (on credit). Both of these activities are heavily promoted as financial services, and they mutually reinforce one another. As Cook *et al.* (2009: 136) put it:

> With a flexible mortgage at the interface, housing wealth may be *saved and spent*: linking debts secured against the home to a wider range of long and short-term household transactions.

Moreover, this adds to the understanding of financialisation in terms of the diet paradox, addressing why households both save and spend simultaneously. And, at a systemic level, the representation of finance as obese is not only apt but also commonplace as a metaphor, including fat cat salaries and bloated consumer credit, both individually and systemically.

Yet, in the world of saving and spending (and financialisation), all are equal but some are more equal than others. In this respect, the mcf is *Closed*, if not absolutely so, in that, as with finance itself, some participate in its formation more fully and with more influence than others, as well as at different nodes in the circulation of value (from City trader to indebted household) – 'All construals are equal, some are more equal than others' (Jessop 2015: 88). Such is already apparent from the earlier discussion of knowledge/ignorance and what is known let alone knowable. And, as Montgomerie and Williams (2009) observe, whilst there may have been mass participation in financialisation and, in that sense alone, democratic participation in free markets, interventionism has been increasingly for and by, if not confined to, an increasingly powerful (financial) elite, going far beyond the too big to fail syndrome as symbol of loss of democratic accountability.

More concretely, the closure of policymaking has been indicated by CRESC (2009: 5), finding that those UK bodies reporting on the financial system, and how better to regulate it, drew upon a membership of '662 years of work experience and 75% of those years were spent in City [the London financial centre] occupations or servicing City needs'. Further, '90% of its witnesses came from finance or consultancy with revenue links to finance'.[14] Indeed:

> Membership contained no non-financial businesses and their trade associations, no trade unions despite the unionisation of retail finance workers, no NGOs to represent consumers or press social justice agendas, no mainstream economists or heterodox intellectuals, very few politicians or civil servants. (CRESC 2009: 23)

Significantly, even as witnesses, the representation of the public sector was notable for its absence.

What is both striking and disturbing is the extent to which different constituencies other than those attached to finance have been marginalised or subordinated, almost as second nature, within both the institutions and processes of government. This is part and parcel of the politics of neoliberalism more generally, a hollowing out of those institutions that challenge the dictates of the amorphous market. Nonetheless, any closure in the mcf cannot be self-contained and totally exclusionary, and it is necessarily *Contested*, if only on conditions not necessarily made by (all of) the contestants, or equally so. For Dodd (2016: 269), neatly combining contestation with construal:

> Culture is important to understanding the ways in which people shape money for themselves, bending it to their own purposes and resisting its capacity to homogenize everything it touches. This idea ought to be compelling … not least because culture influences what money actually does.

Or in more mundane terms, we can highlight the slogan 'Quantitative Easing for the People'.

What is striking of such contestation, however, especially in the wake of the crisis, is how much it is not only muted but also transformed in view of the commodification and closure attached to financialisation. To some degree, this can again be understood by parallel with consumption, and the distinction drawn between the consumer and the citizen. As argued in Fine (2005, 2013), both these categories are limited in expressing conflicts of interest as all are both consumers and citizens. Nonetheless, the reduction of citizenship to financialised consumerism tends both to depoliticise and to disempower as will tend to occur with financialisation and individual responsibilisation. Or contestation can be driven to extremes, or out of the ordinary, as with street protests, the Occupy Movement (and its telling symbol of the 1 per cent).

That financialisation is contested raises the elusive issue of power – what it is and how it is exercised. As Moran and Payne (2014: 33) observe:

> Making sense of the power of financial markets faces what we might now do better to think of as 'the political science of political economy' with three big problems: the conceptualization of power itself; the conceptualization of markets; and the conceptualization of financial systems.

What does not seem to work analytically (possibly for financialisation and otherwise), however, is to seek out independent solutions for these issues, not least because conceptualisations of markets and financial systems already embody, at least implicitly, their own conceptualisations of power. Accordingly, Johal et al. (2014: 403) seek to pinpoint power through the bricolage of four (abstract) elements, 'the power of decision, the power of nondecision, the power of (narrative) hegemony and the power of learned self-discipline'. They then apply this to a history of the power of the UK's City during the past century, suggesting the exercise of different forms of power at different times as finance has sought to finesse both democratically elected governments and the competitive workings of financial markets.[15]

Yet, it is far from clear to what extent the same power is being exercised and the same finance is exercising it, given the changes in the nature of each as well as the contexts within which they have operated. What is clear, though, is that contestation is inevitably *Collective*, especially if it is to be successful, whether collectivities promote financialisation (as with the newly emerged and/or strengthened financial elites) or resist it, however indirectly or effectively in street protests or through opposition to commercialisation. Of course, it might be argued that irrationally breaching a budget constraint is a form of dissent, a strike against Foucauldian governance, a material counter-culture. However, irrespective of its longevity and impact, it does in its own way conform to the mcf rather than transform it.

And last, and by no means least, the mcf is *Chaotic* in the sense of drawing together a multiplicity of practices and influences across a multiplicity of dimensions, with those being reflected upon by households themselves as they go about their daily lives, provisioning for life prospects and beyond. As Langley (2007: 82) puts it:

> The subject position of the investor that is summoned up in neoliberal governmentality is represented as a paradoxically monolithic and disconnected economic identity. Indeed, the very isolation of the 'the investor' provides the anchor point in representations of close relationships between the financial markets on the one hand and individual freedom and security on the other. Such isolation, of course, cannot hold, as investors are also simultaneously workers and consumers.

As a result, it follows that, 'Drawing attention to the contradictions present in the assembly of investor subjects is particularly important' (85). To impose a simple, or even complex, logic on the mcf (the optimising or even behaviourally enriched punter) does seem inappropriate not least if reference is made to the telling examples of those experts, regulators, traders and scholars of the financial system itself let alone its humble customers. Yet, the mcf ranges far beyond knowledge to the totalities of economic and social reproduction, on which financialisation has exerted an impact whether directly or indirectly.

Concluding remarks

Elsewhere it has been argued that financialisation lies at the heart of neoliberalism and explains its longevity (Fine et al. 2015). But, of course, the material cultures of neoliberalism extend far beyond that of mere money. Or does it? In The Grapes of Wrath, Steinbeck observes, 'this tractor does two things – it turns the land and turns us off the land', and his novel charts the material cultures of those dispossessed. But the author also makes clear that behind the tractor and the land lies the banker whose bottom line must be met irrespective of the economic and social costs. The mcf is no different except that it exerts a longer, broader and deeper reach into our lives, however well this is acknowledged by those who gain and lose by it.

Not all of us can so skilfully as Steinbeck articulate the material and the cultural with narrative and imagery. This, though, has motivated the hunter/gatherer exercise that yielded the 10Cs, drawing upon the weapons of theoretical reflection and the instruments of case studies to solicit ways of framing material culture that avoid the Scylla of structural reductionism at one extreme and Charybdis of free-floating semiotic readings at the other.

Each of the 10Cs has the potential, contingent upon the object of study, to straddle the material and the cultural, albeit with different balances and content – consider the contradictory determinants of culture as opposed to its derived chaotic meanings for example. The studies that follow apply the 10Cs selectively, illustrating its elements across the diverse subject matters covered with, for example, commodification in practice of greater significance in underpinning owner-occupation and its corresponding cultures than delivery and content of financial literacy programmes although the latter would surely be different if inhabiting a world where money and credit matters less in light of decent wages, employment and public services free at the point of delivery.

Notes

1. See Fine (2013) for a recent account of its origins and evolution and various contributions. See also Bayliss *et al.* (2013).
2. But see, for example, Isakson (2014).
3. This being drafted during the height of the horse meat scandal!
4. Although the SoP approach has also been applied to public provision, or public sector systems of provision, pssop.
5. See especially Christophers (2013).
6. See Langley (2008: 143) for whom:

   > instrumental rationality cannot be assumed to be an inherent feature of all modern monetary relations and all manner of financial networks. Rather, what we see are multiple monetary and financial networks in which the appearance of scientific rationality has to be secured and remade in specific forms, and remains contingent, contested, and open to (re)politicization.

   From his perspective of financialisation as everyday (performative) life, there are resonances with the 10Cs approach as he ranges across financial inclusion and exclusion, inequality and networks, power, identity and dissent. Unsurprisingly, the implicit and, at times, explicit, presence of the 10Cs is pervasive across the literature.
7. See also Svetlova (2012).
8. On financial literacy, see Santos and Costa (2013), Santos (2017) and Gabor and Brooks (2017), and Fine (1998) for food.
9. See also Engelen *et al.* (2010) and Dixon and Ville-Pekka (2009) for pension provision as bricolage, and also Dorn (2012) and Thompson (2010). With his retrospective as Governor of the Bank of England replete with references to the importance of 'radical uncertainty', King (2016: 123) asks, 'Why are we so reluctant to accept that the future is outside our control?' His own analysis is founded on four universals of the human condition, those of disequilibrium, radical uncertainty, cooperation (prisoners' dilemma) and trust – that might, as opposed to being specific to the second millennium's financial system, equally be applied to war through to marital breakdown!
10. As Executive Director for Financial Stability at the Bank of England. See also Haldane (2009, 2010) and Cornford (2012).
11. This is implicit in his use of metaphors to paint his picture, not only dogs catching frisbees but also sudoku, SARS, and so on (Haldane 2012). See also Davies and McGoey (2012).
12. See Davies and McGoey (2012).
13. For financialisation and the Polanyian pendulum, or not, in the context of financialisation, see Watson (2009) and Konings (2009).
14. For the Bischoff and Wigley Reports, respectively.
15. But see Binderkrantz *et al.* (2015), who emphasise the increasing coincidence of power across government, media and bureaucracy.

Disclosure statement

No potential conflict of interest was reported by the author.

Funding

This study was supported by the project Financialization, Economy, Society and Sustainable Development (FESSUD), which is funded by the European Union under Framework Programme 7 (contract number 266800).

References

Bayliss, K., Fine, B. and Robertson, M. (2013), *From Financialisation to Consumption: The Systems of Provision Approach Applied to Housing and Water*, FESSUD, Working Paper Series, No. 02, Available from: http://fessud.eu/wp-content/uploads/2013/04/FESSUD-Working-Paper-021.pdf [accessed 15 December 2015].

Bayliss, K., Fine, B. and Robertson, R. (2017), 'Introduction to Special Issue on the Material Cultures of Financialisation', *New Political Economy*. doi:10.1080/13563467.2017.1259304

Beggs, M., Bryan, D. and Rafferty, M. (2014), 'Shoplifters of the World Unite! Law and Culture in Financialized Times', *Cultural Studies*, 28 (5), pp. 976–96.

Binderkrantz, A., Christiansen, P. and Pedersen, H. (2015), 'Interest Group Access to the Bureaucracy, Parliament, and the Media', *Governance*, 28 (1), pp. 95–112.

Brassett, J., Rethel, L. and Watson, M. (2009), 'Introduction to the Political Economy of the Sub-prime Crisis in Britain: Constructing and Contesting Competence', *British Journal of Politics and International Relations*, 11 (3), pp. 377–81.

Christophers, B. (2013), *Banking Across Boundaries: Placing Finance in Capitalism* (Chichester: Wiley-Blackwell).

Cook, N., Smith, S. and Searle, B. (2009), 'Mortgage Markets and Cultures of Consumption', *Consumption, Markets and Culture*, 12 (2), pp. 133–54.

Cornford, A. (2012), 'Of Dogs, Frisbees and the Complexity of Capital Requirements'. Available from: http://www.networkideas.org/news/jan2013/pdf/Andrew_Cornford.pdf [accessed 15 December 2015].

CRESC. (2009), *An Alternative Report on UK Banking Reform, Jointly Authored by a Working Group of Practitioners and Academics Based at the ESRC Centre for Research on Socio Cultural Change, University of Manchester*. Available from: http://www.cresc.ac.uk/publications/documents/AlternativereportonbankingV2.pdf [accessed 15 December 2015].

Davies, W. and McGoey, L. (2012), 'Rationalities of Ignorance: On Financial Crisis and the Ambivalence of Neo-Liberal Epistemology', *Economy and Society*, 41 (1), pp. 64–83.

Dixon, A. and Ville-Pekka, S. (2009), 'Institutional Change and the Financialisation of Pensions in Europe', *Competition and Change*, 13 (4), pp. 347–67.

Dodd, N. (2016), *The Social Life of Money* (Princeton, NJ: Princeton University Press).

Dorn, N. (2012), 'Knowing Markets: Would Less Be More?' *Economy and Society*, 41 (3), pp. 316–34.

Engelen, E., *et al.* (2010), 'Reconceptualizing Financial Innovation: Frame, Conjuncture and Bricolage', *Economy and Society*, 39 (1), pp. 33–63.

Engelen, E., *et al.* (2012), 'Misrule of Experts?: The Financial Crisis as Elite Debacle', *Economy and Society*, 41 (3), pp. 360–82.

Erturk, I., *et al.* (eds) (2008), *Financialization at Work: Key Texts and Commentary* (London: Routledge).

Fine, B. (1993), 'Resolving the Diet Paradox', *Social Science Information*, 32 (4), pp. 669–87.

Fine, B. (1995), 'Towards a Political Economy of Anorexia?' *Appetite*, 24 (3), pp. 231–42.

Fine, B. (1998), *The Political Economy of Diet, Health and Food Policy* (London: Routledge).

Fine, B. (2002), *The World of Consumption: The Cultural and Material Revisited* (London: Routledge).

Fine, B. (2005), 'Addressing the Consumer', in F. Trentmann (ed.), *The Making of the Consumer: Knowledge, Power and Identity in the Modern World* (Oxford: Berg), pp. 291–311.

Fine, B. (2013), 'Consumption Matters', *Ephemera*, 13 (2), pp. 217–48. Available from: http://www.ephemerajournal.org/contribution/consumption-matters [accessed 15 December 2015].

Fine, B. (Forthcoming), 'From Performativity to the Material Culture of Legal Expertise?' *London Review of International Law*. doi:10.1093/lril/lrw009.

Fine, B. and Lapavitsas, C. (2000), 'Markets and Money in Social Theory: What Role for Economics?' *Economic and Society*, 29 (3), pp. 357–82.

Fine, B., et al. (2015), Thirteen Things You Need to Know about Neoliberalism, FESSUD, Working Paper Series, No. 155. Available from: http://fessud.eu/wp-content/uploads/2015/03/13-Things-you-need-to-know-about-Neoliberalism-working-paper155.pdf [accessed 30 September 2016].

Finlayson, A. (2009), 'Financialisation, Financial Literacy and Asset-based Welfare', British Journal of Politics and International Relations, 11 (3), pp. 400–21.

Fischler, C. (1980), 'Food Habits, Social Change, and the Nature/Culture Dilemma', Social Science Information, 19 (6), pp. 937–53.

Fischler, C. (1988), 'Food, Self, and Identity', Social Science Information, 27 (2), pp. 275–92.

Gabor, D. and Brooks, S. (2017), 'Financial Inclusion', New Political Economy. doi:10.1080/13563467.2017.1259298.

Haiven, M. (2014), Cultures of Financialization: Fictitious Capital in Popular Culture and Everyday Life (Basingstoke: Palgrave MacMillan).

Haldane, A. (2009), 'Rethinking the Financial Network', Presented at the Financial Student Association, 28 April. Available from: http://www.bankofengland.co.uk/publications/speeches/2009/speech386.pdf [accessed 15 December 2015].

Haldane, A. (2010), 'The $100 Billion Question', Presented at the Institute of Regulation and Risk, Hong Kong, 30 March. Available from: http://www.bis.org/review/r100406d.pdf [accessed 2 October 2016].

Haldane, A. (2012), 'The Dog and the Frisbee', Speech Given at the Federal Reserve Bank of Kansas City's 36th Economic Policy Symposium, 'The Changing Policy Landscape', Jackson Hole, Wyoming, 31 August. Available from: http://www.bankofengland.co.uk/publications/Documents/speeches/2012/speech596.pdf [accessed 15 December 2015].

Happer, C. (2017), 'Financialisation, Media and Social Change', New Political Economy. doi:10.1080/13563467.2017.1259301.

Haug, W. (1986), Critique of Commodity Aesthetics: Appearance, Sexuality and Advertising in Capitalist Society (London: Polity Press).

Isakson, S. (2014), 'Food and Finance: The Financial Transformation of Agro-food Supply Chains', The Journal of Peasant Studies, 41 (5), pp. 749–75.

Jessop, B. (2015), 'Neoliberalism, Finance-dominated Accumulation and Enduring Austerity: A Cultural Political Economy Perspective', in K. Farnsworth and K. Irving (eds), Social Policy in Times of Austerity: Towards a New International Political Economy of Welfare (Bristol: Policy Press), pp. 87–112.

Johal, S., Moran, M. and Williams, K. (2014), 'Power, Politics and the City of London After the Great Financial Crisis', Government and Opposition, 49 (3), pp. 400–25.

Karacimen, E. (2014), Dynamics Behind the Rise in Household Debt in Advanced Capitalist Countries: An Overview, FESSUD, Working Paper Series, No. 9. Available from: http://fessud.eu/wp-content/uploads/2013/04/Dynamics-behind-the-Rise-in-Household-Debt-FESSUD-Working-Paper-09-1.pdf [accessed 15 December 2015].

King, M. (2016), The End of Alchemy: Money, Banking and the Future of the Global Economy (London: Little Brown).

Konings, M. (2009), 'Rethinking Neoliberalism and the Subprime Crisis: Beyond the Re-regulation Agenda', Competition and Change, 13 (2), pp. 108–27.

Langley, P. (2007), 'Uncertain Subjects of Anglo-American Financialization', Cultural Critique, 65 (Fall), pp. 67–91.

Langley, P. (2008), The Everyday Life of Global Finance: Saving and Borrowing in Anglo-America (Oxford: Oxford University Press).

Lapavitsas, C. (2003), Social Foundations of Markets, Money and Credit (London: Routledge).

MacKenzie, D. (2008), An Engine, Not a Camera: How Financial Models Shape Markets (Cambridge: MIT Press).

Mellor, M. (2016), Debt or Democracy: Public Money for Sustainability and Social Justice (London: Pluto).

Montgomerie, J. and Williams, K. (2009), 'Financialised Capitalism: After the Crisis and Beyond Neoliberalism', Competition and Change, 13 (2), pp. 99–107.

Moran, M. and Payne, A. (2014), 'Introduction: Neglecting, Rediscovering and Thinking Again about Power in Finance', Government and Opposition, 49 (3), pp. 331–41.

Payne, C. (2012), The Consumer, Credit and Debt: Governing the Modern Economy (London: Routledge).

Robertson, M. (2017), '(De)constructing the Financialised Culture of Owner-occupation in the UK, with the Aid of the 10Cs', New Political Economy. doi:10.1080/13563467.2017.1259303.

Santos, A. (2017), 'Cultivating the Self-reliant and Responsible Individual: The Material Culture of Financial Literacy', New Political Economy. doi:10.1080/13563467.2017.1259302.

Santos, A. and Costa, V. (2013), Financial Literacy and Consumer Protection in the Midst of Financial Crisis: Underlying Presuppositions and Alternative Approaches, mimeo.

Svetlova, E. (2012), 'On the Performative Power of Financial Models', Economy and Society, 41 (3), pp. 418–34.

Thompson, G. (2010), 'The Global Regulatory Consequences of an Irrational Crisis: Examining "Animal Spirits" and "Excessive Exuberances"', Globalizations, 7 (1–2), pp. 87–103.

Watson, M. (2009), 'Headlong into the Polanyian Dilemma: The Impact of Middle-Class Moral Panic on the British Government's Response to the Sub-prime Crisis', British Journal of Politics and International Relations, 11 (3), pp. 422–37.

Zelizer, V. (1994), The Social Meaning of Money (New York: Basic Books).

Zelizer, V. (1996), 'Payments and Social Ties', Sociological Forum, 11 (3), pp. 481–95.

Zelizer, V. (1998), 'The Proliferation of Social Currencies', in M. Callon (ed.), The Laws of the Market (Oxford: Blackwell), pp. 58–68.

Zelizer, V. (2000), 'Fine-tuning the Zelizer View', Economy and Society, 29 (3), pp. 383–9.

Material cultures of water financialisation in England and Wales

Kate Bayliss

ABSTRACT
The ownership structure of the water and sewerage sector has changed substantially in England and Wales (EW) since the 10 companies were listed on the London Stock Exchange in 1989. The majority of firms are now delisted and a number of companies are now owned by financial investors via special purpose vehicles. In some cases, revenue streams from customer water bills have become securitised for decades into the future not only to raise funds for investment, but also for finance distributions to shareholders. The high financing costs associated with these highly leveraged corporate structures are passed on to customers. The regulator, Ofwat, tasked with protecting the interests of consumers, operates largely within a system of price controls intended to mimic a competitive market in the absence of financial speculation. This means that regulation steers away from intervening in the financialised corporate structures that have emerged around some of the water utilities. These manifestations of financialisation are considered to be 'market outcomes'. This paper explores the discourses and narratives that have developed in the provision of water in EW to create a situation where such rentier transfers are normalised. Using the systems of provision approach, the paper shows that the material culture of water finance has been constructed along narrow lines with superficial consumer consultation, while extensive financial engineering to increase shareholder returns continues unimpeded.

Introduction

This paper considers the material culture of financialisation in relation to the provision of water in England and Wales (EW). Since the industry was privatised, ownership stakes have changed hands and some water companies became owned by private equity investors. The sector has evolved considerably in the decades since privatisation. Some companies have become highly indebted and financial engineering has led to substantial returns generated from speculative activities, far removed from the production and distribution of water. Yet this is unchallenged and even normalised through the narrative of efficiency, investment and market outcomes. This paper considers the structures and cultures that underpin this normalisation. It draws heavily on a case study conducted for the European Union-funded Financialization, Economy, Society and Sustainable Development (FESSUD) research programme (see Bayliss 2014 for more details).

Households mostly know little about the heavily financialised structure that lies behind their water consumption. For the vast majority of water consumers in EW, little appears to have changed in the way they consume water since privatisation, by the turn of a tap. While some may now have their consumption metered, many private water companies still have the same name as their public sector predecessors. This superficial continuity conceals substantial changes in the underlying social and economic relations of the sector. Largely, consumers are unaware that they are making significant payments to global financialised capital via their water bills.

This paper draws on the Systems of Provision (SoP) approach to explore the way in which relations between agents in the production and consumption of water interact to promote specific outcomes (for more on the SoP approach, see Bayliss *et al.* 2013). Actors at different stages along the SoP engage in and experience financialisation[1] differently depending on their position in the chain of provision and even their physical location in the country, as there is considerable regional diversity in forms of water delivery. After a brief background review of some of the wider literature regarding water reforms in EW, the paper aims to highlight the ways in which financialisation has become embedded in the provision of water in EW, outlining the financial methods used to increase surplus extraction. Then, the paper explores the attitudes and cultures that are attached to this structure. This requires differentiating between the agents along the SoP. Private investors, the regulator and consumers all have evolved their own understandings and cultures so that financialisation is legitimised.

The paper shows that after more than 25 years of privatisation, the provision of water has fully entered circuits of global capital. Household water bills for decades into the future have, in some cases, become assets of private equity investors and have been repackaged and sold on via offshore jurisdictions. Yet there has been scarcely a murmur of protest from any quarter. This is in sharp contrast with other parts of the world where much weaker forms of privatisation (with a fixed-term concession contract rather than divestiture) have resulted in major protests. In conclusion, the paper considers how an understanding of the material culture of finance for water sheds light on this (lack of) response.

Background

The privatisation of water has been bluntly described as part of a general process of 'accumulation by dispossession', a new round of enclosures of the commons and expansion of primitive accumulation (Harvey 2004, Bakker 2005, Roberts 2008, Ahlers 2010). However, privatisation in practice occurs differently across locations. Water in EW was privatised in 1989 by floating regional water and sewerage companies on the London Stock Exchange (LSE). Prior to this, water sector reforms in EW in the 1970s and 1980s followed a pattern of neo-liberalisation (see Fine *et al.* (2015) for more on neo-liberalism) similar to that adopted across the world with water companies established at 'arm's length' from the government and price setting based on cost recovery principles (Bayliss 2013). However, the way in which privatisation was implemented in EW, with the complete divestiture of state companies, has not been adopted in any other country. In neighbouring Northern Ireland and Scotland, water has remained in public hands. Where privatisation was implemented elsewhere, this has typically followed the French 'affermage' model with the introduction of concession or lease contracts for the operation of the water infrastructure. Sometimes these are for long time periods but, ultimately, ownership of the infrastructure remains with the state. In EW, privatisation by divestiture was intended to be irreversible and to create a class of share-owning investors. Water was one of a number of industries privatised in this way in the UK in the 1980s (Parker 2004). This mode of privatisation has been fundamental to the financialisation that has followed.

Water privatisation was associated with a change in the ethos of water management in common with the expansion of neo-liberalism more widely. Bakker (2005) charts the transition in the provision of water in EW from a post-war, 'state hydraulic' model, where policy emphasis was on the supply led development of water infrastructure with largely state ownership of resources, to 'market environmentalism' where economic efficiency is prized over access or equity. Swyngedouw (2005: 98) describes water privatisation as 'a process through which nature's goods become integrated into global circuits of capital' and privatisation is increasingly linked with financialisation. For example, Leyshon and Thrift (2007) refer specifically to the need for finance to ultimately drill down to real sector activity. Leyshon and Thrift (2007: 98) argue that the 'bedrock' of financial capitalism is 'dependent on the constant searching out or the construction of new asset streams'. Such a predictable stream can be securitised and this allows borrowers to effectively realise their income streams 'early'. They use the example of UK Private Finance Initiatives but, as this paper shows, it equally applies to the water sector. Allen and Pryke (2013) take up the theme of securitisation in their research into Thames Water. They describe a process of financialisation of water where 'households themselves are the financial asset' (2013: 419). Such 'commoditisation' of both people and nature under capitalism increasingly shapes social relationships (LeBaron 2010).[2]

Ekers and Loftus (2008: 706) consider the politics of urban water provision through the lens of Gramsci and Foucault to show how, from a Gramscian perspective, water infrastructure can be considered part of the hegemonic apparatus through which forms of 'common sense' in support of a specific group's interests come to be constituted. Meanwhile, from a Foucauldian approach, 'this entails managing the conduct of people and their relations with the material world, customs, beliefs and ways of acting and thinking'. They posit that everyday relations with water contribute to the maintenance of hegemony and the continuance of subtle forms of rule. Thus, water financialisation can be considered to be part of a wider project of social control.

More specifically, Allen and Pryke assess the model of 'household securitisation' where household water bills become a financial asset of the company through policies such as those adopted by Thames Water. In attempting to understand why this is tolerated, they conclude that this model of financialised household water

> appears to be the subject of a political 'ring-fence' where the regulatory body brokers agreement with investors over domestic water prices, service quality, water efficiency and the like, yet leave untouched the politics of packaging and selling households as a captive revenue stream. (Allen and Pryke 2013: 420)

They stop short, however, of trying to understand why the securitisation of water seems to be off limits for the regulator. This paper attempts to expand on some of these themes using the lens of the material culture of financialisation, and the 10Cs (see Introduction and Fine, this issue) to investigate the processes which have shaped the current system of provision and the cultures that sustain it.

Financialisation in practice

Concern is restricted, though, to the 10 regional companies that provide water and sewerage services across EW.[3] Since the initial privatisation in 1989, the ownership structure has shifted considerably. Only three companies remain listed on the LSE. Owners of these listed companies are mostly institutional investors. For example, more than 95 per cent of Severn Trent shares are owned by financial institutions including insurance companies, nominee companies, banks, pension funds, other corporate bodies, and limited and public companies.[4] Some of the largest investors have a stake in more than one utility (such as investment fund manager Blackrock Inc. which has a stake in Severn Trent and United Utilities).

Of the other seven water companies, one (Welsh Water) is owned by a not-for-profit company, two (Wessex Water and Northumbrian Water) are owned by large Asian conglomerates and four are owned by special purpose vehicles put together by financial investors and, in most cases, listed offshore. Details of the ownership of these companies are provided below:

- **Yorkshire Water**'s ultimate parent company is Kelda Holdings Ltd registered in Jersey and owned by Deutsche Asset & Wealth Management, Corsair Capital (described on the Kelda website as 'a capital custodian for investors in infrastructure companies'), GIC Special Investments, the private equity arm of the Government of Singapore Investment Corporation and M&G Infracapital Investments (part of Prudential Plc);[5]

- **Anglian Water**'s parent company is Anglian Water Group Ltd, registered in Jersey and owned by Colonial First State Global Asset Management (part of Commonwealth Bank of Australia), the Canadian Pension Plan Investment Board, Industry Funds Management (a global asset manager owned by 30 Australian pension funds specialising in infrastructure, private equity, debt investment and listed equity) and 3i (an international investor focusing on private equity, infrastructure and debt management);[6]
- **Thames Water**'s ultimate parent is Kemble Water Holdings Ltd owned by a consortium led by Macquarie European Infrastructure Fund II LP (MEIF2) owned by Australian Macquarie Group, with other stakeholders including Australian and Dutch pension funds, the Abu Dhabi Investment Authority, CIC the Chinese sovereign wealth fund and the BT Pension Scheme;[7]
- **Southern Water** was bought from the Royal Bank of Scotland (RBS) in 2007 by a consortium known as Greensands Holdings Ltd registered in Jersey with owners including IIF International SW UK Investments Limited (advised by JP Morgan Investments Inc.), the Northern Trust Company (Australian asset management firm), Phildrew Nominees (a subsidiary of UBS Global Asset Management), Sumaya Investments Ltd and various others including a Superannuation Fund from Papua New Guinea.[8]

Since privatisation, the sector has seen a marked increase in indebtedness of water companies. The level of gearing (the ratio of debt to equity) has increased substantially, although this has been more pronounced in some companies than others. The different company ownership structures have been associated with equally diverse financial practices. Typically, the delisting of a company from the LSE is associated with a reduction in public scrutiny of the operations of the firm, as the value of the share price gives an indication of how the market values different companies. But the delisted companies owned by infrastructure conglomerates (Wessex and Northumbrian Water) appear to have more in common, in terms of corporate structures, with the companies that remain listed on the LSE than with the delisted companies owned by financial investors.

A detailed review of the structure of the corporate groups, within which the regulated water utility is situated, indicates that the companies owned by infrastructure conglomerates and those listed on the LSE are associated with a 'flatter' group structure with just one or two intermediaries between the regulated company and the ultimate registered parent. The finance-owned companies, by contrast, have a long ladder of companies between the regulated water provider and the ultimate parent company. Most of these rungs in the ladder do little apart from receiving and paying out interest and dividends to other companies in the group. Figure 1 shows an abbreviated diagram of the flow of such funds associated with Thames Water. Dividends and interest paid by the regulated utility on intergroup loans flow up the corporate chain before reaching the ultimate shareholders. The reality is more complicated than shown here. Research published in 2014 revealed nine companies between the regulated utility and the ultimate parent, Kemble Water Holdings Ltd, as opposed to the four in this diagram (Bayliss 2014).

A similar pattern can be observed in the corporate group structures of the other financially owned companies (Anglian, Yorkshire and Southern Water). Another common feature of these four companies is that they have all carried out a process known as Whole Business Securitisation (WBS). This is a complex financial operation whereby finance is raised on the basis of future cash flows, the revenue stream from the payment of water bills in this case. These are packaged into a tradable financial asset and sold to investors. WBS requires certain covenants to be put in place to protect investors such as ring-fencing of the business segment that relates to the revenue stream. With these established, the creditworthiness of the firm is enhanced and they are able to increase their gearing levels while maintaining their credit rating. WBS is only possible where there is an extremely stable revenue stream, for which the EW water companies are ideal.

Ironically, WBS was first used in the water sector to enable the not-for-profit Glas Cymru to take over Welsh Water, using debt to finance the acquisition in 2001. An additional part of this transaction required that a subsidiary group company be set up in the Cayman Islands in order to overcome the

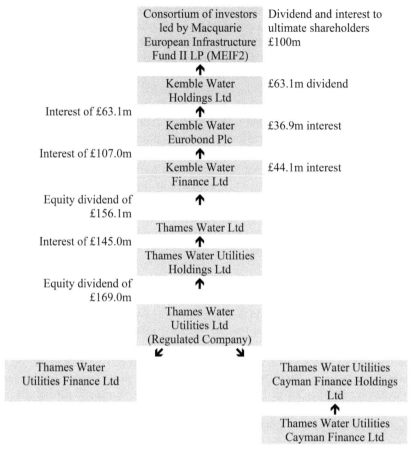

Figure 1. Thames Water Utilities Ltd group structure and flow of funds. Source: Thames Water Utilities Ltd Annual Report (2015: 33).

restrictions of UK corporate law regarding the raising of debt to facilitate an acquisition. This model was then followed by Anglian, Thames, Southern and Yorkshire Water. Using WBS and with a Cayman Island group company, these investors were able to buy water companies in large part using debt finance, which was then added to the debts of the company (rather than staying with the investors). Since then, Welsh Water has paid off a considerable portion of its debt. Meanwhile, the finance-owned companies are now the ones with the highest gearing levels and the lowest credit ratings of the sector, although they are still a couple of notches above investment grade (Table 1), so they stay within the bounds of regulatory requirements on this criterion.

Table 1. Credit ratings and gearing levels for WaSCs.

Credit rating[a]	Outlook	Company	GEARING – Net debt/RAV
A3	Stable	Dwr Cymru (Welsh Water)	61.7
A3	Stable	United Utilities Water Plc	62.7
A3	Stable	Severn Trent Water Ltd	66.7
A3	Stable	Wessex Water	68.1
Baa1	Stable	Northumbrian Water Ltd	70.4
Baa1	Stable	Thames Water Utilities Ltd	79.0
Baa1	Stable	Anglian Water Services	80.4
Baa1	Stable	Yorkshire Water Services Ltd	82.6
Baa2	Negative	Southern Water Services Ltd	81.3

Source: Moody's (2013).
[a]Based on corporate family and not class of debt. WaSCs, water and sewerage companies.

The consolidation of acquisition debt is one reason for the increase in water company debts. Another reason is that these firms have also raised loans in order to pay dividends. Bayliss (2014) provides a detailed account of the transactions for Anglian, Yorkshire, Thames and Southern Water which have all increased gearing and delivered associated special dividends as a payout to shareholders, this often coinciding with the initial takeover. It is a theme that has been raised in several accounts of the sector, although often only in passing (such as PWC (2013: 15); RiskMetrics (2008: 7); Allen and Pryke (2013: 426) and Turner (2013)).

Finally, another reason to increase debt is that interest is tax deductible (while dividends are not), so companies have an incentive to finance investment with borrowing rather than equity. These companies pay little tax due in part to their high interest payments, and the amount they pay in interest has soared since privatisation. This incentive is enhanced further where the loans are from shareholders at high rates of interest. The 2013 (81) accounts of the ultimate parent of Southern Water, Greensands Holdings Ltd, show interest of £67.9 million payable to the shareholders on loans of £633.9 million. The 2013 accounts of Thames Water Utility Ltd (the regulated company) show that interest was paid to shareholders of £17.5 million (TWUL Annual Report 2013: 75). In part, then the debts incurred are a means to provide further distributions to shareholders through (tax-deductible) interest payments.

The above considerations demonstrate then that there is a heavily financialised structure to the production in some areas of water provision, but that this varies across investor types. For consumers, though, the experience of financialisation is largely unseen. Few of the 15 million Thames Water customers, for example, will have any idea that paying their water bill connects them to one of the largest Australian investment banks via a portfolio of European infrastructure funds. They are, however, beholden to these investors. Average household bills have increased by 40 per cent in real terms since privatisation (NAO 2013). Over the 2010–15 price review period, nearly 27 per cent of the average customer bill of £360 was paid for 'return on capital' (Ofwat 2011a: 8, 2011b: 9). This is just to cover financing costs of interest and dividends and not actual investment. The water SoP generates a substantial transfer of revenue from households.

Material cultures of water financialisation

The privatisation and financialisation of water create a shift in the relations of economic and social reproduction. The transitions are experienced differently by the agents in the SoP. This section explores the way in which the ethos of financialisation is incorporated into the cultures of the stakeholders in the SoP. In so doing, the paper makes selective use of the 10Cs set out in the Introduction to this volume in framing the material culture of water financialisation.

The discussion shows that the agents in the SoP have *Contested* priorities in the operation of the water sector. For investors, the provision of water is seen in terms of a source of profit. For consumers, water is an essential service and an item of household expenditure. While the consumer has an interest in an efficient and effective water supply, when it comes to pricing, the interests of these agents diverge. The regulator is supposedly tasked with mediating between these agents, but the interests of investors would appear to be prioritised. This is justified on the grounds that what is good for investors is good for consumers. For example, according to Ofwat (2008: 1): 'A regulatory system that gives incentives to companies to be efficient, and to make profits, is in the best long-term interests of customers'. Thus, the regulatory discourse is *Construed* so that the interests of consumers are merged with those of investors and the conflicts between agents overlooked.

Water companies

Water in EW is an attractive investment with an almost guaranteed revenue stream and a sympathetic regulator. In part this stems from the material culture of water which is vital for life and is an important input into other production processes. It often has no substitutes; provision is capital-intensive and largely monopolistic due to the high sunk investment costs. Furthermore, it is not a sector of rapid technological progress. Once a water system is established, it can generate regular long-term financial inflows over a period of decades.

However, in many countries, water privatisation has not been widespread. Opposition to water privatisation usually stems from the strategic nature of water and its importance for social repro-duction. In developing countries, privatisation efforts have been disappointing with firms reluc-tant to invest, in part because of fears of the contract being cancelled due to political pressure. There are no such concerns in EW. The culture of water privatisation is long-established and is replicated across other sectors such as energy and transport. The UK is planning to attract more infrastructural investment from the private sector in the coming decades; so it is important that this is seen as an attractive destination for investment finance. This strengthens the position of water company investors as many also have stakes in other areas of infrastructure, whether in the UK or globally. This unique *Context* has proved to be a fertile breeding ground for financialisation.

For private equity investors, water companies offer particularly profitable opportunities. Such buyers have a reputation for buying up firms and turning them around to make a quick profit using debt rather than equity investment as far as possible (for example, Cooper 2015). The 'sweating' of assets and raising debts to pay a special dividend to shareholders are common practice for such investors, and the same goes for adding acquisition debt to the company (Shaxson 2013).[9] This was the approach adopted in the water sector and has led to considerable returns for investors. The finan-cial gains are not always obvious. As mentioned above, shareholders received substantial 'special dividends' during the acquisition process, but distributions are also realised through shareholder loans to the companies and with profits made on the sale of ownership stakes. Macquarie, for example, has sold off small parts of its stake in Thames Water for 'undisclosed sums'. These share-holder returns are not easily traced in standard financial reports. The high profits that can be earned from water investments are revealed in the high price that investors are willing to pay to acquire stakes in the companies, over and above the regulated asset value (RAV). Southern, Thames and Anglian Water were sold in the 2000s for 20–25 per cent over RAV, while Yorkshire Water fetched a 34 per cent premium (Utility Week 2009). In 2013, Severn Trent rejected a bid esti-mated to be a 27.8 per cent premium on the RAV (Bloomberg Business News 2013). For shareholders of listed water companies, such a takeover offers considerable financial rewards. The listed water utility United Utilities saw its share price 'leap' in September 2015 when a broker indicated that it was an attractive acquisition target for a pension or infrastructure fund (Telegraph 2015). For these firms, then, EW water companies are profitable investments and regulation presents obstacles that at most need to be worked around. As Hildyard (2012) points out, for investors, the term infrastruc-ture means a revenue stream rather than bricks and mortar.

The regulator: Ofwat

The Water Services Regulation Authority, Ofwat, was established at the time of privatisation. The primary tasks of Ofwat are designated to be to protect the interests of consumers, to make sure that water and sewerage companies carry out their functions observing the terms of their licence and to secure that the companies are able to finance their operations (known as 'financeability').[10] The main regulatory tool is price-cap regulation, devised in the 1980s and originally applied to the privatised telecoms and electricity industries. Prices are set in advance for a five-year period. Cur-rently, the 2015–20 regulatory period has just started with prices that were set in the 2014 price review process (PR14). Prices for 2010–15 were set in the 2009 Price Review process (PR09). The maximum price that each company can charge is multiplied each year by a factor, known as K, as well as the increase in the retail price index (water prices are inflation-proof).

Price-cap regulation is supposed to encourage and harness efficiency in a way that other regulat-ory methods, such as rate-of-return regulation, do not. The idea is that where the price is fixed for a five-year period, companies have an incentive to increase productivity as they can retain the additional profits generated. At the end of the five years, the regulator incorporates productivity improvements into the next price-setting process so the gains are subsequently shared with customers. Rate-of-return regulation in contrast is considered to stifle innovation and productivity gains and instead incentivises firms to increase their costs with profits following in proportion.

The framing of the regulatory framework is in terms of intervening to weaken the scope for monopolistic exploitative practices. For example, Ofwat is required to promote effective competition wherever appropriate to protect consumer interests. The regulatory tools are intended to act as market forces might ideally perceived to do. By fixing prices in advance, water companies are supposed to be forced to act as price takers as they would be in an imaginary competitive market. Similarly, price controls are affected by firm performance against targets for meeting customer service standards. Where these are not met, firms see a reduction in the price they are allowed to charge. This is supposed to reflect the loss in revenue that would occur if customers were able to use an alternative source of supply.

However, this regulatory framework in practice involves mediating between agents with competing interests and contradictory objectives. Any solution has winners and losers, and regulation is not neutral. The competing interests in the sector come out in the contestation over the value of K, the factor by which prices can be adjusted. A small change in the value of K can have a significant effect on water prices and a large impact on company revenue. The calculation of K is highly complex and involves assumptions about future financing needs and costs as well as past performance against targets. The 2009 price review (where prices were set for 2010–15) took place in the wake of the financial crisis, and there were concerns that financing costs would rise significantly. This is fed into the setting of K. In practice, however, interest rates have remained extremely low and firms have benefitted from prices based on an assumed cost of capital that was higher than actual. In fact, the past 3 price reviews (covering a 15-year period) have been generous to water companies. The cost of debt has consistently been below that assumed in the price reviews by Ofwat (2013a), although the latest review (PR14), which set the prices from 2015 to 2020, looks set to lower prices slightly.

The role of Ofwat is presented as an external enforcer of rules, but in practice the regulatory structure itself affects the ability of firms to meet the regulatory requirements, so the relationship is not so simple. For example, Ofwat has a responsibility to ensure financeability, which means that prices need to be set at a level at which firms can still raise sufficient funds to finance investment. Firms also have a requirement to maintain a credit rating that is 'investment grade' as determined by external credit rating agencies (Standard and Poors, Moody's and Fitch). But if firms increase their debts, this puts downward pressure on their credit ratings. Does the regulator then have to allow price increases to protect credit ratings? The boundaries of responsibility are blurred and complicated further because the regulatory framework itself has a major impact on the perceived creditworthiness of the water companies. The ability of firms to repay debts built on securitised water bills requires a highly predictable regulatory framework. The credit rating agency Moody's raised concerns in the build-up to PR14 that cuts in allowed returns for water companies would be 'credit negative' and the highly geared water companies (Anglian, Thames, Yorkshire and Southern Water) were the most vulnerable.[11] The regulator is not external to the credit rating process and there are suggestions that the high debts of some companies offer protection against tighter regulation. According to Bloomberg Businessweek: 'The debt mountain at UK water companies is their best defence against politicians seeking to cut the cost of living' (Bloomberg News 2013). Research by OXERA, cited in Turner (2013: 48), also indicates that 'a significant number of investors believed that if companies took on more debt the regulator would be less likely to take action against them as action would be more likely to lead to the company experiencing financial difficulty'. There is a sense in which such water companies have become too indebted to be properly regulated!

The interplay of these complex relations then has a bearing on the outcomes of regulation which is far from a simple mechanical exercise of allowing for costs, incentivising innovation and sharing its benefits. Indeed, the regulator is effectively caught in a trap of allowing for financialised rewards to its companies or having the industry face increased financial costs with corresponding implications for subsequent pricing (with rewards going to lenders instead).

The mandate of the regulator to protect the interests of consumers and ensure financeability for companies is, however, conveniently broad and unspecific. In practice, the regulator intervenes selectively in some areas and steps back completely in others. One example of such selective intervention is the Revenue Correction Mechanism (RCM). The RCM highlights some of the contradictions emerging from attempting to force the provision of water into a 'market' structure. Across the sector, there is a policy to increase the proportion of consumers that access water with a meter. This is intended to reduce water consumption, particularly in parts of the country that are water stressed (Ofwat 2013b). But where company revenue is earned on units sold, such a reduction leads to a fall in turnover and profits. In EW, this is overcome by the RCM. Under this policy, the price of water is adjusted in a price review period to account for over- or underconsumption in the previous period. If consumption falls, the price is increased in the next period. This is designed to overcome the disincentive that firms face to encourage households to reduce their water consumption.

This is, unsurprisingly, not made obvious to consumers, who are advised on how to keep their bills down. The Consumer Council for Water (CCW) provides guidance on how to cut water bills by being water efficient. Advice includes installing a 'save-a-flush' device in the toilet cistern; taking a shower instead of a bath; avoiding overfilling the bath and turning off the tap when brushing teeth (CCW 2013). But consumer advice should come with the caveat that while your bill may fall in the current price review period, it will be increased in the next period so that water companies are not out of pocket.

While this seems to be a clear regulatory intervention to protect investors, the regulator opts elsewhere not to intervene, for example, in the capital structures of highly leveraged firms. The very high debts of securitised water companies are potentially vulnerable to shocks and a threat to sustainability as there is no space to increase borrowing if necessary, quite apart from the interest costs to end users. Given that Ofwat is charged with protecting the interest of consumers, it is difficult to see any way in which this rent extraction by private equity firms is of any benefit to consumers.

But Ofwat (2011b) does not want to intervene to prevent these 'market-led structures'. In a speech by the Chairman of Ofwat, Jonson Cox, it was stated: 'The regulator has previously taken the view that the capital structure of the companies (and consequent risks) is for the boards and shareholders to determine'. And this view continues as long as the water utility is not put at risk (Ofwat 2013a: 9). On the contrary, rather than being alarmed by the rapid increase in gearing, this is seen as evidence of the strength of the regulatory regime, demonstrating a high level of confidence in the sector: 'Stakeholders have acknowledged this stable and transparent regulatory framework as a factor that has allowed the companies to sustain a relatively high level of gearing, but still maintain investment grade credit ratings' (Ofwat 2011b: 37).

Essentially, the regulator is permissive when it comes to financialisation. As long as the regulated utility meets its targets, what happens to financial structures is considered irrelevant. However, this amounts to tacit support for financialisation. Ofwat's position here is driven in part by a cultural attachment to incentive-based regulation, even though, as shown above, the incentive created has been to increase profit via financial rather than productive innovation. But, second, Ofwat is not, and does not see itself, in a position to regulate these financial dealings. It is challenging enough monitoring the activities of the water utilities. Attempting to control the machinations of global private equity is beyond its scope and ambition. As Ofwat (2011b: 38) states, it is not designed to assess future financial failure as if a credit rating agency itself. Finally, the culture of financialisation is greatly strengthened by the 'revolving door' between the industry and regulator. The Chairman of Ofwat, Jonson Cox, was awarded a payout of almost £10 million when he left Anglian Water in 2010 in recognition of the increase in shareholder value during his time at the company (see, for example, Daily Express 2010). Cox was Chief Executive at the company when Anglian was taken over by private equity investors in 2006 when a special dividend of £215 million was paid to shareholders and gearing increased to 83 per cent.[12] Cox is, therefore, unlikely to challenge other firms operating in the same manner, unless he were to become a poacher turned gamekeeper.

Financialised consumption and consumers

The privatisation of water is associated with a shift in relations of social reproduction. For Bakker (2005: 548), 'consumer access is legitimated not by a citizen's entitlement to water as a service but by a customer's purchase of water as a quasicommodity. A reconfiguration of the hydrosocial contract between users and their environment is required'. However, most consumers have very little involvement in the industry beyond paying their bill, and water providers are largely invisible. A study on consumer attitudes to water, based on a series of workshops with water customers, found that most respondents had no idea who owned their water company (and many thought the owners were French). The corporate structure was largely unknown, not a high priority for respondents and was not felt to impact on perceptions of value for money (Creative Research 2013).

Consumers are in no position to understand the financial practices taking place in the sector or their role in paying for this. The information is difficult to find and is obscured by a greater emphasis on superficial forms of customer engagement. For example, in extensive customer surveys conducted by the Regulator and the consumer body, the CCW,[13] customers are asked questions such as how satisfied they are with their water. This generates findings, for example, that 75 per cent of customers are satisfied with value for money. Where customers feel that the water price they pay is unfair, this is mainly because it is perceived as 'expensive' or has risen. But customers are lacking information on which to base their views as they cannot know the costs on which their bill is based, and they are in no position to determine if the price they pay is fair. Such opinions are more likely to be derived from media campaigns and public relations efforts of companies, or simply that the tap works at relatively low cost compared to other necessities.

The issues of finance are out of reach for most consumers, instead being collectively organised by a tight (Closed) group of agents including the water companies, the regulator and financial advisors. While the CCW has achieved some success in navigating the complexities of finance on behalf of consumers, for example in providing input into consultations on the weighted average cost of capital in PR14 (ECA 2014), consumers are not invited to engage in debates on capital structures or securitisation or directors' remuneration. Consumer Challenge Groups (CCGs), established by water companies to approve company business plans for 2015–20, were not equipped to engage in any discussion on corporate finances. The CCG for Southern Water, when asked to comment on whether or not the shareholders are making returns which are fair, responded that they were not in a position to judge: 'the CCG is not the best body to answer this question' (SWCCG 2013: 24).

The result then has been a highly successful narrowing of Contestation to a manageable set of issues for companies. The glossy presentation gives the appearance of a customer focus with firms responding to customer needs. Water is increasingly Commodified and packaged as a consumer good. For example, in a survey for CCW, households are asked how likely they would be to recommend their water provider to friends and family in order to calculate what is termed a 'Net Promoter Score' (NPS). The overall NPS for water is 23. This is compared with results for Apple (69), First Direct (61), Sky (14), Churchill Insurance Company (−8) and the RBS (−19) (CCW 2015). Thus, water is reinvented as a consumer good with customers a little less happy with their water than they are with their technology provider, but happier than they are with the scandalised bank, RBS. This survey information is gathered, analysed and presented even though there is no choice of water provider. But this kind of consultation has contributed to the cultural Construal of water as a Commodity like any other and the consumer as a customer.

There are, however, some increasing concerns about affordability, with the proportion of households spending more than 5 per cent of their disposable income on water bills increasing from 8 per cent in 2002/03 to 12 per cent in 2011/12 (NAO 2013), amounting to about 2.7 million households. Those that have trouble paying for water are, on the whole, the poorest and there is a statistically significant relationship between debt and deprivation (Ofwat 2011g:28). Analysis by the debt charity StepChange (2014) found that water bill arrears were higher for female clients, for households with children and especially for lone parents. For the water companies and the Regulator, however, indebtedness is seen purely in business terms. Bad debts now add £15 to the average bill. There is some means-tested support for those that have problems paying. Water companies are now able to introduce 'social policies' in water pricing, but this is subject to narrow provisos, including that the cost of social provision must not be more than the revenue saved from the introduction of such measures.

Although it is known that those who fail to pay their bills are on the whole the most deprived, non-payment is depicted to some degree as profligate, as for example in the title of the Ofwat web page, 'A drain on society – what can be done about water debt?'[14] The angle taken by Ofwat is that:

> Consumer debt makes it more difficult and expensive for companies to finance investment in services. It also means that customers who pay their bills promptly are effectively subsidising those who do not. This raises difficult issues about fairness, particularly for those on low incomes who do manage to pay their bills.

Paying for water has become tinged with moral responsibility, with non-payment of bills *Construed* as depriving the sector of investment and exploiting hard-working households – as opposed to under-pinning bloated returns to globally organised investment funds.

Consumers are crucial (if passive) agents in the financialisation of water. It is their regular payment of bills on which the whole architecture of securitisation rests. They are now financing significant payments to the financial sector in the payment of their water bills. The average water bill was £396 in 2014/15 (Ofwat 2014). Out of this, interest and dividend payments are around £100 a year per household.[15] With 23 million households (ONS 2011) in EW, that amounts to over £2 billion each year transferred from households to pay for returns on debt and equity for water companies (excluding non-household consumers). This is what feeds the global circuits of capital referred to by Swyngedouw (2005) and where speculative activity is anchored in real activity as outlined by Leyshon and Thrift (2007), attaching households to private financiers around the world. Yet consumers have no awareness of this. They are unwitting agents in the processes of financialisation. That consumers pay higher bills that provide revenue to finance securitisation and financialisation is not unique to water. However, the previous discussion shows that the sector is dominated by a culture of 'market outcomes' which is structurally skewed against consumers both in their bills proximately funding the costs of financialisation and their lack of access to knowledges of such practices. The regulatory function is inherently compromised by the need to remain investor-friendly combined with the weight and complexity of financial activity within the sector which takes place at an unobserved distance from the bills that appear through the letter box.

Conclusion

Opposition to water privatisation has sometimes sparked riots, most notably in Bolivia. Protests and poor delivery around the world have led to a number of privatisation contracts being terminated and water being renationalised (Kishimoto *et al.* 2014). In contrast, the lack of dissent around the financialisation of water in EW is striking. This paper has attempted to provide some insights into the cultures and structures that have allowed and even encouraged this feature of EW's water financialisation.

The *Context* has been significant. The way in which water was privatised, and the culture of privatisation across many sectors of the economy, has facilitated financialisation. In addition, the private water industry is long-established in EW. Hence, investors have been able to rely on regulatory stability to boost securitisation revenues. The complexities of the sector are such that consumers have little option but to place faith in the regulator to protect their interests. In some respects, consumers appear to have benefitted from the privatised water SoP over the years, receiving a good quality, regular water supply. The 2014 price review will bring prices down by around five per cent (before inflation) over the next five years.

However, this obscures the complexities of the underlying financial activities, as discussed above. *Contestation* has been channelled along the lines of narrow, superficial consumer consultations, and regulation is skewed to address specific issues such as capital costs, leakage and customer services at the expense of others. In particular, the securitisation of household bills and the influence of the financial sector remain unquestioned. But even if Ofwat wanted to control the financial extraction of private equity firms, it is questionable if this would be possible, given the immense challenges that financial regulation raises in the wider economy.

The financialisation of water has also been noticeably absent from political debates. Some campaigners are supporting the renationalisation of the railways and energy companies, but most are silent when it comes to water. This could be due to the success of the water companies and Ofwat in emphasising the positives of privatisation in terms of the increases in investment and quality of water. According to Ofwat, water companies are currently investing around £80 million a week in maintaining and improving assets, and services and consumers have access to drinking water of excellent quality.[16] There are also political issues involved. Stakeholders in water companies have interests in other infrastructure investments. For example, the Chinese government has a stake in Thames Water and is being courted for further infrastructure investments in the UK, not least the new nuclear power stations at Hinkley Point and beyond.

An additional factor may be that the complexities of ownership are too challenging and costly to unravel. For example, in March 2014 the total debts of the Kemble Water Finance Group, which owns Thames Water, came to over £10.5 billion (next to an operating income for Thames Water of just £23.6 million in 2014) and incorporate numerous bond issues made by different group companies, some located in the Cayman Islands and some with a maturity date as far off as 2062.[17] In the current economic climate, there is unlikely to be any political appetite for devoting public funds to water renationalisation. This paper, then, shows the power of finance in shaping sector outcomes and that this is maintained by instilling cultures that normalise such practices. This hegemony is preserved with the consumer distanced from the financial operations of the sector and rent extraction treated as a 'market outcome' which can be interpreted as the new 'common sense', in the spirit of Ekers and Loftus (2008), discussed above.

To return to the theme of the 10Cs raised in the Introduction to this volume, and at various points, above, the material culture of water finance is *Constructed* around financialisation but *Construed* as if regulated market outcomes suffice with no grounds for these to be *Contested* despite private firms pushing for ways to extract surplus in the form interest and dividends. But decision-making around financing decisions is *Closed* with only token involvement of consumers, and water heavily *Commodified*, presented as a good like any other, and with the regulator seeking to ensure that consumers *Conform* to this new form of water culture. Payment for water is *Construed* as a moral obligation, with non-payment depicted as depriving the sector of investment finance and exploitative of the obedient customers who pay their bills. The *Context* is significant with no other country operating their water in this way. Finally, water pricing is presented as a technical exercise, but there are underlying *Contradictory* pressures that emerge from water conceived both as an essential commodity for all households and as a source of profit for financial investors. The setting of tariffs is not neutral, but results in specific distributional outcomes.

Notes

1. For a discussion on the meaning of the term 'financialisation', see Introduction and Fine, this issue.
2. See Introduction to this issue for a more detailed specification of these processes of commodification with reference to the distinction between this and commodity form and commodity calculation.
3. In addition, there are nine smaller water-only companies, five local companies providing either water or sewerage services or both, but these do not form part of the analysis of this paper.
4. http://www.severntrent.com/investors/shareholder-centre/shareholding-analysis.

5. http://www.keldagroup.com/about-us/our-investors.aspx.
6. http://www.awg.com/investors/.
7. http://www.thameswater.co.uk/about-us/7565.htm and Bayliss (2014).
8. Bayliss (2014).
9. Shaxson describes the darker side of private equity investment, using the example of a hypothetical shoe company to show how cost cutting or asset sweating can save the company money and this cost saving can be used to raise debt. Then the debt is used to pay the owners a 'special dividend' and firms use other means of financial engineering to direct the company cash flow to shareholders while minimizing equity investment: 'And here's the fun part: you haven't taken on that debt, it's the shoe company that's now saddled with it'.
10. This is an extreme simplification and for more on the role of Ofwat, see www.ofwat.gov.uk.
11. https://www.moodys.com/research/Moodys-Highly-leveraged-UK-Water-Sector-companies-most-exposed-to--PR_292728.
12. Anglian Water Services Limited Annual Report and Accounts (2007).
13. https://www.ofwat.gov.uk/regulating/aboutconsumers/sim.
14. Available at https://www.ofwat.gov.uk/publications/prs_web_1002baddebt [accessed 26 October 2015].
15. According to Ofwat (2011a: 8, 2011b: 9), about 26.8 per cent of the average customer bill is paid for 'return on capital'.
16. https://www.ofwat.gov.uk/industryoverview/today/achieve [accessed 22 October 2015].
17. Kemble Water Finance Limited Investors Report for year ended 31 March 2014.

Disclosure statement

No potential conflict of interest was reported by the author.

Funding

Research for this paper was supported by the project FESSUD, which is funded by the European Union under Seventh Framework Programme contract number 266800.

References

Ahlers, R. (2010), 'Fixing and Nixing: The Politics of Water Privatization', *Review of Radical Political Economics*, 42 (2), pp. 213–30.
Allen, J. and Pryke, M. (2013), 'Financialising Household Water: Thames Water, MEIF and 'Ring-fenced' Politics', *Cambridge Journal of Regions, Economy and Society*, 6 (3), pp. 419–39.
Bakker, K. (2005), 'Neoliberalizing Nature? Market Environmentalism in Water Supply in England and Wales', *Annals of the Association of American Geographers*, 95 (3), pp. 542–65.
Bayliss, K. (2013), 'The Financialisation of Water', *Review of Radical Political Economics*, 20 (10), pp. 1–16.
Bayliss, K. (2014), 'The Financialisation of Water in England and Wales', FESSUD Working Paper No. 52. Available from: http://fessud.eu/wp-content/uploads/2015/03/Case-study-the-financialisation-of-Water-in-England-and-Wales-Bayliss-working-paper-REVISED_annexes-working-paper-52.pdf [accessed 26 October 2015].
Bayliss, K., Fine, B. and Robertson, M. (2013), 'From Financialisation to Consumption: The Systems of Provision Approach Applied to Housing and Water', FESSUD Working Paper No. 2. Available from: http://fessud.eu/financialisation-consumption-systems-provision-approach-applied-housing-water-2/ [accessed 26 October 2015].
Bloomberg Business News. (2013), 'Severn Trent Rejects Sweetened Canadian, Kuwaiti Offer', 3 June. Available from: http://www.bloomberg.com/news/articles/2013-06-03/severn-trent-rejects-sweetened-bid-from-canada-and-kuwait-group [accessed 26 October 2015].
Bloomberg News. (2013), 'Debts Keep Water Firms Off-Limits for Politicians: UK Credit', 18 October. Available from: http://www.businessweek.com/news/2013-10-18/debts-keep-water-firms-off-limits-for-politicians-u-dot-k-dot-credit [accessed 26 October 2015].
CCW. (2013), 'How to Cut Your Water and Sewerage Bills by Being Water-efficient, Advice for Domestic Customers', Information from Consumer Council for Water, Birmingham. Available from: http://www.ccwater.org.uk/wp-

content/uploads/2013/12/How-to-cut-your-water-sewerage-bills-by-being-water-efficient.pdf [accessed 26 October 2015].

CCW. (2015), 'Water Matters: Household Customers Views on their Water and Sewerage Services 2014', Report prepared by DJS Research for the Consumer Council for Water, Birmingham.

Cooper, C. (2015), 'Accounting for the Fictitious: A Marxist Contribution to Understanding Accounting's Roles in the Financial Crisis', *Critical Perspectives on Accounting*, 30 (July), pp. 63–82.

Creative Research. (2013), 'Value for Money: A Report on Drivers of Satisfaction in the Water and Sewerage Industry', Report prepared for the Consumer Council for Water by Creative Research Ltd, London. Available from: http://www.ccwater.org.uk/wp-content/uploads/2013/12/Value-for-money-A-report-on-Drivers-of-Satisfaction-in-the-Water-and-Sewerage-Industry.pdf [accessed 26 October 2015].

Daily Express. (2010), 'Jonson Cox's £10m Payoff from Anglian Water', 15 November. Available from: http://www.express.co.uk/news/uk/211537/Jonson-Cox-s-10m-payoff-from-Anglian-Water [accessed 26 October 2015].

ECA. (2014), 'Recommendations for the Weighted Average Cost of Capital 2015–20', Report submitted to the Consumer Council for Water by Economic Consulting Associates. Available from: http://www.ccwater.org.uk/wp-content/uploads/2014/07/ECA-CCWater-Cost-of-Capital-summary-report.pdf [accessed 27 October 2015].

Ekers, M. and Loftus, A. (2008), 'The Power of Water: Developing Dialogues Between Foucault and Gramsci', *Environment and Planning D: Society and Space*, 26 (4), pp. 698–718.

Fine, B., *et al.* (2015), 'Thirteen Things You Need to Know about Neoliberalism', FESSUD, Working Paper Series, No 155, Available from http://fessud.eu/wp-content/uploads/2015/03/13-Things-you-need-to-know-about-Neoliberalism-working-paper155.pdf [accessed 30 September 2016].

Harvey, D. (2004), 'The 'New' Imperialism; Accumulation by Dispossession', *Socialist Register*, 40, pp. 63–87.

Hildyard, N. (2012), 'More than Bricks and Mortar Infrastructure as Asset Class: A Critical Look at Private Equity Infrastructure Funds', Report for The Corner House. Available from: http://www.thecornerhouse.org.uk/resource/more-bricks-and-mortar [accessed 26 October 2015].

Kishimoto, S., Lobina, E. and Petitjean, O. (2014), 'Remunicipalisation as a Global Trend', Report by Transnational Institute, PSIRU and Multinationals Observatory. Available from: https://www.tni.org/files/download/heretostay-en.pdf [accessed 26 October 2015].

LeBaron, G. (2010), 'The Political Economy of the Household: Neoliberal Restructuring, Enclosures and Daily Life', *Review of International Political Economy*, 17 (5), pp. 889–912.

Leyshon, A. and Thrift, N. (2007), 'The Capitalization of Almost Everything: The Future of Finance and Capitalism', *Theory, Culture and Society*, 24 (7–8), pp. 97–115.

Moody's. (2013), 'UK Water Sector: Stable Outlook for Sector but Individual Companies Will Face Challenges', Industry Outlook, Moody's Investors Service, London.

NAO. (2013), *Infrastructure Investment: The Impact on Consumer Bill* (London: National Audit Office), Report by the Comptroller and Auditor General.

Ofwat. (2008), *Water Charges and Company Profits: Position Paper* (Birmingham: Ofwat). Available from: http://www.ofwat.gov.uk/consumerissues/chargesbills/pap_pos_watchrges20080604.pdf [accessed 26 October 2015].

Ofwat. (2011a), *Cost of Capital and Risk Mitigants – A Discussion Paper* (Birmingham: Ofwat). Available from: http://www.ofwat.gov.uk/future/monopolies/fpl/pap_tec1106cocrisk.pdf [accessed 26 October 2015].

Ofwat. (2011b), *Financeability and Financing the Asset Base – A Discussion Paper* (Birmingham: Ofwat). Available from: http://www.ofwat.gov.uk/future/monopolies/fpl/prs_inf1103fpl_financeability.pdf [accessed 26 October 2015].

Ofwat. (2011g:28), 'Affordability and Debt 2009–10: Current Evidence', Report by Ofwat, Birmingham.

Ofwat. (2013a), 'Observations on the Regulation of the Water Sector', Lecture by Jonson Cox. Ofwat Chair Royal Academy of Engineering, March. Available from: http://www.ofwat.gov.uk/mediacentre/speeches/prs_spe20130305jcrae.pdf [accessed 26 October 2015].

Ofwat. (2013b), 'Water Meters – Your Questions Answered: Information for Household Customers'. Available from: http://www.ofwat.gov.uk/mediacentre/leaflets/prs_lft_101117meters.pdf [accessed 26 October 2015].

Ofwat. (2014), Press Release, PN09/12, 12 December 2014. Available from: http://www.ofwat.gov.uk/mediacentre/pressnotices2008/prs_pn20141212finaldet [accessed 26 October 2015].

ONS. (2011), Office of National Statistics 2011 Census.

Parker, D. (2004), *The UK's Privatisation Experiment: The Passage of Time Permits a Sober Assessment* (Munich: Centre for Economic Studies), CESifo Working Paper No. 1126.

PWC. (2013), 'Cost of Capital for PR14: Methodological Considerations', Report for Ofwat. Available from: https://www.ofwat.gov.uk/pricereview/pr14/rpt_com201307pwccofc.pdf [accessed 26 October 2015].

RiskMetrics. (2008), 'Infrastructure Funds: Managing, Financing and Accounting – In Whose Interests?', Report by RiskMetrics Group. Available from: http://www.maynereport.com/images/2008/09/01-13GEDV97N00.pdf [accessed 26 October 2015].

Roberts, A. (2008), 'Privatizing Social Reproduction: The Primitive Accumulation of Water in an Era of Neoliberalism', *Antipode*, 40 (4), pp. 535–60.

Shaxson, N. (2013), 'The Zombies of Mayfair', *New Statesman Business Blog*, 4 July.

StepChange. (2014), *Statistics Yearbook: Personal Debt 2014* (London: StepChange Debt Charity). Available from: http://www.stepchange.org/Mediacentre/Researchandreports/PersonalDebtStatisticsYearbook2014.aspx [accessed 26 October 2015].

SWCCG. (2013), 'Southern Water Customer Challenge Group Report to Ofwat', *Worthing*.

Swyngedouw E. (2005), 'Dispossessing H_2O: The Contested Terrain of Water Privatization', *Capitalism Nature Socialism*, 16 (1), pp. 81–98.

Telegraph. (2015), 'Takeover Chatter Sends United Utilities Higher', *The Telegraph*, 7 September. Available from: http://www.telegraph.co.uk/finance/markets/ftse100/11848608/Takeover-chatter-sends-United-Utilities-higher.html [accessed 26 October 2015].

Turner, G. (2013), 'Money Down the Drain: Getting a Better Deal for Consumers from the Water Industry', *Report for Centre Forum*. Available from: http://www.centreforum.org/assets/pubs/money-down-the-drain.pdf [accessed 26 October 2015].

TWUL Annual Report. (2013), 'Annual Report and Financial Statements for Year Ended 31 March 2013', Thames Water Utilities Ltd.

TWUL Annual Report. (2015), 'Annual Report and Financial Statements 2014/15', Thames Water Utilities Ltd.

Utility Week. (2009), 'Ofwat Will Need the Wisdom of Solomon for PR09', *Utility Week*, 8 April.

(De)constructing the financialised culture of owner-occupation in the UK, with the aid of the 10Cs

Mary Robertson

ABSTRACT

Taking owner-occupation as the quintessential form of financialised housing provision, this paper investigates how housing cultures, understood as a set of shared behaviours and beliefs about housing, have been (re)shaped in the UK in a way that favours owner-occupation, and the implications of this shift for agents' subjectivities. Utilising the systems of provision/10Cs approach, which takes as its starting point that the norms and meanings associated with homeownership are complex and conditioned by the contradictory interaction of cultural and material factors, the paper shows how the rise of owner-occupation reflected changes in socially shared images and meanings around housing as well as material benefits associated with the tenure. However, the complex analysis of material culture facilitated by the 10Cs reveals that the culture of owner-occupation is not hegemonic. While housing policy since the 1980s has given material and cultural impetus to owner-occupation in Britain, the reflexive and resistive capacities of consumers, when coupled with the competing meanings attached to housing and the growing dysfunctionality of the current housing model, have constrained the dominance of the ethos of owner-occupation and render its future vulnerable.

1. Introduction

Whether through the elevation of real estate in international financial markets due to securitisation (Gotham 2009, Sassen 2009, Wainwright 2009) or through its wider role in emerging financialised growth and welfare regimes (Schwartz and Seabrooke 2008, Crouch 2009, Montgomerie and Büden-bender 2015), housing has been central to financialisation. At the macroeconomic level, the creation and trade in residential mortgage-backed securities have been at the core of financialised forms of capital accumulation. The wedding of such forms of accumulation to the US subprime mortgage market, culminating in the 2007–9 financial crisis, confirmed for many, 'the ineluctability of housing to any comprehensive account of contemporary political-economic dynamics and trans-formation' (Christophers 2013: 886). Underpinning these systemic transformations has been an inter-national restructuring of the ways in which housing is provided, accessed and consumed. Notwithstanding cross-country variation in forms and structures of provision, we are, as Robertson (2015) documents, witnessing an international convergence towards relying on owner-occupation, supported by mortgage borrowing, as the dominant, if far from exclusive, means of accessing housing. While national differences in economic, social and political context, as well as in pre-existing forms and conditions of housing, mean that the shift towards owner-occupation has emerged in different ways and to different degrees across countries, homeownership has increased in all developed countries except for Germany (Froud et al. 2010, European Mortgage Federation Hypostat 2011). Increased homeownership has served to expand household debt and asset ownership, advancing households' involvement in, and reliance upon, financial markets. More broadly, housing has been placed at the forefront of attempts to 'reprivatis[e] ... social reproduction' (Roberts 2013: 22) and reconstitute citizens as market-oriented saver-investors, in what is often described in terms of a "welfare trade-off" whereby reduced welfare provision is accepted in exchange for use of housing 'as a means to wealth, by which individuals and families can store and accumulate capital' (Seabrooke 2010: 56).

Housing is, therefore, variously implicated in financialisation, with mortgage-dependent owner-occupation constituting the quintessential feature of financialised housing provision. This article leaves aside the systemic or macroeconomic dimensions of the financialisation-housing nexus and uses the system of provision, or SoP, approach and associated 10Cs (Bayliss et al, this issue; Fine, this issue) to look at this shift from the perspective of the subject, primarily but not exclusively the housed, asking how the expanded presence of finance in housing, and the role of housing in a financialised growth and different welfare systems, have affected and relied upon changes in the way in which people consume their housing. In other words, how have housing cultures, understood as a set of shared behaviours and beliefs about housing, been (re)shaped in a way that favours owner-occupation, and with what implications for agents' subjectivities? In line with the growing recognition from different perspectives that manifestations of financialisation are variegated across countries (Lapavitsas and Powell 2013, Bayliss et al. 2015), and that consumption cultures, as captured by the 10Cs are *Contextual*, I do not try to answer this question across the international level, but focus on Britain, where 'homeownership has become both politically and culturally salient' (Stanley 2014: 900).

The growing prominence of a culture of homeownership in Britain dates back to the 1980s and the Conservative Government's promotion of owner-occupation at the expense of social housing. Its rise was, therefore, bound up with the *Commodification* of social housing, which saw owner-occupation shift from being one (albeit majority from 1970) tenure within an essentially mixed system to being regarded as the pre-eminent, default tenure:

> owner-occupation in the UK, most obviously since the advent of the Thatcher administrations in the early 1980s ... has been promoted and protected by policy as the "natural" housing tenure to which the vast majority of people ought to aspire (Hiscock et al. 2001: 55).

Hiscock captures the way in which the architects of this shift sought to portray policy as helping people to realise a pre-existing, even innate, desire for homeownership. However, I follow the SoP approach in seeing consumption cultures as contingent and malleable, emerging out of the material structures and processes through which goods are provided (Bayliss et al. 2013). On this view, the culture of owner-occupation emerged from a number of transformations that the British housing system underwent in the 1980s. The Right to Buy attached a financial incentive to switching from socially rented to owner-occupied dwellings. Accompanying restrictions on councils borrowing to replace lost stock diminished the availability of alternative tenure forms. The break-up of building society cartels over mortgage lending, along with increased international capital flows and, from the late 1990s, low interest rates, increased the availability and affordability of mortgage credit. These factors were compounded by past social and economic patterns of housing provision, which meant that owner-occupied property tended to affirm its being more desirable in terms of quality and location (Merrett and Gray 1982).

All this suggests that the culture of owner-occupation was rooted in the material benefits of homeownership in Britain. However, it is integral to the SoP approach that consumption has an irreducibly cultural component because there is often 'a gap between the commodity as it is and the commodity as it has been perceived' (Fine 2007:2), and hence that people's consumption behaviour is *Constructed* by symbols and images as well as by material conditions:

> Consumption does not merely arise in response to fundamental human needs or use values (utility); it is social activity that integrates consumers into a specific social system and commits them to a particular social vision (Ozanne and Murray 1995: 522).

The culture of owner-occupation reflects changes in socially shared images and meanings around housing as well as use values.

The aim of this paper is to investigate this discursive aspect of the creation of the culture of home-ownership in Britain, and its transformative impact on individual subjectivity. In doing so, I borrow from Gurney (1999) who examines the role of naturalising discourses in creating the image of home-ownership as normal and desirable. Gurney's work is rooted in Foucault, and hence dovetails with Foucauldian accounts of neoliberalism, which view it as producing new subjectivities (see, for example, Dardot and Laval 2013). However, while able, in virtue of this framework, to document the subjective transformations associated with the financialisation of housing, he is unable to explain them adequately. Gurney's Foucauldian conception of power leaves him short of an account of the sources and influence of the naturalising discourses that he so ably identifies. This is redressed by a number of authors (Watson 2008, 2009, Crouch 2009, Finlayson 2009, Van Gent 2010, Payne 2012) who attribute the discursive shift to an intentional state project to reconstitute individual subjectivities. These authors are able to explain the origin and, to some degree, the efficacy of naturalising discourses in terms of the social, economic, and political power of the state. However, there is a tendency to focus on policy initiatives while neglecting the barriers to their success. While housing policy since the 1980s has given material and cultural impetus to owner-occupation in Britain, the reflexive and resistive capacities of consumers, when coupled with the competing meanings attached to housing and the growing dysfunctionality of the current housing model, have constrained the dominance of the ethos of owner-occupation and render its future vulnerable. These complexities within the material culture of owner-occupation are captured throughout by the SoP approach's 10Cs: Constructed, Construed, Conforming, Commodified, Contextual, Contradictory, Closed, Contested, Collective and Chaotic (Bayliss et al, this issue; Fine 2013 and this issue).

In the next section I provide an exegesis of Gurney's analysis of naturalising discourses about homeownership, while critically assessing its explanatory power. In the following section, I draw on a range of work that situates the discursive promotion of homeownership within the state's broader transformative policy agenda. As mentioned, this literature pays undue attention to the intentions of policy at the expense of assessing the extent to which they have been realised. Hence, in section four, I articulate the complex reality of the culture of owner-occupation in Britain in terms of the 10Cs. Section five concludes.

2. Naturalising discourses around owner-occupation

Drawing on landmark government policy documents and ethnographic interviews with working class owner-occupiers, Gurney (1999) provides a helpful documentation of how homeownership has been 'normalised' in public discourses about housing. He identifies three discrete normalising discourses. First, the emotional and evocative term 'home' is used much more frequently[1] in relation to owner-occupied housing than privately or socially rented housing.[2] Second, home-ownership is associated with a set of desirable attributes characterising a 'good citizen'. So, for example, a 1981 Department of the Environment (DoE) report states that owner-occupation 'encourages a personal desire to improve and modernise one's own home, enables parents to accrue wealth for their children, and stimulates the attitudes of independence and self-reliance that are the bedrock of a free society' (DoE, quoted in Gurney 1999:176), while the interviewees associate social renters with lack of pride, self-respect and care and responsibility (Gurney 1999:177). Third, homeownership and associated desires and behaviours are treated as normal and natural: 'There is in this country a deeply ingrained desire for home-ownership' (Department of the Environment quoted in Gurney 1999:176), a view mirrored by the interviewees' use of the terms 'human nature' and 'instinct' in association with homeownership.

Gurney highlights the *Constructed* nature of the culture of owner-occupation. He not only provides documented evidence that owner-occupation has come to be discussed as the 'natural' housing tenure, and shows that this attitude is evident among both government and the public. He also observes that these discourses have the effect of disciplining and conditioning individuals by creating 'a whole new set of exclusionary processes' that are cultural and linguistic rather than merely economic or political:

> There is some evidence to suggest that current homeowners, whose parents were homeowners and who have never owned themselves have been subject to a 'tenure-socialisation' producing pronounced tenure prejudice sustained by stereotypical allegories and aphorisms which construct non-owners as a stigmatised out-group (Gurney 1999: 165).

The risk of stigmatisation from not owning a house may help shape people's attitudes and desires towards homeownership. Gurney also recognises that this disciplining effect is highly complex because normalising discourses are reflexively *Construed* by agents. Gurney rejects approaches in which 'homeowners are … portrayed as either passive recipients of hegemonic projects or as passive respondents to innate desires' (Gurney 1999:163). In other words, Gurney refuses to accept either that the public who adopt normalising discourses about homeownership are passively duped into adopting the rhetoric of governments seeking to promote owner-occupation, or that desire for homeownership is, indeed, natural.

Gurney contributes to our understanding of the cultural aspect of how housing preferences are formed by identifying the ways in which public discussion of housing embodies the idea that owner-occupation is superior. However, his attempt to explicate how and why these discourses have such an influence over the attitudes and beliefs of individuals who are not passive dupes is more problematical. Gurney adopts a Foucauldian conception of power meaning that, for him:

> power is understood as the name given to the particular and complex situation constituted by the forces and tactics which socially construct homeownership as a majority housing tenure (Gurney 1999: 166).

In other words, power is something that achieves efficacy through a set of circumstances and processes rather than through an agent or group of agents. In Foucault's own words, 'power relations are rooted deep in the social nexus, not reconstituted "above" society as a supplementary structure' (Foucault 1982:791). For Foucault, power is not necessarily the direct and explicit domination of one agent or agency over another, but a much more multifaceted, widely distributed, and amorphous force that indirectly narrows and conditions an individual's fields of actions.

The Foucauldian influence leads Gurney to argue that our focus should be on the processes and outcomes of power rather than on the source of power and who exercises it. Such an approach captures the important point that, if individuals are formally free, reflexive and contemplative beings who will not simply believe what they are told, the channels through which they are influenced by discourses are both flexible and possibly nebulous. However, in trying to avoid 'arguments in which housing consumers are passive actors in the face of structural … forces' (Gurney 1999:180) or accounts in which individual attitudes are shaped by crude exercises of authority, and in trying to redress what he sees as an over-emphasis on political and economic processes by stressing the power and efficacy of cultural and linguistic practices, Gurney goes too far in dismissing the significance of structural economic and political processes and is left with little to say about why the discourses emerged in the first place or the configurations of power underpinning them.

It sometimes seems as if Gurney thinks that the normalisation discourses are a result of the owner-occupation tenure form itself. He says, for example, that 'tenure is imbued with a disciplinary power which normalises homeowners' (Gurney 1999:166). But this begs the question of how and why owner-occupation generates such discourses, and why, as Gurney acknowledges, they did not appear in the 1960s when owner-occupation was sizeable, leaving us stuck in explaining why owner-occupation has expanded. Furthermore, if discourses that normalise owner-occupation spontaneously emerge and expand with that tenure form, then the disciplining and regulatory effects of those discourses that Gurney makes so much of are reduced to mere epiphenomena of owner-occupation and robbed of causal content.

What is missing from Gurney's account is that governments and individuals relate to the material practices that underpin cultural discourses differently. Gurney treats his evidence base – seminal government documents on housing and in-depth interviews with working class homeowners – as on a par with each other, two types of evidence that normalisation discourses have taken hold of in the public and private realms, respectively. But it is naive to suppose, as Gurney does, that cultural and linguistic practices can be separated from politics. It is not treating people as passive actors to acknowledge that agents are not equal in their capacity to shape and interpret discourses. Governments have outlets and opportunities to set agendas and shape public opinion that few other actors have (see Happer, this issue). Even Foucault recognised that 'power relations have been progressively governmentalised (in the restricted sense of the word government)' (Foucault 1982:793) meaning that:

> In contemporary societies the state is not simply one of the forms or specific situations of the exercise of power – even if it is the most important … in a certain way all other forms of power relation must refer to it (Foucault 1982: 793).

Cultural discourses do not spontaneously appear or exist in the abstract. They are created through channels of public discourse, which some actors have a greater ability to influence than others, making consumption cultures relatively *Closed*. Thus it is more plausible to suppose that government representations shape private attitudes more than the reverse is true, and that Gurney's resistance to engaging with the sources and exercise of power is misplaced.

3. Situating discourses in neoliberal policy agendas

In this respect, Gurney can be contrasted with evidence that achieving cultural change was an intentional part of the Thatcherite project. In her own words:

> 'economics are the method: the object is to change the soul' (Thatcher, quoted in Butt 1981)

> 'I came to office with one deliberate intent: to change Britain from a dependent to a self-reliant society — from a give-it-to-me, to a do-it-yourself nation. A get-up-and-go, instead of a sit-back-and-wait-for-it Britain' (Thatcher 1984)

There is a body of work that explains and analyses the emergence of naturalising discourses in these terms. For example, Britain has been the inspiration for literature on housing asset-based welfare (Watson 2008, 2009, Crouch 2009, Finlayson 2009, Van Gent 2010), which argues that over the last thirty years states have attempted to shift from a model of direct, universal welfare provision to an individualised asset-based model in which individuals or households bear the risk and responsibility for their own welfare by accumulating assets and borrowing against them. The growth of owner-occupancy is thought pivotal to such reform because housing is most households' largest asset. The intentional transformation of the culture of housing consumption is central to this story:

> Through neo-liberal ideological constructions the relationships between households, markets and state are restructured in two ways. First, higher owner-occupancy rates facilitate the spread of neo-liberal ownership ideologies, which emphasise the role of markets and the opportunities for households to make capital gains from their assets. Second, the ideology undermines expectations of universal citizenship rights to welfare goods and services by promising individuals gains through markets and resisting the 'moral hazard' of collective provision and the inefficiency and taxes of public spending (Van Gent 2010: 740).

A similar account is provided by Payne (2012) who, like Gurney, borrows from Foucault, but focuses on his concept of governmentality, that is, the processes by which individual behaviour is regulated and changed – the 'conduct of conduct' (Payne 2012:5). He argues, first, that neo-liberalism should be understood as a rationale for how to govern the economy and, second, that the neo-classical consumer, by which he means a consumer that is rational, entrepreneurial and asset-building, has been central to this rationale. He then argues that the Thatcher Government tried to reconstitute individuals' subjectivity by encouraging them to behave like neo-classical consumers, and made economic policy with such consumers in mind.[3]

Unlike Gurney, Payne locates the naturalisation of owner-occupation within broader political and economic changes taking place at the time, making its emergence comprehensible. Payne sees the promotion of owner-occupation as one aspect of the neo-liberal challenge to the Keynesian consensus that had prevailed in the 1960s but began to break down in the 1970s. Thus neoliberal governments, such as Thatcher's, problematised the Keynesian consensus that preceded them in terms of its having stifled entrepreneurial behaviour and consumer sovereignty, and sought to inculcate and solicit the behaviour befitting such a conception of individuals to counter Keynesian-induced deformities.

This literature suggests the basis for explaining the naturalisation of owner-occupation as one aspect of the changing relationship between the economy, the state and the individual that came out of the breakdown of the Keynesian consensus. If Gurney identifies and unpicks elements of the cultural shift that accompanied the material causes of the rise of owner-occupation, Payne and the asset-based welfare literature address the question of from where this cultural impetus came. Their answer – that the culture of owner-occupation was part of Thatcher's attempt to use housing to change the character of the individual and their role in the economy – takes us beyond the question of which tenure form is dominant and into the ways in which people relate to and consume their housing, and how this fits in with broader societal welfare provision.

This literature has two additional advantages. First, unlike Gurney, it recognises that the attitudes and beliefs that actors adopt must *Conform* to their material experiences, noting that, as well as adopting rhetoric that encouraged individuals to behave like entrepreneurs, the Thatcher Government tried to induce changes in people's behaviour by changing the material circumstances in which they acted. Thus, Payne says, Thatcher's Government decided economic policy on the basis of what the enterprising consumer needed to flourish – choice, independence, and, most importantly, the availability of credit to borrow and assets to purchase – because 'it was taken for granted that if credit could be made available for consumers and households then it would follow, naturally, that the population would take up the chance to borrow' (Payne 2012:152). The Right to Buy and limitations put on local authorities' capacity to build more council housing should also be mentioned here, as should the prolonged above-inflation house price increases that Britain experienced from the early 1990s, as they helped to confirm housing's potential as an appreciating asset. For Crouch (2009), these house price increases were the fall-out from a reliance on credit to stimulate demand in the context of falling welfare spending and stagnant wages, though Robertson (2014) reminds us that it also took aspects of the UK housing SoP, most notably, a restrictive planning system and speculative housebuilders, to channel credit into house prices rather than housebuilding. Interestingly, discourses promoting owner-occupation have relied on excluding discussion of the chronic undersupply of housing, despite it providing a crucial material basis for the success of such discourses in the UK context. This highlights another sense in which the culture of owner-occupation is *Closed*.

Second, Payne and the asset-based welfare literature bring out more deeply the essentially *Constructed* nature of consumer behaviour by emphasising that what use-values people want from their housing is also something that is created and, therefore, *Contextually* contingent. Most notably, the literature stresses that thinking about their housing as an asset is something that people had to be induced to do. Again, it is important to remember that this inducement had rhetorical and material dimensions.

These strengths notwithstanding, a limitation of the literature is that it takes as its subject matter the policy agendas of successive governments and how they have been presented, rather than the extent to which these agendas have been realised, and *Contested*, in practice. It is clear from the quote above that Van Gent focuses his analysis on ideology and policy constructs and takes as his subject matter policy debates and discourses. Similarly, Watson (2008) says 'the *government* has challenged the legitimacy of passive welfare receipts in favour of establishing a welfare system based on incorporating the individual into an active asset-holding society' and that 'the housing market has taken on a new *political* significance as a means for individuals first to acquire assets and then to accumulate wealth on the back of asset ownership' (Watson 2008:285, my emphases). Finlayson (2009) explicitly takes government policy, and the way in which it is marketed, as his focus, though he recognises some of the contradictions that arise in the course of implementation. Crouch (2009) argues that 'privatised Keynesianism' as intentional government policy followed rather than led its emergence but, nonetheless, the attempt to reconstitute subjectivities is tied to this policy intent. And Payne's analysis does not extend to an investigation of the extent to which neo-liberal restructurings of the relationships between households, markets and state has actually occurred.

This focus on policy is problematic because, as Fine (2013) points out, behaviour is not a straightforward response to ideology or policy, but the result of the combination of, and relationship between, material conditions and how they are perceived. Van Gent recognises this as an issue, saying 'whether housing market gains are indeed sufficient to allow people to freely choose welfare or whether people are actually willing to trade down their homes for extra income is a separate debate in housing literature' (van Gent 2010:736). However, it is a debate that is crucial to understanding the culture of owner-occupation, especially given the manifold barriers to its becoming hegemonic.

4. Tensions, limitations, and barriers – analysing the culture of owner-occupation in terms of the 10Cs

Material cultures do not arise automatically or uniformly from SoPs and dominant discourses. Rather they are the result of agents' reflexive interpretation of these discourses in light of their experiences. Fully comprehending the material culture of owner-occupation in the era of financialisation, therefore, requires moving beyond a one-sided focus on the content of dominant discourses and the restructuring of provision, and looking at the interaction of these reflexive processes. Doing so reveals tensions within the culture of owner-occupation arising from both the meanings attached to homeownership and the way it has been provided.

First, the asset-based welfare literature's focus on the way in which housing has come to be seen as an asset does not sit comfortably with the part of Gurney's discourse analysis that focuses on the invocation of ideas of homeliness in relation to owner-occupation. The first suggests adaptable and independent consumers relating to their homes as one way of building their personal balance sheets, while the second suggests rooted individuals seeking from their homes a place of comfort and constancy. This is a *Contradiction* within the modern idea of owner-occupation itself, rooted in the clash of use and exchange value. In short, owner-occupation has been promoted for reasons that were 'economic and tangible and reasons that are emotional and intangible' (President Clinton, quoted in Payne 2012:155). Owner-occupation has been sold to the public simultaneously as a form of shelter that, compared to other tenures, is particularly equipped to provide comfort and security and as an investment vehicle for accumulating wealth and managing spending. While the former implies that people relate to their homes through constancy and attachment, the latter requires that they relate to it in a much more objective and calculating way, valuing financial value and tradability.

These contradictory imperatives make the culture of owner-occupation somewhat *Chaotic*, reflecting differences in the way people relate to their housing. An extreme manifestation of housing being treated as an asset is provided by international investors buying housing in central London from afar and often without any intention of living in it. This is pure case of housing functioning as a cash cow – as one commentator put it, the London property has become a 'global reserve currency' (Green and Bentley 2014:5). The buy-to-let market presents an intermediate case, as it has served as a means for homeowners to use the equity in their existing property to buy – and secure the capital gains associated with – additional dwellings. However, buy-to-let loans currently account for only 13.4% of total mortgage lending, indicating that most homeowners have not chosen to use their homes as leverage to access more wealth (Council of Mortgage Lenders 2015). Further, interestingly, the contradictory ethos of owner-occupation as family home and as financial asset places the buy-to-letter in a culturally *Contradictory* position. On the one hand, buy-to-let is the very essence of financial literacy, the heroic financial agent able and willing to take advantage of economic opportunities afforded by the wider availability of mortgages. On the other hand, there is the despised property owner, depriving others of access to owner-occupation and forcing them to rent both by their buying available property and forcing up house prices. Significantly, despite the extraordinary revival of the private rented sector, it has been far from celebrated by official discourse in deference to the ethos owner-occupation and antipathy to social housing.[4]

Another measure of how housing is being treated as an asset is the extent to which mortgage equity withdrawal (MEW) is used to increase consumption and welfare spending. The evidence here is inconclusive. The Bank of England downplays the role of MEW in fuelling consumption on the grounds that MEW does not go above 10% of disposable income up until the early 2000s (when their data end) (Benito et al. 2006). The Bank further argues that the bulk of this MEW occurred through trading down or final sale which, according to Benito and Power's (2004) analysis of the 2003 Survey of English Housing, is less likely to be used for immediate spending than in situ MEW:

> Those who sell a property without purchasing another one and those who trade down are more likely to pay off debt or save withdrawn equity than spend the proceeds. Remortgagors and those who obtain further secured advances are likely to spend the equity, but we estimate that their equity constitutes only about a quarter of total gross withdrawals (Benito and Power 2004: 302).

However, the Bank's results concern the significance of spending out of MEW at the aggregate level. Measures of changes in the behaviour of households with mortgages place more weight on the use of housing wealth for consumption. For example, Lowe et al. (2011) find from the British Household Panel survey that one-third of households with mortgages withdraw equity in any one year and conclude from this that in situ MEW has become routine. This is compatible with the Bank's finding that MEW is small relative to total consumer spending and that in situ MEW for consumption is small relative to gross MEW, but leaves moot the question of whether spending out of housing wealth has been normalised or not. What is clear from both measures is that only a minority of homeowners engage with MEW. Thus, even in a context in which the capital gains to housing have been prolonged and substantial, vindicating housing's potential for accumulating wealth, the material practice of using housing as an asset has not become hegemonic.

The second tension in the culture of owner-occupation is that a growing section of the population is excluded from homeownership. The 1980s saw a policy shift towards treating owner-occupation as the default tenure form, but the corresponding shift in tenure dynamics has not endured. Owner-occupation's share in the total housing stock was rising from the 1980s, largely at the expense of council housing, but it peaked in 2005 at 72% and has since shrunk to 63% (DCLG 2015:11). At the root of this decline is the problem of affordability – long-term trend above-inflation house price increases, the product of credit-inflated demand in the context of an accumulated undersupply of housing, are putting homeownership out of reach of a growing portion of the population (Robertson 2014). As a result, we are witnessing the historic return of the private rented sector, PRS, after a century of decline, and the corresponding emergence of housing counter-cultures. More young people are spending longer in the PRS or living with their parents, with projections that they may never be able to buy (Ramesh 2012). This *Collective* experience of exclusion from owner-occupation has entered public discourses under the rubric "Generation Rent", but 'the bedrock desire for home-ownership appears to be persisting, with all age groups having a dominant preference for home-ownership longer-term' (Council of Mortgage Lenders 2012:1). This suggests that the culture which views owner-occupation as the default tenure form still holds sway, with any serious clash with the dominant discourse latent rather than manifest. However, the patterns of inequality that underpin that discourse raises doubts about how long this can last.

Montgomerie and Büdenbender (2015:391) note that housing asset-based welfare 'relies on a disaggregated notion of "the household sector" as equivalent to households, which erases all the significant inequalities between households'. This is problematical because the aforementioned house price and affordability issues are giving rise to growing inequalities in housing wealth. Those on the housing ladder have benefitted from windfall capital gains, while the rest face escalating housing costs. Without a decisive change in supply structures – a possibility which seems remote in light of current policy directions – house price inflation and inequality are set to continue, with housing wealth transferred across generations through bequests and parental assistance with purchase (Robertson 2014). However, there are signs that housing inequality is fuelling discontent and politicising housing counter-cultures. The last few years have seen an upsurge in political struggles around housing, with the culture of owner-occupation increasingly *Contested*. The assignation "Generation Rent" has developed from cultural signifier to political slogan in a campaign for better rights and conditions in the PRS (Generation Rent 2014). Meanwhile, a series of high-profile social housing movements are challenging the narrative of failure and self-responsibility that was attached to social housing as an appendage of the culture of owner-occupation (Williams 2015) with a new discourse of housing as a socio-economic right (Townsend and Kelly 2015). Reflecting the way in which conceptions of the financialised subject 'ignore and thereby perpetuate gender-based inequalities labour markets, in asset ownership and in the division of unpaid labour' (Roberts 2013: 23), the prominence of women has been a notable feature of these movements.

In sum, the material culture of owner-occupation cannot be read off from the discourses and conditions that have created it. Not only are naturalising discourses inconsistent, households have not fully internalised them in their housing consumption behaviour. Only a proportion of the population own their own home and only a proportion of those withdraw equity from it to feed current consumption. Further, the system of housing provision in which owner-occupation is dominant is increasingly dysfunctional, inciting resistance and putting pressure on current housing norms.

As has been argued throughout, the 10Cs can usefully characterise this more nuanced reading of the material culture of owner-occupation. First, the culture of owner-occupation in Britain is *Contextual*. Although the trend towards homeownership is international, the culture of owner-occupation in Britain was shaped by specific developments in that country, including the Right to Buy and enduring above-inflation house price increases, which made homeownership financially attractive to those who could access it. This has inspired asset-based welfare models of housing, with some but by no means hegemonic application. Second, the culture of owner-occupation emerged through the *Commodification* of social housing, and associated reinterpretation of housing as an asset instead of a basic right. Third, the culture of owner-occupation is *Constructed,* arising from discourses promulgated as part of an intentional project to reconstitute agents' subjectivities. Fourth, however, different agents have unequal and differentiated roles in shaping discourses, making them *Closed*. Most notably, the state yields extensive influence while the experiences and voices of people in other tenures have tended to be marginalised and stigmatised. Fifth, dominant discourses are not unquestioningly imbibed by agents, but are reflexively *Construed* in light of their experiences, knowledge, and competing beliefs. Sixth, discourses, therefore, have purchase in part by *Conforming* to material changes taking place in the housing SoP, including easier access to credit, house price inflation, the Right to Buy and the resulting depletion of alternative tenures.

Seventh, the content given to the cultural systems often exercise *Contradictory* pressures. For example, owner-occupation is promoted as a field for entrepreneurial, asset-building behaviour and as a place of safety and comfort in an increasingly volatile world, while the buy-to-let homeowner is simultaneously celebrated and denigrated. Eighth, as a result of these *Contradictions*, as well as the manifold influences on agents' interpretations, which are drawn from multiple dimensions of daily life, the culture of owner-occupation is *Chaotic*, combining, for example, the conflicting instincts to use housing to nest and make money. Ninth, the inequalities arising from a housing SoP in which owner-occupation is the default tenure and house prices continue to rise as the result of a housing shortage mean that the culture of owner-occupation is increasingly *Contested* by Generation Rent and other market excluded groups. These contestations are, finally, *Collective*, having emerged from the realisation that experiences outside of the dominant tenure form are shared.

5. Conclusion

I began this paper with two observations: first, that the expansion of owner-occupation has been an important facet of the financialisation of the housing sector because it is associated with a rising demand for mortgages and the creation of financialised subjectivities; second, that over the last thirty years in Britain, owner-occupation has not only expanded numerically, but has also come to be regarded as the default and 'natural' tenure form, giving rise to what I called 'the culture of owner-occupation'. I then set out to explain the discursive origins of this culture of owner-occupation, arguing that any adequate attempt to theorise a consumption culture must identify and explain the use-values and the image(s) associated with the product in question, and explore their interplay in a way that is socially and historically specific.

Contrary to the idea contained within the culture of owner-occupation that the desire to own one's own home is natural and innate, it is relatively new, contingent and created. Gurney's deconstruction of housing discourses documented their role in naturalising homeownership. However, explaining the emergence and efficacy of such discourses required situating changes in the culture of housing within broader changes to the material and cultural functioning of the British economy. The promotion of owner-occupation was part of Thatcher's broader neoliberal project, which included replacing collectivised welfare provision with greater reliance on the market and encouraging individuals to bear more risk and exercise more choice. Payne makes explicit the way rhetoric is accompanied by material incentives such as easy credit, house price inflation and the residualisation of social housing, and how broader economic changes fed the culture of owner-occupation by creating needs that owner-occupation was thought to fulfil. For example, the individualisation of welfare made ownership of personal assets more important at the same time as the capital gains available through homeownership were being promoted.

The rise of the culture of owner-occupation has corresponded to significant changes in the way that housing and housing wealth is accessed and consumed. Nonetheless, these changes have been partial and tension-ridden rather than complete and comprehensive. The culture itself contains competing imperatives. Thus the extrinsic value of generating capital gains co-exists with the way in which the home is valued for its intrinsic properties as a site of constancy and safety, despite the one encouraging behaviour (speculation, climbing up the property ladder) incompatible with the other (stability, home-making). As a result, the salient idea of housing as cash cow has not translated into a wholesale revision of how people use their housing, with only a minority engaging in buy-to-let markets or MEW. Furthermore, political discontent arising from the inequalities created by the housing SoP to which the culture of owner-occupation is attached are straining the dominance of that culture.

The current material culture of housing in Britain was captured in these complexities by the 10Cs, helping to draw out the ways in which the material culture of housing is constructed by the SoP to which it is attached. Doing so helped to underpin the more general conclusion that international convergence towards owner-occupation is and must be variegated because owner-occupation is more than a particular legal form of residing in a house. That narrow definition conceals multifaceted SoPs to which are attached a range of sometimes contradictory meanings by particular groups of people in particular times and places.

Notes

1. In the DoE (1995) White Paper 'Our Future Homes' for example, the 'density' (number of uses divided by length of chapter in terms of number of lines) of the term 'home' is three times higher in the chapter on owner-occupation than in the chapter on private renting, and four-and-a-half times higher than in the chapter on social renting.
2. Gurney also identifies differences between how the two types of rented tenure are discussed, with private rentals usually being regarded as a helpful stepping stone to owner-occupation and social rentals being restricted to notions of decency.
3. Gurney's attempt to reduce neo-liberalism and the Thatcher government to a rationale for governance centred on a particular conception of the consumer is too narrow, not least because it ignores the dynamics of profit-making. But it is sufficiently insightful into an aspect of neo-liberal governance to be useful here.
4. There is an interesting parallel here between the private landlord and those working in finance given how each has been promoted and benefitted by government but, especially in the wake of crisis, are subject to hostile public attitudes (see Happer, this issue).

References

Bayliss, K., Fine, B., and Robertson, M. (2013), 'From Financialisation to Consumption: The Systems of Provision Approach Applied to Housing and Water', FESSUD Working Paper Series, No. 2. Available from: http://fessud.eu/wp-content/uploads/2013/04/FESSUD-Working-Paper-021.pdf [accessed 28 May 2015].

Bayliss, K., et al. (2015), 'A Series of Thematic Country Synthesis Papers on Relevant Themes', Leeds, UK: FESSUD project, (Deliverable D8.27).

Benito, A. and Power, J. (2004), 'Housing Equity and Consumption: Insights from the Survey of English Housing', Bank of England Quarterly Bulletin House Prices Articles, Autumn. Available from: http://www.bankofengland.co.uk/publications/Documents/quarterlybulletin/qb040303.pdf [accessed 28 May 2015].

Benito, A., et al. (2006), 'House Prices and Consumer Spending', Bank of England Quarterly Bulletin House Prices Articles, Summer 2006. Available from: http://www.bankofengland.co.uk/publications/Documents/quarterlybulletin/qb060201.pdf [accessed 28 May 2015].

Butt, R. (1981), 'Mrs Thatcher: The First Two Years', The Sunday Times, 3 May, from Thatcher Archive. Available from: http://www.margaretthatcher.org/document/104475 [accessed 28 May 2015].

Christophers, B. (2013), 'A Monstrous Hybrid: The Political Economy of Housing in Early Twenty-First Century Sweden', New Political Economy, 18 (6), pp. 885–911.

Council of Mortgage Lenders (2012), 'Maturing Attitudes to Homeownership', Housing Finance, (2). (London: Council of Mortgage Lenders).

Council of Mortgage Lenders (2015), 'CML Members Adopt New Statement of Practice on Buy-to-Let Mortgage Lending', Council of Mortgage Lenders press release, 7 April 2015. Available from: https://www.cml.org.uk/news/press-releases/4179/ [accessed 28 May 2015].

Crouch, C. (2009), 'What Will Follow the Demise of Privatised Keynesianism?', The Political Quarterly, 80 (S1), pp. S302–15.

Dardot, P. and Laval, C. (2013), The New Way of the World: on Neoliberal Society (London: Verso).

Department for Communities and Local Government (2015), English Housing Survey: Headline Report 2013-14, (London: DCLG). Available from: https://www.gov.uk/government/uploads/system/uploads/attachment_data/file/406740/English_Housing_Survey_Headline_Report_2013-14.pdf [accessed 28 May 2015].

European Mortgage Federation Hypostat (2011), 'A Review of Europe's Mortgage and Housing Markets', (Brussels: European Mortgage Federation Hypostat). Available from: http://www.hypo.org/PortalDev/Objects/6/Files/HYPOSTAT_2013.pdf [accessed 28 May 2015].

Fine, B. (2007), 'From Sweetness to McDonald's: How Do We Manufacture (the Meaning of) Foods?', The Review of Social & Economic Studies, 29 (2), pp. 247–71.

Fine, B. (2013), 'Consumption Matters', Ephemera, 13 (2), pp. 217–248.

Finlayson, A. (2009), 'Financialisation, Financial Literacy, and Asset-Based Welfare', The British Journal of Politics and International Relations, 11 (3), pp. 400–421.

Foucault, M. (1982), 'The Subject of Power', Critical Enquiry, 8 (2), pp. 777–795.

Froud, J., et al. (2010), 'Escaping the Tyranny of Earned Income? The Failure of Finance as Social Innovation', New Political Economy, 15 (1), pp. 147–164.

Generation Rent (2014), 'The Renters' Manifesto' (London: Generation Rent). Available from: https://d3n8a8pro7vhmx.cloudfront.net/npto/pages/723/attachments/original/1403006644/Renters_Manifesto_web.pdf?1403006644 [accessed 28 May 2015].

Gotham, K. F. (2009), 'Creating Liquidity Out of Spatial Fixity: The Secondary Circuit of Capital and the Subprime Mortgage Market', International Journal of Urban and Regional Research, 33 (2), pp. 355–371.

Green, D. G. and Bentley, D. (2014), Finding Shelter – Overseas Investment in the UK Housing Market (London: Civitas).

Gurney, C. M. (1999), 'Pride and Prejudice: Discourses of Normalisation in Public and Private Accounts of Home Ownership', Housing Studies, 14 (2), pp. 163–183.

Hiscock, R., et al. (2001), 'Ontological Security and Psycho-Social Benefits from the Home: Qualitative Evidence on Issues of Tenure', Housing, Theory, and Society, 18 (1-2), pp. 50–66.

Lapavitsas, C. and Powell, J. (2013), 'Financialisation Varied: A Comparative Analysis of Advanced Economies', Cambridge Journal of Regions, Economy, and Society, 6 (3), pp. 359–379.

Lowe, S. G., Searle, B. A., and Smith, S. J. (2011), 'From Housing Wealth to Mortgage Debt: The Emergence of Britain's Asset-Shaped Welfare State', Social Policy and Society, 11 (1), pp. 105–116.

Merrett, S. and Gray, F. (1982), Owner-Occupation in Britain (London: Routledge).

Montgomerie, J. and Büdenbender, M. (2015), 'Round the Houses: Homeownership and Failures of Asset-Based Welfare in the United Kingdom', New Political Economy, 20 (3), pp. 386–405.

Ozanne, J. and Murray, J. (1995), 'Uniting Critical Theory and Public Policy to Create the Reflexively Defiant Consumer', American Behavioural Scientist, 8 (4), pp. 516–525.

Payne, C. (2012), The Consumer, Credit, and Neo-Liberalism: Governing the Modern Economy (London: Routledge).

Ramesh, R. (2012), 'UK Housing Shortage Turning Under-30s into "Generation Rent"', The Guardian, 13 June 2012. Available from: http://www.theguardian.com/society/2012/jun/13/generation-rent-uk-housing-shortage [accessed 28 May 2015].

Roberts, A. (2013), 'Financing Social Reproduction: The Gendered Relations of Debt and Mortgage Finance in Twenty-First-Century America', New Political Economy, 18 (1), pp. 21–42.

Robertson, M. (2014), 'Case Study: Finance and Housing Provision in Britain', FESSUD Working Paper Series No. 51. Available from: http://fessud.eu/wp-content/uploads/2013/04/Case-Study_-Finance-and-Housing-Provision-in-Britain-working-paper-51.pdf [accessed 28 May 2015].

Robertson, M. (2015), 'Synthesis Report: The System of Provision for Housing in Selected Case Study Countries', Leeds, UK: FESSUD project, (Deliverable D8.26).

Sassen, S. (2009), 'When Local Housing Becomes an Electronic Instrument: The Global Circulation of Mortgages – A Research Note', International Journal of Urban and Regional Research, 33 (2), pp. 411–426.

Schwartz, H. and Seabroke, L. (2008), 'Varieties of Residential Capitalism in International Political Economy: Old Welfare States and the New Politics of Housing', Comparative European Politics, 6 (3), pp. 237–231.

Seabrooke, L. (2010), 'What do I Get? The Everyday Politics of Expectations and the Subprime Crisis', New Political Economy, 15 (1), pp. 51–70.

Stanley, L. (2014), 'We're Reaping What We Sowed': Everyday Crisis Narratives and Acquiescence to the Age of Austerity', New Political Economy, 19 (6), pp. 895–917.

Thatcher, M. (1984), 'Speech to Small Business Bureau Conference', Thatcher Archive. Available from: http://www.margaretthatcher.org/document/105617 [accessed 28 May 2015].

Townsend, M. and Kelly, L. (2015), 'Thousands Gather in London to Protest Against Lack of Affordable Housing', The Guardian, 31st January. Available from: http://www.theguardian.com/society/2015/jan/31/hundreds-gather-london-march-for-homes-protest-city-hall-affordable-housing [accessed 28 May 2015].

Van Gent, W. P. C. (2010), 'Housing Policy as a Lever for Change? The Politics of Welfare, Assets and Tenure', Housing Studies, 25 (5), pp. 735–753.

Wainwright, T. (2009), 'Laying the Foundations for a Crisis: Mapping the Historico-Geographical Construction of Residential Mortgage Backed Securitisation in the UK', International Journal of Urban and Regional Research, 33 (2), pp. 372–388.

Watson, M. (2008), 'Constituting Monetary Conservatives via the 'Savings Habit': New Labour and the British Housing Market Bubble', Comparative European Politics, 6 (3), pp. 285–304.

Watson, M. (2009), 'Planning for a Future of Asset-Based Welfare? New Labour, Financialised Economic Agency, and the Housing Market', Planning, Practice and Research, 24 (1), pp. 41–56.

Williams, Z. (2015), 'The Tories' Message on Social Housing Is that the State Is for Losers', The Guardian, 5th July. Available from: http://www.theguardian.com/commentisfree/2015/jul/05/tories-social-tenant-council-housing?CMP=share_btn_fb [accessed 5 August 2015].

Cultivating the self-reliant and responsible individual: the material culture of financial literacy

Ana C. Santos

ABSTRACT

This paper analyses the promotion of financial education by many national and international organisations around the world. Drawing on the material culture of financialisation, financial education policy is perceived as part of a broader neoliberal project to extend commodification and (re)construct social and economic reproduction in ways favourable to the financial sector. It argues that, while numerous contradictions inherent in financial education programmes jeopardise the goal of improving individual financial decisions through education, the ideological goal of these initiatives is not compromised. It is the neoliberal cultural project of cultivating self-reliance and individual responsibility at the expense of collective forms of provision across new areas of economic and social life.

Financial literacy and the material culture of financialisation

Financial education has turned into a global policy agenda.[1] This agenda involves concerted action of major international organisations, such as the World Bank and the OECD, and the commitment by an ever-growing number of governments to implement so-called national strategies for financial education.[2] The spectacular and growing numbers of international and national agencies advancing financial education provide indisputable evidence for the magnitude of on-going material changes and their demand for corresponding profound cultural changes in how people both interact with, and perceive, various dimensions of financialisation.

This worldwide interest in individual and household financial knowledge and understanding is symptomatic of the financialised configurations of contemporary capitalist societies, that is, of financialisation,[3] which have increasingly integrated individuals and households into financial markets. The retrenchment of the welfare state is identified as a relevant factor explaining the penetration of finance into ever more areas of economic and social life as social reproduction has become more and more dependent on the financial sector (for example, Barba and Pivetti 2009, Montgomerie 2009, Froud et al. 2010). This has meant that individuals and households have become increasingly responsible for their future financial security through expanding demand for financial products and services that are to supplement or replace public provision, as in the area of pensions, and have increasingly relied upon credit to provide for housing, education, health or consumption in general. This growing involvement of individuals and households with the financial system has been accompanied by the extraordinary expansion and innovations of the financial sector, supplying a myriad of more complex and hard to understand financial products and services, demanding more financial knowledge and understanding on their part. But, more than the logical corollary of the growing demands on individual and household financial decision-making, the financial education agenda is part of a broader neoliberal project to extend (re)commodification and (re)construct social and economic reproduction in ways favourable to the financial sector.

Drawing on the material culture of financialisation, and associated 10Cs (Fine 2017), this paper argues that financial education aims at ensuring suitable *Conformity* of understandings and meanings (or *Construals*) of financialisation to the material processes, structures and relations that guarantee finance's continued expansion (or *Commodification*) and, in the aftermath of the crisis, the transfer of the costs of the problems finance itself created onto individuals and households. It aims, in particular, at the cultivation of 'a corresponding (neoliberal) culture of individual, or individualised, responsibility, at the expense of the collective across ever-expanding terrains of economic and social life' (Fine 2017). The paper shows that the numerous *Contradictions* informing financial education policy support the view that to improve individual and household financial well-being through better financial knowledge and understanding is not its sole goal. More relevant is the ideological goal of cultivating the values of self-reliance and willingness to bear risks in place of values such as the collective provision of certain human needs and the observation of substantive conceptions of equality. This is so because self-reliance and willingness to bear risks are perceived as critical to legitimise the expansion of the financial sector into domains of social life where collective forms of provision previously prevailed and potentially prevail. Finally, the absence of genuine *Contestation* by relevant *Collectives* is taken as a sign of the success of both material and cultural practices of the neoliberal project.

Financial education as a global policy agenda for financialised worlds

Already before the 2008–2009 international financial crisis, international and national agencies, such as the World Bank, the OECD, the European Commission, governments and financial regulators, were actively advancing national strategies for financial education. Even though these strategies were not framed in this way by their proponents, the increasingly financialised configurations of the economy and society, imposing added financial decisional burdens on individuals and households, are evoked to justify the need for promoting financial education at the national scale.[4] Pervasive in official documents are the challenges posed by on-going and necessary future reforms of the welfare states, implying the transfer of the responsibility and risk from the collective to the individual, and by the extraordinary expansion of the financial sector, supplying to individuals and households an ever wider range of complex financial products and services.

This overall background is very clearly presented in OECD official documents and publications, as one of the leading organisations in placing financial education on the political agenda, especially in the developed world.[5] The OECD project on financial education started in 2002, very revealingly, under the aegis of the Financial Markets and the Insurance and Private Pensions Committees (OECD 2005a). In 2008, it set up the International Network on Financial Education (INFE) to encourage and guide the launching of financial education programmes among its members. In 2015, more than 240 public institutions from more than 110 countries had already joined the network.[6] While their implementation began in the early 2000s (mostly in developed economies such as, the Netherlands, the UK and the USA), this policy gained momentum after the financial crisis of 2008–2009 (OECD/INFE 2009). In 2011, 26 countries had designed or implemented their strategies (Grifoni and Messy 2012), a number that rose to 45 in the following two years (OECD 2013a), and more countries are expected to launch their national programmes in the future.

The, ongoing and future, reform of welfare states is the point of departure for the financial education agenda (OECD 2005a: 28). The reform of pension systems, which is reducing state- and firm-supported pensions and introducing private pre-funded schemes, is a case in point. It implies that workers have increasingly the responsibility to save for their retirement, involving increased financial decision-making and the transfer of investment risks to individuals. Workers now need to make decisions about whether to contribute, how much to contribute, how to allocate contributions across investment options and be willing to accept that their retirement income is to be determined by the saving and investment decisions made during their working lives. The relevance of financial education is further magnified by the increasing number and complexity of financial products provided by a growing number of heterogeneous financial institutions.

The financial crisis of 2008–2009 intensified these trends, as the resolution of the crisis through austerity has implied a generalised weakening of public support, turning financial literacy into 'an important individual life skill' (OECD/INFE 2012: 2–3). The crisis was thus used to consolidate the inevitability of reforms that imply a greater transfer of responsibility and risk to individuals, making financial literacy a more relevant and necessary life skill.

The role that subprime had in setting off the financial crisis was used to push further the financial education agenda, namely by exposing the consequences of 'uninformed' credit decisions, especially those relating to mortgage loans, which represent a significant individual or household financial commitment. The crisis was thus taken as a 'teachable moment' as 'its direct, stressful and potentially significant long lasting consequences on individuals' wealth and well-being have incited households to become more concerned and interested in financial issues' (OECD 2009: 7–8).

But financial education policy is not only targeted at the unsophisticated consumers. It is targeted equally at those on low incomes to 'avoid the [high] cost charged for financial transactions' and those with money to invest by supplying them with 'more specific information about the advantages and disadvantages of particular types of investments' (OECD 2005a: 13), and this irrespective of the stage one finds him/herself in life. In the words of the European Commission (EC 2007: 4):

> Financial education can help children to understand the value of money and teach them about budgeting and saving. It can give students and young people important skills for independent living, for example in managing and repaying student loans. It can assist adults in planning for major events like buying a home or becoming parents. It can help citizens make better financial provision for unforeseen situations, invest wisely and save for their retirement.

If doubts remain about the ambition of financial education programmes, the launch, in 2012, of the first large-scale international test to assess financial literacy among 15-year-olds (included in the OECD Programme for International Students Assessment, known as PISA), suffices to dispel them. The test's stated goal is to assess the extent to which young people are 'prepared for the new financial systems that are becoming more global and more complex', which are expected to be substantially different from those known by older generations. This anticipates greater exposure to global and complex financial markets as younger generations 'are more likely to have to bear more financial risks in adulthood than their parents', including 'more responsibility for the planning of their own retirement savings and investments, and the coverage of their healthcare needs'. The diagnosis is thus the need to educate younger generations about financial matters as early as possible because efforts to improve financial knowledge in adulthood 'can be severely limited by a lack of early exposure to financial education and by a lack of awareness of the benefits of continuing financial education'. In newly financialised worlds, where access to a wide range of goods and services requires financial decision-making, financial literacy becomes one condition for 'equality of opportunity', as with any other type of literacy, assigning to schools the responsibility for advancing 'financial literacy among all demographic groups and reduc[ing] financial literacy gaps and inequalities' (OECD 2013b: 142–3).

Notwithstanding the important role of the crisis in advancing the financial education agenda, the main targets are not those blamed for taking out loans they could not afford or signing contracts without fully understanding the terms (or those promoting and selling them). The targets are those that are to renew engagement with finance as borrowers, investors and insurers so as to provide responsibly for their present and future needs.

Financial education and the construction of market society

Financial education is praised for its contribution to the improvement of the functioning of financial markets and the economy more generally. By demanding products more responsive to their needs, financially literate consumers, it is argued, encourage providers to develop new products and services, increasing competition, innovation and quality in financial markets. This is taken to have a positive impact on the economy by increasing overall savings and the efficient allocation of resources and thereby investment and economic growth.

This emphasis on the role of financial education in the workings of financial markets and the economy has been explicitly and repeatedly underlined by various agencies, denoting the hegemony of neoliberal ideology favourable to market expansion through de-regulation. The OECD (2005a: 35) envisaged already at the outset that by being 'in a better position to protect themselves on their own and to report possible misconducts by financial intermediaries to the authorities', financially educated consumers 'facilitate supervisory activity', which 'might in principle allow for lower levels of regulatory intervention', reducing the 'regulatory burden on firms' and allowing governments 'to spend fewer resources on enforcement of regulations and on the investigation and prosecution of fraud'. In the UK, the National Strategy for Financial Capability too, under the aegis of the Financial Services Authority (FSA), was grounded on the presumption that 'better informed, educated and more confident citizens, [are] able to take greater responsibility for their financial affairs and play a more active role in the market for financial services'. They will then become more 'active consumers', fostering competition and 'helping UK financial services firms to become more efficient, innovative and globally competitive'. The expectation is that 'in time, higher levels of financial capability could mean lower business acquisition costs for firms, greater persistency and less need for regulatory intervention' (HM Treasury 2007: 7). Along the same line, the Swedish Minister for Financial Markets, Mats Odell, underlined the imperative of 'households' ability to manage their personal finances' to the good of the financial sector since '[o]nly then will we get the savvy consumers the Swedish financial sector deserves and need to face tougher competition' (Odell, cited by Bay et al. 2014: 39). Explicitly referring to OECD's Recommendations (2005b), and with the hindsight of the financial and economic crises, in 2011, the Portuguese National Council of Financial Supervisors (CNSF 2011: 5–6) underlines also the role of financial education in ensuring financial stability insofar as 'well informed citizens, through the choice of financial products suited to their risk profile and needs, help to monitor the markets, thus contributing to the greater stability of the financial system'.

The empowerment discourse of financial education is therefore of a radically different nature from that of traditional consumer policy. A new regulatory project is in the making in which the emphasis is on protecting financial markets and institutions from households (Williams 2007). Regulators thus 'appear to reverse the idea of market failure posing a risk to consumer welfare, focusing instead on the risk of consumer "failure" jeopardizing the health of financial markets' (243). The financial education agenda thus launches a new regulatory project whereby the literate or capable financial consumer becomes a 'regulatory subject', who is responsibilised for the good functioning of financial markets through 'managing her present consumption to provide for future needs' (248). That is, rather than focusing on problems that asymmetric information poses to consumers' welfare, within the neoclassical economics framework of 'market failures', financial education policy focuses instead on the problems deficient decision-making poses to well-functioning markets.

While apparently akin to traditional consumer protection policy, potentially contributing to consumer empowerment through helping individuals understand financial risks and make decisions better adapted to their personal circumstances, the financial education policy agenda is substantially distinct: where 'consumer protection puts the burden on the financial institutions and the legal system', with 'financial education the burden is on the individual' (OECD 2005a: 21); and where 'consumer protection emphasises legislation and regulation designed to enforce minimum standards, require financial institutions to provide clients with appropriate information, strengthen the legal protection of consumers when something goes wrong, and provide for systems of redress', financial education provides instead 'information, instruction and/or advice' to help the individual 'to make informed choices, to know where to go for help, and to take other effective actions to improve their financial well-being and protection' (OECD 2005a: 26).

In reducing the problems to be tackled to deficient financial literacy, financial education policy essentially assumes the good workings of financial markets as it passes on the idea that consumers need only be financially literate to make welfare-improving decisions. This inversion of the terms of discussion is instrumental in advancing market solutions to pressing societal problems, especially those stemming from the alleged unsustainability of the welfare states rationalising greater demand for financial products and services. This confidence in 'the market', which is not discussed, and in the capacity of individual decision-making, if properly instructed, serves to reduce the issues at stake to a technical and de-politicised discussion, and to reduce the terms of these in turn to responsible individuals. Financial literacy can then be unquestionably acknowledged as 'an essential life skill for individuals' and financial education as a policy that contributes to both financial stability and individuals' financial well-being (OECD 2013a: 16). In so doing, the financial education agenda obfuscates the role of socioeconomic structures, especially financial ones, that both embed individual and household decisions and how they are to translate into individual and aggregate outcomes.

This conforms to the neoliberal view of market society as a 'natural' and inexorable state, and of the market as solution to all sorts of problems, including those they themselves create, which exempt financial institutions from responsibility for economic and social problems while transferring it to the individual (Fine 2009, 2011, Mirowski 2009, 2013). It also conforms to the neoliberal conception of individual freedom, understood in the negative sense as the absence of coercion. Financial education is simply to help the consumer make more adequate choices based on her preferences and personal circumstances. They assist the consumer to choose for herself, avoiding other forms of intervention that would limit the range of options available, say through prohibition of extremely risky financial products. These are deemed intrusive obstructions as they would reduce the choice available to the rational decision makers who could benefit from them, impairing the efficient outcomes of free functioning of markets.

However, the faith in both the 'free' market and individual 'rational' decision-making stands in sharp contrast to the concerted action of international organisations and hundreds of public institutions around the globe that underlie the large-scale and synchronic design and implementation of national strategies of financial education. Interventions to 'educate' both belie faith in all-powerful, self-serving individuals and serve to constitute them as financialised subjects to prepare them for the new financialised worlds in the making.

Construing suitably *conforming* financialised subjects

Financial education policy must be put in the context of contemporary capitalist societies that are engendering a transformation of citizens into consumers where collectively earned individual rights are being replaced by increased access to a wider panoply of commodified products and services. It must be perceived, in particular, as part of a broader strategy that aims at promoting the expansion of financial markets at the expense of collective forms of provision, based on intensifying household relations with financial markets as borrowers, investors and insurers.

Financial education contributes to this endeavour by intervening, and responding to, the formation of the material cultures of financialisation (Fine 2017). It does so by ensuring suitable *Conformity* of understandings and meanings (or *Construals*) of financialisation to the material processes that guarantee finance's continued expansion and, in the aftermath of the crisis, subtly rationalises the transfer of the costs of the problems finance itself created onto individuals and households. This implies the neoliberal cultural project of moulding individual and collective values in the direction of greater individual responsibility.

Financialisation is at the heart of three decades of neoliberalism being a key defining characteristic of the world economy, deploying 'the ideology of non-intervention and efficacy of market forces as a rationale for considerable intervention by the state, especially to promote the interests of private capital in general and of finance (and financialisation) in particular' (Fine 2011: 9). Financial literacy is part of this neoliberal strategy, belonging to a second phase where state intervention is not so much concerned with the release of the role of financial markets through privatisation and deregulation but with the management of prior interventions with 'the imperative of sustaining and not just ameliorating the process of financialisation' (Fine 2009: 8). In the aftermath of the crisis, this phase 'has been more overtly extensively interventionist in order to sustain the process of financialisation both, and primarily, on its own terms and through soliciting a modicum of acceptability given the extreme inequalities and iniquities to which it has given rise' (ibid). The most striking difference between the two phases is thus that 'rather than the state withdrawing to allow for the expansion of private capital, it was increasingly required to intervene to promote private capital', diverting discourse from the old dichotomy between the state and market towards 'the state making the market and globalisation work' (Fine 2011: 9).

In present neoliberal financialised times, state intervention implies, in particular, 'extending deeper into individual life'. As Finlayson (2009: 407) aptly summarises the process in the UK context:

> Liability is transferred from the collective via the state to individuals and as responsibilities that once fell primarily on the state are shifted to individuals the state takes up the task of ensuring that those individuals will be capable of carrying out their responsibilities. Just as the state seems to withdraw from one area of social life it extends deeper into individual life seeking to engender within people what are believed to be the appropriate aspirations. In this sense the interventionist welfare state, having been delegitimated and 'rolled back', finds a way to reinvent itself, intervening into and acting upon new objects in new domains.

Neoliberals acknowledge that market society requires state intervention to ensure neoliberal legitimacy, requiring continual attention to the interaction between market and non-market institutions and the values they nurture, specifically for their impact on the designs and design of market society. This is so because market society draws upon and induces a set of motivational and moral background conditions. These include the values of self-reliance and the willingness to bear risks, considered integral to the more or less tacit acceptance by individuals of the rules that frame markets and its underlying 'discipline' containing and veiling the role of the state (Mirowski 2009, 2013, Amable 2011, Rodrigues 2012, 2013).

A pessimistic intuition endangers neoliberal legitimacy: the potential popular rejection of the projected neoliberal version of the state. This renders imperative 'conscious intervention to change a culture in a direction more favourable to the neoliberals', constituting a fundamental tension in neoliberal thought (Mirowski 2013: 57). For the pretence of freedom as the absence of coercion ultimately must come to terms with the likely democratic rejection of neoliberal society. This partly explains why, as Mirowski (2013: 58) suggests, '[n]eo-liberals seek to transcend the intolerable contradiction of democratic rejection of the neo-liberal state by treating politics as if it were a market, and promoting an economic theory of democracy'. On Mirowski's view, this conflation of politics and economics finds its most clear expression precisely in the replacement of the notion of citizen by that of consumer of state services. This neoliberal angst offers an additional vantage point from which to assess financial education, one that envisages strong resistance to the withdrawal of collective forms of provision, which may lead to the re-emergence of deliberate efforts to reorganise the provisioning process in non-commodified ways, and based on a different range of principles, such as the satisfaction of certain human needs and the observation of substantive conceptions of equality.

The challenge for the neoliberal project is then to conceive social policy so that it cultivates the required values for the sustenance of the neoliberal market society, namely the values of self-reliance and the willingness to bear risks, considered integral to the more or less tacit acceptance by individuals of the rules that frame markets and underlying 'discipline'. As Amable (2011: 6) puts it:

> Public intervention is far from being prohibited [by neoliberals] but must be justified by reference to the promotion of individual competition … As a consequence, redistribution, that is *ex post* change in income distribution, or social protection, that is an attempt to limit the rigour of competition, is considered illegitimate.

> The individual is left exposed to economic risks and should not expect any guarantee of unconditional support, nor, of course, be granted any collective rights, because this would be morally reprehensible, provided that public intervention ensures that competition is fair, which means that every individual is exposed to it and no protection against competition is granted by the state.

This is exactly the logic behind financial literacy: to favour a culture where individual exposure to risk is acceptable and collective protection against it is undermined. Financial literacy programmes are well-placed to accomplish this since taking responsibility for the self can be realised through the intermediation of the financial sector. Individuals and households are precisely invited to engage responsibly and autonomously with finance to provide for housing, education, healthcare and income after retirement. And, as many have already noted, drawing on Foucauldian accounts of governmentality (such as Langley 2008), embroilment with finance involves the cultural embrace rather than fear of financial risks and rewards through entrepreneurial borrowing and investment for those with the right calculative skills and attitudes towards risk. Financial markets thereby become more and more prevalent in social and economic reproduction, further facilitating the take-up of associated risks.

The *contradictions* of financial education policy

The numerous *Contradictions* informing the financial education agenda support the view that to improve individual and household financial well-being through better financial knowledge and understanding is not its sole goal and role. It is also the ideological objective of cultivating the values of self-reliance and willingness to bear risks required for the extension of neoliberal financialised market society.

First, this policy aims at further entangling individuals and households into financial markets, as added responsibility for present and future well-being implies rising financial participation as borrowers, investors and insurers. Were improved decision-making and individual welfare the main objectives, financial education policy would need to consider alternatives to finance, or at least admit the possibility that abstaining from financial participation and financialised forms of provision could be preferable. But rather than (collective) financial disengagement, the focus, especially after the crisis, is on managing financial risks through further (individual) participation, often state organised or supported (most notably, for example, in subsidies to financialised forms of provision in support of health, education, pensions and so on). While the putative objective is to ensure that households are financially safe, safety is acquired 'not by withdrawing from financial contracts, but by trading actively' (Beggs et al. 2014: 984).

Second, the rationale for the financial education policy agenda is not empirically grounded, in the sense of demonstrating that it achieves its objectives. Granted that this may partly be due to the still incipient state of research on evaluating financial education policies, 'the overall picture, confirmed by other commentators', as O'Connell (2008: 17–18), an OECD consultant, summarises 'is that the evaluations so far have shown mixed and inconclusive results'. As a result, '[a] positive impact from financial education has not been unambiguously proven in all cases; nor has a clear picture emerged of what works best and why'. However, the prospects are not necessarily optimistic as the evaluation of these programmes is riddled with methodological difficulties pertaining to the establishment of clear-cut causal relations between financial education and financial behaviour due to the multidimensional and systemic natures of both personal finances and financial outcomes (see also Willis 2008b).

Third, and unsurprisingly, the effectiveness of financial education policies is now questioned by the very same sources that inspired it, through bandwagoning upon increasingly influential, and opportunistically appropriated behavioural economics research programmes, with the World Bank and the OECD in the lead (Fine et al. 2016). For example, a study commissioned by the British FSA to investigate the application of behavioural economics research to financial education has challenged the view that people may effectively improve their financial decision-making by learning how to do it. It identified many, varied, reasons for people making poor choices other than their lack of knowledge and understanding of financial concepts and terms, suggesting that 'low financial capability is more to do with psychology than with knowledge' (de Meza et al. 2008: 4). The compilation of these psychological traits by behavioural researchers has inspired the 'nudge' approach to policy making, through which the design of 'choice architectures' allows the neoliberal policy-maker to choose for the individual (Thaler and Sunstein 2008), whilst apparently respecting freedom of choice.

Save More Tomorrow is one of the most celebrated policies, which aimed at increasing the American 401(k) employee saving plans (Benartzi and Thaler 2007). It was set out to promote the automatic escalation of employees' contributions, by synchronising the upward adjustment of employees' savings rates to pay rises, circumventing the psychological traits of aversion to income reduction and inertia. Thus, rather than providing information and training and letting people choose for themselves, a default option was designed to be selected in case employees failed to make a choice. This was deemed to respect individual choice, as employees had the option to opt out of the scheme. The programme was successful to the extent that it led to higher saving rates, under the assumption that people were under-saving.

This is not to say that behavioural economics is antagonistic to the neoliberal programme (Santos and Rodrigues 2014). Nudge policies may offer effective ways of engaging households with finance by dispensing with the need of persuading political actors to set up and implement the required institutions to produce the behaviourally desired transformations. Gabor and Brooks (2017) offer another eloquent illustration of such policies, now targeted at the inclusion of the financially excluded in developing contexts. With the aid of digital technology, financial inclusion is to be pursued through the mapping of the behavioural profile of costumers to tailor-deliver them the most adequate financial products.

Fourth, and perhaps more revealingly, the financial literacy agenda is challenged by literacy research more generally, accusing it of being erroneously based on the assumption that financial literacy is a 'singular capability that, when gained, automatically affects people's financial practices'. Indeed, it is as if such literacy is akin to the learning of a foreign language that capacitates the individual for its various uses. Financial literacy, however, much more fundamentally 'needs to be [socially] situated and studied in practice because the characteristics that constitute financial literacy, or those that apply to it, vary with time and place' (Bay et al. 2014: 37).

Fifth, some commentators have gone as far as to claim that financial education is actually an impossible project due to 'the velocity of change in the financial marketplace', which creates an insurmountable 'gulf between current consumer skills and those needed to understand today's complex non-standardised financial products' (Willis 2008a: 197). Moreover, financial institutions, which may gain from people's mistakes, can always be 'at least one step ahead of even cutting-edge personal-finance programs', meaning that 'financial-literacy education is chasing a moving target it will never reach' (Willis 2008b: 219). The generally low levels of financial literacy, the complexity of financial products, the specific circumstances and needs of consumers, and the speed of change in financial markets, together imply that 'effective financial education would need to be extensive, frequent, and personalized for each consumer', which would 'outstrip any public education campaign ever attempted' (Willis 2011: 5–6).

Sixth, and not least, the uncertainty intrinsic to financial decisions comprises another set of insurmountable difficulties that makes it virtually impossible to calculate the risks involved in financial decision-making, which are fundamentally unknowable (for example, Erturk et al. 2007 and Fine 2017). This has to do with the inter-temporal dimension of household financial decisions which are about managing income and expenditure through time, requiring taking into account: the evolution of employment and wage income; the likelihood of personal and social contingencies such as sickness, unemployment, family breakdown; the evolution of house prices; changes in public provision and events such as the crisis itself.

Finally, and summing up, financial literacy is doomed to failure due to the unbridgeable gulf between what it can deliver and the rational and moral demands on the neoliberal subject, and also the material and moral conditions of neoliberal market society. If, on the one hand, financial literacy can never promise knowledge of the unknowable, or attribute the individual responsibility for the systemic; on the other, financial markets can never promise individual and collective security. The recent incursions of resilience metaphors into financial literacy campaigns further expose this gulf by shifting the focus from predicting the future to the unavoidable need to absorb and accommodate its unexpected effects. In so doing, as Clarke (2015: 270) underlines, 'the resilience doctrine foreshadows the inevitable failure of successfully learning the content of FLE [financial literacy education] because people will always face crises of economic security and well-being'.

The non-*contested* nature of financialisation

The recent promotion of financial education for wide segments of the population is symptomatic of the dominance of neoliberal policies that involve new forms of state intervention, promoting the expansion of finance within both the market economy and systems of social provision (Bayliss et al. 2013). The greater individual and household involvement with the financial sector not only means that individual and social welfare depends more and more on financial decisions (for example, credit to buy a house, saving for retirement), it also means that more aspects of individual and household lives have become prone to volatility from financial instability (for example, evolution of interest rates, housing prices, profitability of pension funds, let alone wages and working conditions, and so on).

The financial crisis has revealed how dramatic these effects can be on households, ranging from insolvency problems, due to the combination of rising interest rates and falling housing prices, to the loss of a lifetime's savings due to stock markets crashes or even fraudulent practices on the part of financial institutions. Governments have then been called upon to deal with social problems generated by the disproportionate growth of finance. Surprisingly, what we have been witnessing is the public shaming of consumers for not having sufficient financial knowledge to provide security for themselves and their families. The speech of President Obama in launching the 2010 National Financial Literacy month exemplifies what has been a globalised trend:

> In recent years, our Nation's financial system has grown increasingly complex ... many Americans took out loans they could not afford or signed contracts without fully understanding the terms ... While our government has a critical role to play in protecting consumers and promoting financial literacy, we are each responsible for understanding basic concepts: how to balance a checkbook, save for a child's education, steer clear of deceptive financial products and practices, plan for retirement, and avoid accumulating excessive debts ... Our Nation's future prosperity depends on the financial security of all Americans ... Together, we can prevent another crisis and rebuild our economy on a stronger, more balanced foundation (Obama 2010: 1–2).

In 2016, eight years after the global financial crisis and ensuing institution of austerity as a permanent condition, the culture of individual responsibility thrives. Based on the UK, Montgomerie and Tepe-Belfrage (2016) show that financial (and non-financial) literacy programmes applied to the most destitute likewise cast 'poor families as lacking of essential skills to live in the world' (12), and thus propose tackling poverty by teaching indebted poor households 'to exercise prudence and temperance', and 'troubled families' to 'turn their lives around' (2). They underline the moral impacts of such literacy campaigns, which further marginalise the vulnerable by attributing their condition to bad decisions and morally deviant behaviours, and specifically their gendered effects as these policies tend to target poor women and thereby convey the idea that 'women's morality is what ultimately needs reforming' (3).

The gap between financial literacy discourses, responsibilising the individual for her financial vulnerability and for the financial crisis itself, sidelining socio-economic causes and the systemic factors that underpin financial market instability, raises the question of why the shift of responsibility, that once fell primarily on the state, to the individual is not being seriously *Contested*; especially as it occurs in tandem with degrading levels of social protection, resulting in a deterioration of living conditions with the rise of unemployment, the deterioration of labour protection laws, stagnating income and growing inequality. While many resistance points have emerged, the fact of the matter is that finance continues expanding and individual and household financial engagements already show signs of recovering to pre-crisis levels.[7]

The absence of genuine *Contestation* by relevant *Collectives* might in itself be the result of the material and cultural transformations produced by three decades of neoliberalism. It is partly the result of the discourse of the financial education agenda that reduces citizenship to financialised consumerism, depoliticising and disempowering citizens as they become more and more responsibilised as consumers. Indeed, as citizens qua consumers are blamed for the dire circumstances in which they find themselves, financial hardship is increasingly perceived as one's own responsibility, irrespective of the reasons that led to reduced income, unsustainable indebtedness, insufficient saving for a child's education or for retirement. In addition, financial education agenda articulates with other narratives disseminated by other agents and through other means, which sideline alternative understandings and solutions to economic problems from public debate, precluding much of the potential for effective resistance to the interests of finance (See Stanley 2014, Happer 2017).

More fundamentally, and as mentioned, financialisation processes themselves, by replacing collective forms of provisions by individualised ways of securing basic household needs, render finance an ever more integral part of everyday life and its pervasiveness becomes increasingly naturalised. This means not only that those hindered by financialisation are increasingly perceived and publicly shamed for failing to provide for themselves and their families; but also that those who have succeeded through increased engagement with finance are perceived as financially educated and skilled, as well as responsible citizens, constituting new role models, that of the financialised subjects as specific examples of the neoliberal entrepreneur.

Finally, and relatedly, the fragmented nature of household engagements with finance may also help explain the lack of effective resistance to the interests of finance as 'contestation is inevitably *Collective*, especially if it is to be successful' (Fine 2017). In addition to unbalanced power relations in favour of the newly emerged and/or strengthened financial elites, fragmentation is occurring at the level of the working and middle-class households, most visible in the evolution of homeownership. As is now clear, including in countries other than the Anglo-Saxon world, financialisation has been a means through which particular groups have benefited from the accumulation and use of housing wealth, even if subject to temporal, spatial and social contingencies (Montgomerie and Büdenbender 2015). This has meant that some social groups have strengthened their relative advantage, reproducing and consolidating corresponding inequalities, producing 'a growing divide between the "haves" (on the housing ladder; higher income; older households) and "have nots" (not on the housing ladder; lower income; younger households)' (Robertson 2014: 7). That is, by (re)producing inequalities, benefiting one segment of the population more than others, financialisation has promoted and reinforced private, commodified, individualised forms of provision that are increasingly detrimental to the most vulnerable with ever feebler conditions to exercise successful contestation.

Notes

1. Many definitions of financial literacy and associated notions of financial education coexist in the literature (see Remund 2010). We will follow here the OECD's definition of financial education targeted to the retail consumer/investor, understood as 'the process by which financial consumers/investors improve their understanding of financial products and concepts and, through information, instruction and/or objective advice develop skills and confidence to become more aware of financial risks and opportunities, to make informed choices, to know where to go for help, and to take other effective actions to improve their financial well-being and protection' (OECD 2005a: 26).
2. The OECD defines a national strategy for financial education as 'a nationally co-ordinated approach to financial education' which: 'recognises the importance of financial education – including possibly through legislation – and

defines its meaning and scope at the national level in relation to identified national needs and gaps; involves the co-operation of different stakeholders as well as the identification of a national leader or co-ordinating body/council; establishes a roadmap to achieve specific and predetermined objectives within a set period of time; and provides guidance to be applied by individual programmes in order to efficiently and appropriately contribute to the national strategy' (OECD/INFE 2012: 7).

3. One of the most popular and all-encompassing definitions of financialisation is that offered by Epstein (2005: 3) referring to the 'increasing importance of financial markets, financial motives, financial institutions, and financial elites in the operations of the economy and its governing institutions, both at the national and international levels'.

4. That the term 'financialisation', however defined, is not used is not at all surprising as it has been developed and adopted by critical perspectives on the financialisation of contemporary capitalist economies. See Fine (2011).

5. The World Bank is instead more active promoting financial education in developing countries (see, for example, Rutledge, 2010, and Gabor and Brooks 2017).

6. http://www.financial-education.org/join_INFE.html (consulted on 28 May 2015).

7. The 'occupy' and the 'indignants' movements have certainly caught the public's eye and imagination worldwide, campaigning against the power of finance and austerity's regressive policies. And, while the prospects for important segments of the population continue gloomy, including those for the younger generations who cannot aspire to the living standards of their parents and even less so to climb on to the property ladder, mortgage lending, for example, already shows signs of recovery in many places. See, for example, http://www.ft.com/cms/s/0/8cfddb46-c66f-11e4-add0-00144feab7de.html#axzz3hNx4Ho4s, and http://www.theguardian.com/money/2015/jul/24/mortgage-lending-shows-uk-housing-market-hotting-up, consulted on 29 July 2015.

Acknowledgements

Special thanks are due to Ben Fine, Kate Bayliss and Mary Robertson as well as two anonymous referees for comments on an earlier draft.

Disclosure statement

No potential conflict of interest was reported by the author.

Funding

The research leading to these results has received funding from the European Union Seventh Framework Programme (FP7/2007–2013) under grant agreement number 266800.

References

Amable, B. (2011), 'Morals and Politics in the Ideology of Neo-liberalism', *Socio-Economic Review*, 9 (1), pp. 3–30.

Barba, A. and Pivetti, M. (2009), 'Rising Household Debt: Its Causes and Macroeconomic Implications – A Long-Period Analysis', *Cambridge Journal of Economics*, 33 (1), pp. 113–37.

Bay, C., Catasús, B. and Johed, G. (2014), 'Situating Financial Literacy', *Critical Perspectives on Accounting*, 25 (1), pp. 36–45.

Bayliss, K., Fine, B. and Robertson, M. (2013), 'From Financialisation to Consumption: The Systems of Provision Approach Applied to Housing and Water', FESSUD Working Paper No. 2. Available from: http://fessud.eu/wp-content/uploads/2013/04/FESSUD-Working-Paper-021.pdf [accessed 28 May 2015].

Beggs, M., Bryan, D. and Rafferty, M. (2014), 'Shoplifters of the World Unite! Law and Culture in Financialized Times', *Cultural Studies*, 28 (5), pp. 976–96.

Benartzi, S. and Thaler, R. (2007), 'Heuristics and Biases in Retirement Savings Behavior', *Journal of Economic Perspectives*, 21 (3), pp. 81–104.

Clarke, C. (2015), 'Learning to Fail: Resilience and the Empty Promise of Financial Literacy Education', *Consumption Markets & Culture*, 18 (3), pp. 257–76.

Conselho Nacional de Supervisores Financeiros (CNSF) (2011), *Plano Nacional de Formação Financeira 2011–2015* (Lisboa: BdP, CMVM, ISP).

Epstein, G. (ed.) (2005), *Financialization and the World Economy* (Northampton: Edward Elgar Press).

Erturk, I., *et al.* (2007), 'The Democratization of Finance? Promises, Outcomes and Conditions', *Review of International Political Economy*, 14 (4), pp. 553–75.

European Commission (EC) (2007), *Communication from the Commission: Financial Education* (Brussels: EC). Available from: http://eurlex.europa.eu/LexUriServ/LexUriServ.do?uri=COM:2007:0808:FIN:EN:PDF [accessed 28 May 2015].

Fine, B. (2009), 'Neo-Liberalism in Retrospect? – It's Financialisation, Stupid', paper presented to the Conference on 'Developmental Politics in the Neo-Liberal Era and Beyond', 22–24 October, Centre for Social Sciences, Seoul National University. Available from: http://eprints.soas.ac.uk/7993/ [accessed 28 May 2015].

Fine, B. (2011), 'Financialisation on the Rebound?'. Available from: http://eprints.soas.ac.uk/12102/ [accessed 28 May 2015].

Fine, B. (2017), 'The Material and Culture of Financialisation', *New Political Economy*. doi:10.1080/13563467.2017.1259299.

Fine, B., *et al.* (2016), 'Nudging or Fudging: The World Development Report 2015', Development and Change, 47 (4), pp. 640–63.

Finlayson, A. (2009), 'Financialisation, Financial Literacy and Asset-Based Welfare', *British Journal of Politics & International Relations*, 11 (3), pp. 400–21.

Froud, J. *et al.* (2010), 'Escaping the Tyranny of Earned Income? The Failure of Finance as Social Innovation', *New Political Economy*, 15 (1), pp. 147–64.

Gabor, D. and Brooks, S. (2017), 'The Digital Revolution in Financial Inclusion: International Development in the Fintech Era', *New Political Economy*. doi:10.1080/13563467.2017.1259298.

Grifoni, A. and Messy, F. (2012), 'Current Status of National Strategies for Financial Education: A Comparative Analysis and Relevant Practices', OECD Working Papers on Finance, Insurance and Private Pensions, No. 16 (Paris: OECD).

Happer, C. (2017), 'Financialisation, Media and Social Change', *New Political Economy*. doi:10.1080/13563467.2017.1259301.

HM Treasury (2007), *Financial Capability: The Government´s long-term Approach* (London). Available from: http://www.hm-treasury.gov.uk/d/consult_fincap_resp240707.pdf [accessed 28 May 2015].

Langley, P. (2008), *The Everyday Life of Global Finance: Saving and Borrowing in Anglo-America* (Oxford: Oxford University Press).

de Meza, D., Irlenbusch, B. and Reyniers, D. (2008), *Financial Capability: A Behavioural Economics Perspective* (London: Financial Services Authority).

Mirowski, P. (2009), 'Postface: Defining Neo-liberalism', in Philip Mirowski and Dieter Plehwe' (eds), *The Road from Mont Pèlerin: The Making of the Neo-Liberal Thought Collective* (Cambridge, MA: Harvard University Press), pp. 417–55.

Mirowski, P. (2013), *Never Let a Serious Crisis Go to Waste: How Neo-Liberalism Survived The Financial Meltdown* (London: Verso).

Montgomerie, J. (2009), 'The Pursuit of (Past) Happiness? Middle-Class Indebtedness and American Financialisation', *New Political Economy*, 14 (1), pp. 1–24.

Montgomerie, J. and Büdenbender, M. (2015), 'Round Houses: Homeownership and Failures of Asset-Based Welfare in the United Kingdom', *New Political Economy*, 20 (3), pp. 386–405.

Montgomerie, J. and Tepe-Belfrage, D. (2016), 'A Feminist Moral Political Economy of Uneven Reform in Austerity Britain: Fostering Financial and Parental Literacy', *Globalizations*, 13 (6), pp. 890–905.

Obama, B. (2010), 'National Financial Literacy Month, 2010'. Available from: http://www.ebri.org/pdf/PresProcl2010.pdf [accessed 28 May 2015].

O'Connell, A. (2008), 'Evaluating the Effectiveness of Financial Education Programmes', *OECD Journal: General Papers*, No. 3 (Paris: OECD).

OECD (2005a), *Improving Financial Literacy: Analysis of Issues and Policies* (Paris: OECD).

OECD (2005b), *Recommendations on Principles and Good Practices for Financial Education* (Paris: OECD).

OECD (2009), *Financial Literacy and Consumer Protection: Overlooked Aspects of the Crisis. OECD Recommendation on Good Practices on Financial Education and Awareness Relating to Credit* (Paris: OECD).

OECD (2013a), *Advancing National Strategies for Financial Education: A Joint Publication by Russia's G20 Presidency and the OECD* (Paris: OECD).

OECD (2013b), *PISA 2012 Assessment and Analytical Framework: Mathematics, Reading, Science, Problem Solving and Financial Literacy* (Paris: OECD).

OECD/INFE (2009), *Financial Education and the Crisis: Policy Paper and Guidance* (Paris: OECD).

OECD/INFE (2012), *OECD/INFE High-Level Principles on National Strategies for Financial Education* (Paris: OECD).

Remund, D.L. (2010), 'Financial Literacy Explicated: The Case for a Clearer Definition in an Increasingly Complex Economy', *Journal of Consumer Affairs*, 44 (2), pp. 276–95.

Robertson, M. (2014), 'Housing Provision, Finance, and Well-Being in Europe', FESSUD Working Paper, No. 14. Available from: http://fessud.eu/wp-content/uploads/2013/04/Housing-provision-Finance-and-Well-Being-in-Europe-Working-paper-14.pdf [Accessed 28 May 2016]

Rodrigues, J. (2012), 'Where to Draw the Line Between the State and Markets? Institutionalist Elements in Hayek's Neo-Liberal Political Economy', *Journal of Economic Issues*, 46 (4), pp. 1–27.

Rodrigues, J. (2013), 'Between Rules and Incentives: Uncovering Hayek's Moral Economy', *American Journal of Economics and Sociology*, 72 (3), pp. 565–92.

Rutledge, S.L. (2010), 'Consumer Protection and Financial Literacy: Lessons from Nine Country Studies', Policy Research Working Paper Series, No. 5326 (Washington, DC: World Bank).

Santos, C.A. and Rodrigues, J. (2014), 'Neo-liberalism in the Laboratory? Experimental Economics on Markets and their Limits', *New Political Economy*, 19 (4), pp. 507–33.

Stanley, L. (2014), 'We're Reaping What We Sowed: Everyday Crisis Narratives and Acquiescence to the Age of Austerity', *New Political Economy*, 19 (6), pp. 895–917.

Thaler, R.H. and Sunstein, C.R. (2008), *Nudge: Improving Decisions about Health, Wealth, and Happiness* (New Haven: Yale University Press).

Williams, T. (2007), 'Empowerment of Whom and for What? Financial Literacy Education and the New Regulation of Consumer Financial Services', *Law & Policy*, 29 (2), pp. 226–56.

Willis, L.E. (2008a), 'Against Financial-Literacy Education', *Iowa Law Review*, 94 (1), pp. 197–285.

Willis, L.E. (2008b), 'Evidence and Ideology in Assessing the Effectiveness of Financial Literacy Education', *Scholarship at Penn Law*, Paper 206.

Willis, L.E. (2011), 'The Financial Education Fallacy', *American Economic Review*, 101 (3), pp. 429–34.

The digital revolution in financial inclusion: international development in the fintech era

Daniela Gabor and Sally Brooks

ABSTRACT

This paper examines the growing importance of digital-based financial inclusion as a form of organising development interventions through networks of state institutions, international development organisations, philanthropic investment and fintech companies. The fintech–philanthropy–development complex generates digital ecosystems that map, expand and monetise digital footprints. Its 'know thy (irrational) customer' vision combines behavioural economics with predictive algorithms to accelerate access to, and monitor engagement with, finance. The digital revolution adds new layers to the material cultures of financial(ised) inclusion, offering the state new ways of expanding the inclusion of the 'legible', and global finance new forms of 'profiling' poor households into generators of financial assets.

Introduction

If we solve these large problems of financial inclusion, it will be with new business models, technologies and innovations. Data allow us to know which innovations work and which don't. (Rodger Voorhies, Bill and Melinda Gates Foundation 2014)

Policy initiatives aimed at 'financial inclusion' (FI) have gathered pace since the global financial crisis. The 2008 World Bank Annual Report, entitled *Finance for All*, stressed the importance of FI in the context of the earlier broader paradigm shift in development towards the Post-Washington Consensus' concern with 'inclusive markets' (Mendoza and Thelen 2008). With this, the focus in pro-poor finance moved from microcredit (as provided by microfinance institutions or MFIs) to FI, a term that encompasses a far broader range of financial products and providers (Soederberg 2013).

Since then, strong political headwinds powered the FI agenda in international development. By 2011, the Alliance for Financial Inclusion (AFI), a network of policy-makers and regulators from 90 developing countries, had been created, with funding from the Bill and Melinda Gates Foundation (BMGF) and endorsement from the G20. Half of its members have since signed the Maya Declaration, a shared commitment to 'reach the world's 2.5 billion unbanked' and put in place national FI strategies in partnership with private sector actors (AFI 2014b: 3). At the AFI's 6th Annual Global Policy Forum conference in 2014, the World Bank revealed that it was 'realigning resources to support Maya [Declaration] commitments' at the country level (AFI 2014a: 27), reflecting the emphasis on a greater role for private finance in the post-2015 era (World Bank Group 2013).

In 2014, AFI announced that 'the Maya Declaration has revolutionized international development cooperation by empowering countries to set their own goals and targets' for FI (AFI 2014b: 3). In parallel, the Better than Cash Alliance was set up in 2012 with one important priority – to digitalise social cash transfers and thus accelerate the inclusion of the 'unbanked' of poor countries. Housed at the UN as the implementing partner for the G20 Global Partnership for Financial Inclusion, the Better than Cash Alliance promises that a 'cash lite' Finance for Development agenda would put the UN's Sustainable Development Goals within reach (Goodwin-Groen 2016). Both AFI and the Better than Cash Alliance are funded by the BMGF and by the Omidyar Network, a philanthropic investment organisation created by Peter Omidyar, the entrepreneur behind eBay.

What might explain the rapid rise of FI as a model for development cooperation? Two distinct explanations have emerged recently. Soederberg (2013) scrutinises the G20s' efforts to energise development through FI through the lens of global finance-led capitalism, a capitalism that obscures in the process its exploitative and speculative nature. The 'invitation to live by finance' (Roy 2010 citing Martin 2002: 3) and its spread from high-income countries (including segments of the population considered 'subprime') to the core of the international development agenda should be understood in relationship to broader dynamics of financialisation (see Bayliss *et al.* 2017; also Finlayson 2009, Bryan and Rafferty 2014, Montgomerie and Budenbender 2015). The transformation of welfare states in Organisation for Economic Cooperation and Development (OECD) countries that led to the emergence of individualised, asset-based welfare (Finlayson 2009, Montgomerie and Budenbender 2015) is one side of the financialisation–FI nexus. The push for financial – or financialised – inclusion in the developing world is the other. Poverty is understood as a new frontier for profit-making and accumulation (Elyachar 2012, Roy 2012, Soederberg 2013).

In contrast, some anthropologists of newly emerging forms of money view the convergence between philanthropic development and regulatory communities with less suspicion (see Maurer 2012). In this account, financial technologies such as 'mobile money' open up novel and exciting possibilities for democratising monetary and FI. The poor do not always behave as technologies anticipate, but actively (re)shape monetary spaces through innovations such as informal money transfer mechanisms. Indeed, as the 'financial diaries' literature illustrates, far from being excluded, poor households are often accustomed to managing a multiplicity of formal and informal financial instruments (Collins 2005, 2008, Kamath *et al.* 2010). Since such practices can provide new sources of (legitimate) profits from high-volume, low-value transactions, industry participants observe closely how the poor innovate (Costa and Ehrbeck 2015). Philanthropists, development agencies and regulators see unprecedented opportunities for effective development interventions with low infrastructural and investment requirements.

However, we argue in this paper that it is important to examine critically the contours of a fast-evolving fintech–philanthropy–development (FPD) complex. This should be understood against the backdrop of rapid growth of a digital underworld that feeds available data into opaque algorithmic processes that are increasingly used to organise economic life (Pasquale 2015). This reflects a transformation in the field of predictive algorithm design, from anticipating consumer decisions (Agrawal *et al.* 1993) to producing geographies of suspicion in the securitisation of the war on terror (see Amoore 2009), opening up new possibilities to generate a screened economy of (appetite for) risk in low-income countries.

The process of harvesting digital footprints simultaneously involves the poor's use of mobile technologies and the state's increasingly digitalised social transfers, the latter in recognition that the state, through private digital entrepreneurs, can connect (poor) populations to algorithms. The practices of digital-based FI delineate 'at-risk' populations into categories of borrowers (Kear 2013, Kaminska 2015), incorporating the poor into global strategies of capital accumulation through digital footprints, a project particularly apt for (chaotically) shaping financial(ised) subjectivities.

The scholarship on material cultures of financialisation and the associated 10Cs (Bayliss *et al.* 2017) provides a useful lens through which to examine this complex network of discourses and practices. In particular, we are interested in how digital technologies-based FI is *Constructed* through material practices, *Collective* in promoting financialisation and *Closed* in confining policy-making to an increasingly powerful digital elite with little *Contestation* from official development actors. We trace a discursive shift that attributes market failures not to poorly regulated financial markets and institutions, but to *individual* consumers whose behavioural traits can be captured, shaped and 'corrected' through behavioural economics (see World Bank 2013, 2015). This disjuncture is mirrored in development discourses that naturalise 'the market', with a shift in emphasis from correcting market failures ('making markets work for the poor') to creating market *subjects* (Berndt 2015). Cognitively deficient financial subjects must now learn to be 'resilient' to market shocks (Clarke 2015) through financial education (Kear 2013, Marron 2013, Santos, 2017) or, failing that, 'nudge' techniques (Berndt 2015, World Bank 2015). This 'consensus', locating the cause and solution of financial crises in consumer fallibility, has thus spurred a phase in development thinking and practice that seeks to further embed 'commodity calculation' (see Bayliss *et al.* 2017) in everyday household decision-making (see World Bank 2015). Meanwhile, the rapid diffusion of mobile technologies in developing countries provides the technological infrastructure through which financial providers, facilitated by these global networks, can 'reach the unbanked' and shape financial subjectivities.

A defining feature of financial(ised) inclusion as enabled by new information technologies, particularly mobile technology, is what we refer to as the 'commodification' of a new class of financial consumer, or more accurately, of his or her personal data. Central to this vision is the potential of digital technologies to capture the data of the newly 'included' in ways that enable lenders to map, know and govern 'risky populations'. In other words, rather than seeking to reorganise people and things spatially in order to render societies 'legible' (cf. Scott 1998), mobile technologies provide the means to 'administratively re-order' populations in new ways by engaging individual citizens in the process of creating themselves as legible subjects (Ruppert *et al.* 2013). This project of digital legibility is *Closed* in the sense defined by Bayliss *et al.* (2017), as the assumptions underpinning the algorithms of the predictive industry are the proprietary knowledge of an increasingly powerful digital elite, while the development of research methodologies that might render algorithms transparent, for example, through institutional practices and effects, is at a nascent stage (Ruppert *et al.* 2013).

The paper is organised as follows. We first outline the historical emergence of a development agenda focused on FI. We then examine the institutional contours and practices of the FPD complex. We argue that the harvesting and monitoring of digital footprints that feed into behavioural models of 'know thy (irrational) customer', and the growing importance of 'nudging techniques', point to the emergence of a firmly disciplinary trait in the financialisation project in international development. This, we conclude, opens up important research questions of how households and agents *Construe* the processes described, and their emerging techniques of resistance to, and transformation of, the sophisticated range of digital surveillance techniques.

FI: the emergence of an international development agenda

FI was conceived as an analytical lens through which to understand the relationship between finance and the poor (Marron 2013). Early research on financial *exclusion* explored the ways in which financial institutions discriminated against certain socio-economic groups (Dymski and Veitsch 1992, Leyshon and Thrift 1995, 1996). This critical reading explored questions of how the financial sector structurally shapes and sharpens inequality by system(at)ically favouring 'the rich and powerful'. Exclusion was thus the fault and responsibility of financial capital, which conducts 'an insidious and relatively unremarked-upon assault […] upon poorer and disadvantaged groups' (Leyshon and Thrift 1995: 314).

Early proposals to force banks to include the poor were deemed problematic at both ideological and political levels. Exclusion was thus reframed as a question of individual accessibility rather than structural marginalisation, and policies focused on removing obstacles to participation in 'normal' activities (Kempson and Whyley 1999, Johnson and Arnold 2012). Demand-side explanations of individual accessibility – the 'individual turn' in FI studies – took centre stage (Marron 2013). According to these, low-income households could not meet the price of certain financial products, were not aware of others and, ultimately, were 'psychologically' un(der)prepared to see themselves as financial subjects (Kempson *et al.* 2000). Policy focused on persuading banks, without direct regulation, to expand the provision of financial services to the excluded, who would in turn be better educated through financial literacy campaigns. Subsidies, private–public partnerships[1] and market-making regulations would incentivise banks to create new products tailored to the excluded.

By the late 2000s, FI had travelled across borders to anchor a new, finance-based, development paradigm. The World Bank played an important role. Its economists dedicated substantial efforts to demonstrating empirically that financial development leads to (pro-poor) economic growth (see Beck *et al.* 2000, 2004), thus legitimising the World Bank's financial liberalisation agenda. FI helped reframe the early emphasis on microfinance as the market-based solution to poverty (Roy 2010, Soederberg 2013). Celebrated in the 1990s as 'the vaccine for the pandemic of poverty', microfinance initiatives such as the Grameen Bank drew attention to the potential of 'peer lending' through which well-organised groups could access credit by replacing economic collateral with the discipline of peer 'solidarity' through group-based lending, to ensure repayment and thus the financial 'sustainability' of microfinance programmes and institutions.

Yet microfinance, as most other market-based development initiatives, failed to achieve 'success' even on its own terms – that is in fostering the poor's entrepreneurship (World Bank 2008). One oft-cited reason for failure is breach of the principle of financial sustainability expected to govern MFIs. This required that loans be used only for productive activities and extended at market interest rates (Cull *et al.* 2007). Moreover, the attempts to impose market discipline typically meant that microfinance clients had to specialise in activities with high uncertainty, short profit cycles and limited profitability (Shakya and Rankin 2008). Nor did microfinance manage to consistently reach the excluded. Instead, loan officers typically resorted to pressuring existing borrowers to take larger loans on longer terms. By early 2008, concerns with over-indebtedness and scepticism about the development potential of microfinance became pervasive (Duvendack *et al.* 2011).

More fundamentally, the microfinance model did not disproportionately benefit the poor, as was originally claimed. Findings from research in Latin America, Eastern Europe, South and Southeast Asia and South Africa have revealed that a development approach centred on microcredit '*programmatically* disadvantages the poor in the longer run' (Bateman 2014: 100, original emphasis), since it directs resources towards 'very small – often one-person firms of low productivity', which might otherwise have been channelled towards a nascent small and medium-sized enterprise (SME) sector as a foundation for economic growth and employment (also Duvendack *et al.* 2011). In this respect, the microfinance model has been described as 'anti-developmental'; instead of delivering sustainable development, it generated a succession of 'boom to bust' episodes in countries as diverse as Bolivia, Nicaragua, Morocco, Pakistan and Bosnia (Bateman 2014: 102).

In *Finance for All* (World Bank 2008), the Bank side-stepped such pressing questions about the pitfalls of market-based financial sector development. It redirected attention from specialist MFIs to mainstream financial institutions, and to the broadening of the definition of 'pro-poor' financial services to include savings and payment services alongside lending, targeting both households and small businesses. Above all, interventions were to be entirely market-based. The Bank warned governments to avoid repeating earlier 'mistakes' with 'market-substituting' policies (subsidised lending rates or government ownership of financial institutions). Instead, the Bank insisted that governments focus on market-*developing* policies, including macroeconomic stability and financial deepening as supply-side interventions that would create instruments for risk diversification and thus allow banks to engage with higher risk consumers.

The global financial crisis in the same year brought into sharp focus the fragility underpinning projects to extend financial participation, throwing into doubt the wisdom of a major expansion of market-based FI. Scholars argued that 'the orgy of subprime lending' in the USA was a consequence of market-based forms of FI (French *et al.* 2009). The pre-crisis wisdom that exclusion from financial services imposes costs mutated into an overt anxiety that inclusion may do the same, by encouraging banks to generate and manage risky assets from 'subprime' borrowers. The Bank's response was swift, and sought to re-*Construct* the market-based FI agenda as the only way forward. Indeed, the premise behind World Bank's Global Findex database is that the relationship between households' access to finance and development outcomes can only be properly theorised with empirical evidence from cross-country, time-series data (Demirgurc-Kunt and Klapper 2012). In other words, empirical evidence of a particular kind would be necessary to demonstrate that the US subprime moment was anything other than an isolated exception in an otherwise positive account of FI.

The 2014 World Bank's flagship Global Financial Development Report, dedicated to FI, took these scholarly 'cleansing' efforts further. On a macro level, the Report addresses the unavoidable question of the analytical link between FI and financial instability. While recognising that over-indebtedness can lead to financial instability where financial institutions have perverse incentives to embrace a 'finance for all at all costs' approach, the empirical sections of the Report reject any correlation, let alone causality, between FI and financial stability across a large set of high- and low-income countries (see Čihak et al. 2013). In doing so, the Report dismisses evidence in support of state intervention through subsidies and state-owned banks in developing countries – a 'developmental' approach to finance (see Bateman 2014 for example) – and instead pushes for private sector innovation as the source of new products and services that will 'address market failures, meet consumer needs, and overcome behavioral problems' (World Bank 2013: 3).

In other words, despite the lip service paid to the systemic implications of over-indebtedness, the pre-crisis enthusiasm for FI as a market-based panacea for inequality and development remained intact. This allows for state intervention as long as it is of the 'right' kind, as explained by the Bank in its discussions of development financing in the post-2015 era (World Bank 2013). For the Bank, aid should be seen as one of a range of institutional and policy levers used to attract and secure *private finance* for development. Indeed, its own International Finance Corporation (IFC) channels fund directly to financial intermediaries in emerging markets as a strategy to foster 'financial deepening and inclusion for private sector-led growth' (World Bank 2013: 32).

In this context, the power of microfinance as a 'mobilising narrative' has played a central – but paradoxical – role in bridging the microfinance and FI eras in international development (Rankin 2013, Mader 2016). While the 'resilience' of the microfinance model stemmed from its *limited* financialisation as a 'closed ecosystem', the model has more recently been recast as a 'safe investment' in a new push to open up MFIs to global investors. Thus, the emphasis shifted from the financial sustainability imperative to the *profitability* of microfinance instruments, with often devastating consequences for the poorest borrowers (Aitken 2010, Rankin 2013).

The IFC has been a major driver of what Soederberg (2013) calls the 'slice and dice' development approach that prioritises securitisation of microfinance instruments in developing countries. In this context, the term securitisation refers to the conversion and packaging of microloans into liquid securities that can be traded on financial markets, in a similar manner to the asset-based securitisation (ABS) that led to the subprime 'moment' and the global financial crisis. Nevertheless, the IFC portrays ABS as a risk-reducing innovation that could help developing countries meet the growing demand for finance generated by successful FI strategies in conditions of capital scarcity. As 'the world's largest supplier of financial services to private sector entities in the global South', the IFC is attracted to securitisation because it allows it to 'expand its reach without expanding its [own] risk/gamble' (Soederberg 2013: 602).

Mapping the future? The alliance for FI

The promotion of FI as a development paradigm is not unique to the World Bank, but rather a symptom of a much larger shift to market-based FI in development cooperation. Since the global financial crisis in 2008, we have witnessed the emergence of networks of policy-makers in emerging/developing countries, international financial organisations, 'philanthropic investment firms' and fintech companies whose interests are closely aligned in promoting FI.

The most visible institutional structure is the AFI, which unites more than 90 developing and emerging countries in a commitment to mobilise FI as a 'method to unlock human potential'. Half of the participating countries agreed to binding targets through the Maya declaration, targets that are designed and owned by each country, tailored to their conditions. Several participants also envisaged the adoption of national FI strategies that would include specific initiatives to achieve the Maya commitments. The World Bank applauded the impressive coordination effort, energised by the G20, and declared that it would realign resources in its country-level missions towards the Maya priorities.

As the AFI (2015, 2014a, 2013) Annual Reports make clear, the top thematic areas of the Maya commitments include financial literacy, digital financial services (electronic payments, mobile financial services and agent banking), 'proportional' financial sector regulation and FI data. The largest regions with 'unbanked' populations, sub-Saharan Africa, Asia, Latin America and the Caribbean, emphasise digital financial services as a solution to problems of access for the population in rural areas whose 'digital footprint' through the use of mobile phones is significant. According to estimates from the Omidyar Network, by the end of 2015, 1.7 billion of the 2 billion without formal access to finance have a mobile phone (Costa and Ehrbeck 2015).

That AFI would not simply be a new forum for coordinating state institutions in global development initiatives became obvious from its inception. With funding from the BMGF, AFI is administered by Deutsche Gesellschaft für Internationale Zusammenarbeit (GIZ), the German public benefit enterprise that coordinates official German development cooperation. By 2014, the Omidyar Network would become the second philanthropic investment organisation officially partnered with AFI (AFI 2015). Its mission is to combine 'venture capital investments in innovative ideas to advance financial inclusion' with grants that generate 'the knowledge and advocacy necessary for an ecosystem in which these ideas can mature' (Costa and Ehrbeck 2015). The Omidyar Network thus funds and invests in fintech companies that can disrupt high information costs of credit risk assessment for the poor and thus leverage an 'emerging lower-cost' environment through innovative products and services.

For the first few years of its existence, AFI remained a forum accessible exclusively to policy-makers. That changed with the launch of the Public Private Dialogue Platform (PPD) in 2014. The PPD promises policy-makers 'private sector insights' for developing new policies, and the private sector 'an unprecedented opportunity' to connect to policy-makers who are regulating new and high growth markets and, furthermore, a 'highly visible exhibition space in AFI Market Place' (AFI 2015: 1). By June 2015, Mastercard, Visa and Banco Bilbao Vizcaya Argentaria (BBVA) (a global bank headquartered in Spain) had become AFI members, with more partnerships to be formalised in the future. Meanwhile, the AFI acts as an umbrella and incubator for a growing number of global and regional FI programmes such as the United Nations Development Programme (UNDP)-Funded 'Mobile Money for the Poor' (MM4P) and 'Shaping Inclusive Finance Transformations' (SHIFT), among others.

The FPD complex thus sees the growing influence of a digital elite in development interventions with apparently little scope for contestation. Indeed, one key priority for the PPD platform is a dialogue on innovative products, business models and approaches, predicated on the idea that technology and big data can play a critical role in enabling public–private partnerships for FI. Its strategic priorities evoke closely the digital ecosystem envisaged by the Omidyar Network, where innovative ideas can be developed and put into practice with support from 'progressive' regulators (Costa and Ehrbeck 2015) and an emerging scholarship on 'proportionate regulation' (for example, see Tait and Banda 2016). It is here that the politics of FI – or financial*ised* inclusion – anchored in the digital revolution starts to become apparent.

First, as Kaminska (2015) argues, behind such promises lies a threat of 'financial intrusion' and an explicit strategy to generate revenue streams from monetising financial data. As such, the extent of genuine consumer 'choice' is constrained by an underlying requirement that all services *Conform* to the logic of a system of provision designed to generate such income streams. Here the group discipline associated with Grameen-type revolving microcredit loans is superseded by new forms of individual self-governance, facilitated by 'disruptive' digital technologies developed with support from philanthropic organisations such as the Omidyar network. For example, Cignifi Inc., a US-based fintech company, receives funding to further its strategic goal of disrupting traditional credit risk assessment. Headed by a former IFC director, Cignifi first partnered with OI Telecom in Brazil in

2010 and then with Telefonica, a telecom operator with presence across Latin American countries, to test its credit-scoring platform (Cignifi 2014).

Cignifi's business model involves creating credit scores for mobile phone users without a credit history, by predicting behaviour from the patterns of calls and text messages. Credit scores extracted from a behavioural track record can help measure the appetite for financial products among 'emerging customers', as well as default risk (Cignifi 2014). Another Omidyar investment, Revolution Credit, exemplifies how the FPD complex not only tracks, but also creates digital footprints. Potential, 'thin file' borrowers are invited to participate in online games and quizzes that generate behavioural data, which are in turn fed in predictive algorithms (Costa and Ehrbeck 2015). Put differently, data and algorithms become critical to pushing the risk frontier in low-income countries, as fintech companies create, collect and commodify behavioural data, within an 'ecosystem' fostered by networks of philanthropic investors, development finance institutions and donors and policy-makers in participating countries.

Furthermore, the state also plays an important role in the commercial processes of harvesting and commodification of digital footprints. Thus, a spinoff from the AFI, the Better than Cash Alliance, takes the project of (re)-constructing digital footprints even further by accelerating the transition from cash to digital payments globally. Set up in 2012, the Alliance ostensibly promotes a partnership between governments, private sector and international organisations involved in development (the UNDP alongside the International Fund for Agricultural Development (IFAD) and global Non-governmental organisations (NGOs) such as CARE and Concern Worldwide), funded the BMGF and Omidyar Network (with United States Agency for International Development (USAID), Mastercard, Citi Foundation and Visa). Its first case study, written by the Bankable Frontier Associates with advice from the World Bank Payment group, explores Mexico's decision to shift from cash to digital payments for government-to-person payments (salaries, pensions and cash transfers). The greatest promise for FI, it stresses, is to digitalise social transfers, thus reaching the 'unbankable' at a stroke through the long arm of the state. The slow progress in digitalising social cash transfers, it argues, stems from a lack of incentives for governments that can be addressed through the Maya commitments to FI (Babatz 2013).

In its report commissioned by the Better than Cash Alliance, the aptly named Bankable Frontier Associates (2014) made clear what is at stake in the 'journey towards cash lite'. For financial service providers, the opportunities for FI via digital payments do not arise from increasing the use of bank deposits by the previously unbanked, since bank accounts are not 'daily relevant'. Rather, opportunities 'come from financial service providers using the digital information generated by e-payments and receipts to form a profile for each individual customer. This digital profiling then enables providers to offer more appropriate and relevant products. Even beyond the use of e-payment records, businesses are starting to use other "digital footprints", such as mobile phone calling records and social network traffic, to offer credit to the excluded groups' (Bankable Frontier Associates 2014: 8). Thus alongside or in cooperation with private digital entrepreneurs, the state can accelerate global finance's access to the poor's digital footprints, while at the same time rendering off-grid populations 'legible' (Scott 1998), and thus governable, in new ways (cf. Ruppert 2012).

It is no coincidence that, along with its FI portfolio, Omidyar is developing drone technology to confirm and protect property rights in low-income countries. Its deep involvement in AFI and the Better than Cash Alliance will allow it to put such 'transformative technologies' at the centre of initiatives to energise FI, involving a constant monitoring of the assets of borrowers and potentially their movements.[2] Omidyar Network is investing in a broad range of fintech start-ups governed by a 'know thy (irrational) customer' philosophy of harnessing the digital revolution to the aims of FI. For example, Zoona in South Africa stresses that the 'unbankable' consumer exists in a very different world, his or her financial decisions shaped by considerations other than those at play in the offices of fintech companies. Using behavioural economics to map and understand those decisions would thus render a continent with a 'high demographic dividend' and high poverty more attractive to foreign capital.

Indeed, one of the promises that Cignifi makes is to continuously track changes in customer performance as mobile phone data are refreshed. A mobile phone, whose use can feed data capturing the 'move from one behavioral state to another' (Cignifi 2014: 7), would become a new Panopticon for self-regulating financial behaviour in ways that preserve mobile-data-based credit scores. Thus, the 'digital revolution' now increasingly underpinning FI adds new layers to the construction of financial governmentality.

In sum, the fintech vision of FI – know thy (irrational) customer – is a market-led process that harnesses the power of technology, the better understanding of human behaviour and broad political support. It is a vision that celebrates the possibilities for simultaneously achieving positive returns, philanthropy and human development.

Know thy (irrational) customer: digital technologies and financial (self-)government

FI is, therefore, a process not only of bringing the 'unbankable' into the market, and making governable subjects more legible to the state, but also one of deploying the assets they generate for broader strategies of capital accumulation that are far from transparent (Roy 2012, Soederberg 2013). Governing the conduct of 'risky populations' involves finding new ways to securitise income streams from the hitherto excluded through the creation and trading of new types of asset, combined with innovative approaches to 'de-risking people who would otherwise be too risky to lend to' (Kaminska 2015: 1). Paradoxically, just as new technologies and products appear to shorten the distance between global banks and households (Finlayson 2009, Soederberg 2013), new processes of 'distancing' are underway. These obscure the role of the newly included in a system whose inner workings are increasingly complex and opaque (cf. Clapp 2014).

Central to this vision is the potential of digital technologies to capture the data of the newly 'included' in ways that enable lenders to map, know and govern 'risky' populations. In other words, rather than seeking to reorganise people and things spatially in order to render societies 'legible' (cf. Scott 1998), data generated via mobile technologies provide the means to 'administratively re-order' populations in new ways, based on the 'moving target' of behavioural data as opposed to more stable 'background' characteristics. Through processes that are far from transparent, therefore, previously out-of-reach citizens participate 'inter-passively' in becoming legible subjects (Ruppert 2011, Ruppert et al. 2013). Omidyar Network's strategy of establishing a presence (eventually dominant) in the different nodes of the digital ecosystem underpinning FI, in close partnership with state institutions, offers a powerful example of the common project of digital legibility.

This generates data that can be used in two ways: to inform behaviour change strategies used by lenders to 'nudge' individual behaviour in desired directions, and to inform risk management strategies that diffuse risk among various others in an increasingly complex chain of actors (Kaminska 2015). In either case, to be 'included' is to be *excluded* from knowledge of the workings of a *Closed* system into which poor consumers are incorporated as a class of borrowers whose rights to privacy are suspended until such time as full (financial) citizenship is 'earned'.[3]

Meanwhile, a growing body of literature, drawing on tenets of behavioural economics, is at hand to provide further legitimation of this framing of the poor consumer as 'risky subject', not least from the self-named 'knowledge bank' itself. Just as early accounts portrayed the prototypical subprime borrower as the 'single African American woman', distinctly ill-suited to participate in financial markets (Squires 2011), the FI development narrative links financial instability to consumers' 'behavioural problems' (World Bank 2013). Financial education has, therefore, assumed a new importance in the international development field, as Grameen-style group-based discipline and 'solidarity' give way to individualised financial government.

Such interventions are understood in terms of an increasingly pervasive 'resilience doctrine' which views market crises as 'natural' phenomena against which individual citizens and households must become resilient. In this context, then, financial education is a 'training in resilience', or ability to withstand market shocks (Clarke 2015). On the other hand, it is acknowledged that financial literacy alone may be insufficient for the poor to be able to access and benefit from financial services, since 'individuals can have financial knowledge but still make irrational financial decisions' (World Bank 2013: 23). Instead, adequate participation in financial markets necessitates a range of 'psychological traits and motivations associated with financial capability', including self-control. Poor consumers are *Constructed* as more likely to make mistakes, either because they are irrational or because they suffer from cognitive limitations (Firestone, Van Order and Zorn 2007).

This way of envisaging the decision-making processes of the poor finds its clearest expression in the 2015 World Development Report (World Bank 2015, see Fine *et al*. 2016 for a critique). In this Report, poverty 'is not only a deficit in material resources but also a context in which decisions are made. It can impose a cognitive burden on individuals that makes it especially difficult for them to think deliberatively' (World Bank 2015: 13). Instead, poor people are said to rely on 'automatic' decision-making. Financial distress, the Report argues, affects thinking capacity and even IQ. Put another way, poverty imposes a 'cognitive tax'. Solutions are put forward, drawn from 'nudge' theory, involving the use of 'choice architecture' to nudge consumers (or potential consumers) in the direction of 'better' choices (cf. Thaler and Sunstein 2008).

High consumer debt is thus conceptualised as the result of poor consumers thinking 'automatically' rather than deliberatively, justifying a narrow understanding of 'financial education' as channelling behaviour in particular directions without revealing the logic of the system within which such behaviours are deemed necessary. However, this construction of the irrational, financially illiterate and 'excluded' consumer is at odds with that of the more sophisticated individual that emerges from research that draws on poor people's 'financial diaries', charting instances of actual (rather than imagined) financial behaviour (Collins 2005, 2008, Kamath *et al*. 2010). Such accounts, in which consumers of a range of formal and informal financial services engage in complex financial strategies combining acts of borrowing, saving *and* lending, are notable by their absence in the design of programmes for financial education in a development context.

Needless to say, while behaviourism provides the conceptual framework for understanding the borrower, this is not so for the lender (World Bank 2015: 14). The Global Financial Development Report (World Bank 2013) specifically downplays the role of financial actors in creating systemic instability, suggesting that financial institutions can only exploit consumers lacking financial capability. Ultimately, over-indebtedness is a mark of individual behavioural shortcomings rather than structural dynamics in the financial sector. In this context, the decision by the World Bank (2015) to elaborate on insights from the discipline of behavioural economics makes sense as a means to accommodate this *Contradictory* position and 'explain' irrational consumer behaviour without displacing neoclassical economics as the hegemonic discipline, and 'the individual' as the unit of analysis, thus steering the debate well clear of structural explanations of the financial crisis (Fine *et al*. 2016).

From a Foucauldian governmentality perspective that eschews the inclusion/exclusion binary, these developments can be read as a problem of financial *government* which is progressing along with, and through, the production of new subjectivities that are 'eminently governable by financial means' (Kear 2013: 1). This line of enquiry moves the analytical lens onto the (discursive) production of financial subjectivities and the exercise of political power through calculative rationalities (Lemke 2001, see also Bayliss *et al*. 2017). While neo-liberalism involves attempts to universalise the 'homo economicus', since the 'self-regulating capacities of subjects (...) have become key resources' (Miller and Rose 2008: 26), financialisation transforms 'everyday life', creating new financial identities that *Conform* to the requirements of expanding financial markets (Langley, 2008, 2010). FI is thus conceived as a new form of governmentality, rolling out tiered forms of private financial 'government' that produces and relates the financial self(ves) to power (Kear 2013).

Thus, FI discourses mark a broader shift to fostering the individual's ability to deal with contingencies and uncertainties that welfare states had addressed in the past through collective pooling of risk in public pensions, health, housing, education and labour market protection (Kear 2013). From this asset-based welfare perspective (Finlayson 2009), and with the emphasis now firmly on the individual consumer, risk is no longer solely a threat, but can become an opportunity for profit for 'resilient' consumers in possession of the right calculative practices and attitudes to risk (Marron 2013, Bryan and Rafferty 2014, Clarke 2015). FI as a development paradigm, therefore, envisages no material change in the (changing) structures that generate marginality, but rather seeks to channel individual behaviour, through digital surveillance and education, to engage and identify with these structures.

Upgrading the financial subject, Marron (2013: 11) argues, is not solely a question of equipping individuals with the right risk management frameworks. Financial subjects are also expected to 'find meaning, value and self-expression' through their participation in financial activities; if they cannot, they are *Construed* as suffering from 'behavioural problems', issues of 'self-control' and shortages of 'cognitive resources' (World Bank 2015). Here we find the familiar contradictions 'in the assembly of the financial subject' (Langley 2008: 85) that Bayliss *et al.* (2017) attributes to the *Chaotic* nature of the material culture of financialisation.

Before the global financial crisis, FI discourses – promoted by international development agencies – celebrated households' role as risk absorbers of last resort (Bryan and Rafferty 2014: 408). Similarly, global finance saw the poor as being a 'crisis-resilient asset class' with a 'low threshold for risk' (Soederberg 2013: 606, see also Clarke 2015) that held great promise for securitisation. The global financial crisis threw into question this optimism when it revealed that the combination of high unemployment and high food prices left the poor unwilling to prioritise loan repayments over daily subsistence, suggesting that financialisation and its effects may not have gone completely un-*Contested* (see Santos, 2017). The daily monitoring of digital footprints that feed into behavioural models of 'know thy (irrational) customer' and the growing importance of 'nudging techniques' point to the revival of a more disciplinary trait of the financialisation project in international development, with an increasingly sophisticated range of digital surveillance techniques.

However, it would be a mistake to treat these reconfigurations as evidence of the un-*Contestable* nature of financialisation (see Bayliss *et al.* 2017). Indeed, a material culture of financialisation approach raises two questions which merit further investigation. First, it is important to reflect on the practices of resistance that are possible in this new world of rapidly expanding digital technologies. How will we resist dystopian futures of self-governance and discipline where a smartphone or a smartwatch would allow global finance to constantly monitor our everyday lives for signs of irrationality that can threaten the valuation of liquid assets generated through digital footprints? Second, the discourses of the FPD complex give the impression of more control, more reach than occurs in reality. As Maurer (2012) points out, attempts by the financial industry to 'format' the poor into customers have been subverted and transformed precisely because the poor innovate, appropriating technologies in ways that cannot be predicted by algorithms or their creators. Or can they? At present, research methodologies for investigating patterns and processes of digital subjectification, and the potential for innovation and resistance, are at an early stage (Ruppert *et al.* 2013). Nevertheless, just as in the subprime crisis when consumers resisted pressures to prioritise loan repayment, further research is needed to identify and understand evolving practices of adoption, adaptation and resistance at the frontiers of financialisation in developing countries.

Conclusion

The global spread of individualised asset-based welfare (see Robertson in 2017 in the context of housing), FI and the power of global finance, uninterrupted by the financial crisis of 2008 (although not necessarily uniform in its implementation, see Prabhakar 2013), should be understood as connected in tandem with one another. To address their mutual dynamics, therefore, it is important to understand how the subprime 'moment', now perversely being recast as development policy, is being extended to new markets in the South under a 'development' banner. The key words are access via digital footprints – not only the ability of the 'unbanked' to access financial services, but also for financial capital to access new 'risk frontiers', within an institutional and policy framework that enables financial actors to 'de-risk' individual consumers through constant monitoring.

Since the crisis, there has been a convergence of policy and knowledge co-production, and in particular the employment of behaviouralism as justification and guide to future development practice (World Bank 2015). However, these discourses of inclusion (and 'access') obscure the desire and momentum of financial capital to access high-risk/high return markets (Kaminska 2015). In this case, the role of the state is recast to provide 'an enabling environment' for financial capital to flow freely, while allowing the consequences of systemic risks to be transferred to consumers precariously positioned at the 'bankable frontier', while their 'digital footprints' are captured and quantified as evidence of potential income streams against which securitised loans can be made that form the basis for tomorrow's financial 'innovations'.

This analysis of financial(ised) inclusion as a multi-tiered process of financial subject formation (Kear 2013) provides a useful lens for understanding why there should be an absence of genuine *Contestation* (Santos, 2017) in response to the identification of borrowers in need of education – not lenders in need of regulatory reform – as the primary source of risk to the financial system. This article has highlighted how the normalisation of the subprime 'moment' as 'business as usual' worldwide is being facilitated via an ambitious global programme of market-based financial development that has the support of major donors and multilateral development banks.

As an evolving international institutional infrastructure for FI, the FPD complex is extending reach and impact at a rapid pace and, in the process, generating a plethora of finance-based identities and possibilities that are hard to resist. One could conclude that, as predicted by other contributions to this volume, *Contestation* to such a well-resourced programme of incorporation would be limited. However, we would argue that further empirical research is needed to explore in more depth the processes of financial (self-)governance and the (im)possibility of emergent forms of resistance to efforts to induce new populations to *Conform* to the 'ethos of commodity calculation' (Bayliss *et al.* 2017), before drawing conclusions about the ways in which the material cultures of financialisation are *Construed* by diverse actors in FI networks at different sites.

Notes

1. Through initiatives such as (tax-free) Individual Savings Account, stakeholder pensions, insure with rent schemes and the promotion of credit unions.
2. Peru's superintendent of banks and pension funds suggested an even more dystopian disciplining technique for the 'unbanked'. The FI revolution, he argued, would solve employment problems in poor countries when accompanied by psychometric testing for those without formal education. Combined with the World Bank's pathology of the excluded, these would serve to confirm the 'scarcity' of cognitive resources in the poor, and to design behaviour-based approaches for discipline (AFI 2014a).
3. Roy (2010), for example, describes the post-crisis efforts of the Moody's Research Lab, a 'research incubator' recently established within Moody's Corporation and providing credit ratings for debt instruments and securities. The task of the lab is to 'map the risk frontiers associated with hitherto unbanked markets'.

Disclosure statement

No potential conflict of interest was reported by the authors.

Funding

This work was supported by the Seventh Framework Programme [contract number 266800].

References

Aitken, R. (2010), 'Ambiguous Incorporations: Microfinance and Global Governmentality', *Global Networks*, 10 (2), pp. 223–43.

Alliance for Financial Inclusion. (2013), *2013 AFI Global Policy Forum (GPF) Report*. Available from: http://www.afi-global.org/global-policy-forum/2013 [accessed 19 December 2015].

Alliance for Financial Inclusion. (2014a), *2014 AFI Global Policy Forum (GPF) Report: Global Partnerships, National Goals, Empowering People*. Available from: http://www.afi-global.org/library/publications/2014-global-policy-forum-report-global-partnerships-national-goals-empowering [accessed 19 December 2015].

Alliance for Financial Inclusion. (2014b), *Measurable Goals with Optimal Impact: 2014 Maya Declaration Progress Report*. Available from: http://www.afi-global.org/sites/default/files/publications/2014_maya_declaration_progress_report_final_low_res.pdf [accessed 19 December 2015].

Alliance for Financial Inclusion. (2015), *2015 AFI Global Policy Forum (GPF) Report*. Available from: http://www.afi-global.org/global-policy-forum/2015 [accessed 19 December 2015].

Agrawal, R., Imielinski, T. and Swami, A. (1993), 'Mining Association Rules between Sets of Items in Large Databases', *ACM SIGMOD Record*, 22 (2), pp. 207–16. ACM.

Amoore, L. (2009), 'Algorithmic War: Everyday Geographies of the War on Terror', *Antipode*, 41 (1), pp. 49–69.

Babatz, A. (2013), 'Sustained Effort, Saving Billions: Lessons from the Mexican Government's Shift to Electronic Payments', Better Than Cash Alliance Evidence Paper: Mexico Study (New York: Better Than Cash Alliance).

Bankable Frontier Associates. (2014), *The Journey Towards Cash-Lite. Report Commissioned by the Better than Cash Alliance*. Available from: http://www.uncdf.org/sites/default/files/Download/BetterThanCashAlliance-JourneyTowardCashLite.pdf [accessed 19 December 2015].

Bateman, M. (2014), 'South Africa's Post-Apartheid Microcredit-driven Calamity', *Law Democracy and Development*, 8, pp. 92–135.

Bayliss, K., Fine, B. and Robertson, M. (2017), 'Introduction to Special Issue on the Material Cultures of Financialisation', *New Political Economy*. doi:10.1080/13563467.2017.1259304

Beck, T., Levine, R. and Loayza, M. (2000), 'Finance and the Sources of Growth', *Journal of Financial Economics*, 58 (1), pp. 261–300.

Beck, T., Asli Demirgüç-Kunt, E.F. and Levine, R. (2004), 'Finance, Inequality and Poverty Alleviation: Cross-Country Evidence', World Bank Policy Research Working Paper (Washington, DC: The World Bank).

Berndt, C. (2015), 'Behavioural Economics, Experimentalism and the Marketisation of Development', *Economy and Society*, 44 (4), pp. 567–91.

Bryan, D. and Rafferty, M. (2014), 'Political Economy and Housing in the Twenty-first Century–From Mobile Homes to Liquid Housing?', *Housing, Theory and Society*, 31 (4), pp. 404–12.

Čihak, M., Demirguc-Kunt, A. and Ross, L. (2013), 'Financial Development in 205 Economies, 1960 to 2010', *Journal of Financial Perspectives*, 1 (2), pp. 17–36.

Cignifi. (2014), 'Building the Bridge to New Customers in Brazil', White Paper. Available from: http://www.cignifi.com/lead-generation/ [accessed 19 December 2015].

Clapp, J. (2014), 'Financialisation, Distance and Global Food Politics', *Journal of Peasant Studies*, 41 (5), pp. 797–814.

Clarke, C. (2015), 'Learning to Fail: Resilience and the Empty Promise of Financial Literacy Education', *Consumption Markets & Culture*, 18, pp. 257–76.

Collins, D. (2005), 'Financial Instruments of the Poor: Initial Findings from the South African Financial Diaries study', *Development Southern Africa*, 22 (5), pp. 717–28.

Collins, D. (2008), 'Debt and Household Finance: Evidence from the Financial Diaries', *Development Southern Africa*, 25 (4), pp. 469–79.

Costa, A. and Ehrbeck, T. (2015), 'A Market-Building Approach to Financial Inclusion', *Innovations*, 10 (1-2), pp. 1–2.

Cull, R., Demirgüç-Kunt, A. and Morduch, J. (2007), 'Financial Performance and Outreach: A Global Analysis of Leading Microbanks', *Economic Journal*, 117 (517), pp. F107–F133.

Demirguc-Kunt, A. and Klapper, L. (2012), 'Measuring Financial Inclusion: The Global Findex Database', World Bank Policy Research Paper 6025 (Washington, DC: The World Bank).

Duvendack, M., et al. (2011), What is the Evidence of the Impact of Microfinance on the well-being of Poor People? EPPI-Centre, Social Science Research Unit, Institute of Education, University of London. Available from: http://opus.bath.ac.uk/26940/1/Microfinance_2011Duvendack_report.pdf [accessed 18 November 2016].

Dymski, G.A. and Veitch, J.M. (1992), 'Race and the Financial Dynamics of Urban Growth: LA as Fay Wray', in G. Riposa and C. Dersch (eds), City of Angels (Dubuque, IA: Kendall/Hunt), pp. 131–58.

Elyachar, J. (2012), 'Next Practices: Knowledge, Infrastructure, and Public Goods at the Bottom of the Pyramid', Public Culture, 24 (166), pp. 109–29.

Fine, B., et al. (2016), 'Nudging or Fudging: The World Development Report 2015', Development and Change, 47 (4), pp. 640–63.

Finlayson, A. (2009), 'Financialisation, Financial Literacy and Asset-Based Welfare', British Journal of Politics and International Relations, 11 (3), pp. 400–21.

Firestone, S., Van Order, R. and Zorn, P. (2007), 'The Performance of Low? Income and Minority Mortgages', Real Estate Economics, 35 (4), pp. 479–504.

French, S., Leyshon, A. and Thrift, N. (2009), 'A Very Geographical Crisis: The Making and Breaking of the 2007–2008 Financial Crisis', Cambridge Journal of Regions, Economy, and Society, 2 (2), pp. 287–302.

Goodwin-Groen, R. (2016), 'As Development Aid Evolves, Digitising Tax Payments Can Have Dramatic Benefits for Emerging Economies', Huffington Post. Available form: http://www.huffingtonpost.com/ruth-goodwingroen/as-development-aid-evolve_b_12786916.html [accessed 18 November 2016].

Johnson, S. and Arnold, S. (2012), 'Inclusive Financial Markets: Is Transformation Underway in Kenya?', Development Policy Review, 30 (6), pp. 719–48.

Kamath, R., Mukherji, A. and Ramanathan, S. (2010), 'Ramanagaram Financial Diaries: Cash Patterns and Repayments of Microfinance Borrowers', Enterprise Development and Microfinance, 21 (2), pp. 101–17.

Kaminska, I. (2015), 'When Financial Inclusion Stands for Financial Intrusion, FT Alphaville', Financial Times, 31 July. Available from: http://ftalphaville.ft.com/2015/07/31/2135943/when-financial-inclusion-stands-for-financial-intrusion/ [accessed 19 December 2015].

Kear, M. (2013), 'Governing Homo Subprimicus: Beyond Financial Citizenship, Exclusion, and Rights', Antipode, 45 (4), pp. 926–46.

Kempson, E. and Whyley, C. (1999), Kept in or Opted out? Understanding and Combating Financial Exclusion (Bristol: Policy Press).

Kempson, E., et al. (2000), In or Out? Financial Exclusion: A Literature and Research Review (London: Financial Services Authority).

Langley, P. (2008), 'Sub-prime Mortgage Lending: A Cultural Economy', Economy and Society, 37 (4), pp. 469–94.

Langley, P. (2010), The Everyday Life of Global Finance: Saving and Borrowing in Anglo-America (Oxford: Oxford University Press).

Lemke, T. (2001), 'The Birth of Bio-politics': Michel Foucault's Lecture at the Collège de France on Neo-liberal Governmentality', Economy and Society, 30 (2), pp. 190–207.

Leyshon, A. and Thrift, N. (1995), 'Geographies of Financial Exclusion: Financial Abandonment in Britain and the United States', Transactions of the Institute of British Geographers, 20 (3), pp. 312–41.

Leyshon, A. and Thrift, N. (1996), 'Financial Exclusion and the Shifting Boundaries of the Financial System', Environment and Planning A, 28 (7), pp. 1150–56.

Mader, P. (2016), The Political Economy of Microfinance: Financialising Poverty (London: Palgrave Macmillan).

Marron, D. (2013), 'Governing Poverty in a Neoliberal Age: New Labour and the Case of Financial Exclusion', New Political Economy, 18 (6), pp. 785–810.

Martin, R. (2002), Financialisation of Daily Life (Philadelphia: Temple University Press).

Maurer, B. (2012), 'Mobile Money: Communication, Consumption and Change in the Payments Space', Journal of Development Studies, 48 (5), pp. 589–604.

Mendoza, R.U. and Thelen, N. (2008), 'Innovations to Make Markets More Inclusive for the Poor', Development Policy Review, 26 (4), pp. 427–58.

Miller, P. and Rose, N. (2008), Governing the Present: Administering Economic, Social and Personal Life (Cambridge: Polity).

Montgomerie, J. and Büdenbender, M. (2015), 'Round the Houses: Homeownership and Failures of Asset-Based Welfare in the United Kingdom', New Political Economy, 20 (3), pp. 386–405.

Pasquale, F. (2015), The Black Box Society: The Secret Algorithms that Control Money and Information (Boston: Harvard University Press).

Prabhakar, R. (2013), 'Asset-based Welfare: Financialisation or Financial Inclusion?', Critical Social Policy, 33 (4), pp. 658–78.

Rankin, K.N. (2013), 'A Critical Geography of Poverty Finance', Third World Quarterly, 34 (4), pp. 547–68.

Robertson, M. (2017), '(De)Constructing the Financialised Culture of Owner-Occupation in the UK, with the Aid of the 10Cs', New Political Economy. doi:10.1080/13563467.2017.1259303

Roy, A. (2010), Poverty Capital: Microfinance and the Making of Development (London: Routledge).

Roy, A. (2012), 'Subjects of Risk: Technologies of Gender in the Making of Millennial Modernity', *Public Culture*, 24 (1 66), pp. 131–55.

Ruppert, E. (2011), 'Population Objects: Interpassive Subjects', *Sociology*, 45, pp. 218–33.

Ruppert, E. (2012), 'The Governmental Topologies of Database Devices', *Theory Culture Society*, 29, pp. 116–36.

Ruppert, E., Law, J. and Savage, M. (2013), 'Reassembling Social Science Methods: The Challenge of Digital Devices', *Theory, Culture & Society*, 30 (4), pp. 22–46.

Santos, A.C. (2017), 'Cultivating the Self-reliant and Responsible Individual: The Material Culture of Financial Literacy', *New Political Economy*. doi:10.1080/13563467.2017.1259302

Scott, J.C. (1998), *Seeing Like a State: How Certain Schemes to Improve the Human Condition Have Failed* (Boston: Yale University Press).

Shakya, Y.B. and Rankin, K.N. (2008), 'The Politics of Subversion in Development Practice: An Exploration of Microfinance in Nepal and Vietnam', *Journal of Development Studies*, 44 (8), pp. 1214–35.

Soederberg, S. (2013), 'Universalising Financial Inclusion and the Securitisation of Development', *Third World Quarterly*, 34 (4), pp. 593–612.

Squires, C. (2011), 'Bursting the Bubble: A Case Study of Counter-framing in the Editorial Pages', *Critical Studies in Media Communication*, 28 (1), pp. 30–49.

Tait, J. and Banda, G. (2016), 'Proportionate Governance of Innovative Technologies: The Role of Regulations, Guidelines and Standards', *Report to the British Standards Institute*. Innogen Institute, University of Edinburgh. Available from: http://www.innogen.ac.uk/downloads/Innogen_Institute_BSI_Standards_Project_Main_Report.pdf [accessed 17 July 2016].

Thaler, R. H. and Sunstein, C. R. (2008), *Nudge: Improving Decisions about Health, Wealth, and Happiness* (Boston: Yale University Press).

World Bank. (2008), *Finance for All? Policies and Pitfalls in Expanding Access* (Washington, DC: The World Bank).

World Bank. (2013), *Global Financial Development Report: Financial Inclusion* (Washington, DC: The World Bank).

World Bank. (2015), *World Development Report 2015: Mind, Society, Behaviour.* (Washington, DC: The World Bank).

World Bank Group. (2013), *Financing for Development Post 2015* (Washington, DC: The World Bank).

Financialisation, media and social change

Catherine Happer

ABSTRACT
This article uses a circuit of communication framework to examine the role of the media in shaping public debate on the financial system and the way in which this impacts on audience response and related societal impacts. It is founded in debates about neo-liberalism and financialisation which highlight the shift of power from, or through, the state to large corporations. One result of this structural shift is an increasingly integrated political, media and corporate culture which promotes the interests of the 'market' in public and private lives, and operates to limit the information available to audiences. Alternatives to economic policies and solutions to problems are marginalised in public debate, as illustrated by media coverage of the financial crisis. This limiting of alternatives is decisively implicated in the development of sympathetic attitudes to 'preferred' perspectives and related policy moves, which constrain the potential for effective resistance at the level of collective and individual responses.

Introduction

When the global financial crisis broke in 2008, the media played a central role in communicating and interpreting its nature to the wider public. Despite very strong reflection of public anger and blame in the immediate aftermath of the crisis directed at finance, no sustained and effective public challenge to the prevailing economic system has emerged. That the media do not simply reflect social and political change is widely recognised amongst media scholars. However, the ways in which media representations may be decisively implicated in the construction and promotion of social structures, processes and change are the subject of much debate (Curran 2002, Castells 2010, Happer and Philo 2013, Philo *et al.* 2015). The material culture of financialisation, which provides the foundation to this symposium, rests on an understanding that material processes and structures are crucially interdependent on the systems of meanings and beliefs which support (or contest) them (Fine 2013). Further, these meanings develop through the workings of the financial system, and are responded to by audiences in different ways, such as collective support for or resistance to policy moves. As such, media and communications become crucial in discussions about whether the current economic and political system may or may not be sustained.

To understand this more fully, this article draws on a multidimensional model of the circuit of communication (Philo *et al.* 2015) which integrates an analysis of the social and political structures which shape media production, media content and audience response and any societal outcomes. As such, the first section provides an overview of recent structural shifts in the political economy, their relation to the reshaping of the circuit and the way in which these underpin the material cultures of financialisation. It then assesses the role of the media in constructing this financialised culture, with attention to financial journalism and, in particular, the reporting of the crisis and how this marginalised more radical solutions. The final section looks at, first, the degree to which audience members are positioned to contest financialised media representations and, second, the way in which the circuit of communication operates to inhibit the potential for social change.

Financialisation and the transformation of the circuit of communication

Whilst there is broad recognition in the last three decades that societies in the West have moved towards a model of 'neo-liberalism', there is much debate about what this means (Mudge 2008, Fine 2010, Vanugopal 2015). The term has been greatly expanded (Vanugopal 2015) and commentators note that it variously refers to an ideology, a system or set of policies in practice and/or a period or state, such as an era of capitalism (Fine 2013, Davidson 2015). Fine notes that these different elements are continually shifting and often inconsistent, and as such neo-liberalism has, incorrectly, been seen as 'illusory' in nature. A key aspect of this inconsistency is that, whilst theoretically neo-liberalism incorporates the ideological promotion of 'free markets', in practice it has led to the intervention of the state in markets in the direction of increased power of large global corporations (Miller 2010, 2015, Philo et al. 2015). One practical element of this has been the transfer of key sections of the economy from the public to the private sector through privatisation – which the Thatcher government led in the UK and many other (European) countries followed, although in different forms and to varying degrees. Further waves of reform involved the introduction of market-based mechanisms into key aspects of the public sector, such as the health service, education and other government provisions, new markets into which the public are increasingly drawn as consumers. This offered corporations increasing involvement in decision-making in relation to publicly owned services, whilst these have become more weakly subject to democratic processes. This redistribution of power has crucially been accompanied by a structural shift – again supported by governments via deregulation – whereby private profit is increasingly generated 'through financial channels rather than trade and commodity production' (Krippner 2005: 351). Financialisation is a term much referred to in relation to debates about the character of contemporary global capitalism, but here I draw on Fine and Hall's basic characterisation of a political economy which is shaped by the 'excessive expansion and proliferation of financial markets and their penetration into, and influence over, almost every area of economic and social life' (Fine and Hall 2012: 45). It not only incorporates an emphasis on the 'naturalisation' of finance and markets and their prioritisation over political decision-making or regulation (Froud et al. 2012), but also refers to the way in which aspects of everyday experience are quantified and interpreted in financial terms. This conceptualisation underpins the material culture of financialisation, and the 10Cs approach, in which the financial system is *Constructed* through its material structures, relations and processes, in response to which subjects must react. It is *Construed* or interpreted in ways which reflect individuals' experience and knowledge and the range of alternatives on which they have to draw. The *Contradictory* nature of the financial system itself creates the *Context* within which it is *Collectively* interpreted and *Contested*. Despite the latter, the power and centrality of finance, and its integration with communication systems that provide public legitimacy and shape responses to financial outcomes and the crisis in particular, the material culture of finance is *Closed* in who has access to its representation and how, if not absolutely so.

Philo et al. (2015) provide a framework for examining the increasingly complex 'circuit of communication' which integrates the 'diverse range of agencies facilitating the flow of information' (Philo et al. 2015: 446) within a media production, content and reception model. The four key elements of the circuit are the social and political institutions which influence the supply of information; the media and their content; differentiated audience groups and the wide range of decision-makers including politicians, local government and European institutions. Central to the model is that all of these elements interact and are dynamic. They are also not mutually exclusive; politicians, for example, may both feed the supply of information and respond to their understandings of what audiences believe and desire. Digital media support a parallel flow of information that not only interacts with mainstream media to underpin (and *Contest*) content, but also reflect

Collective response. The relationship between the different elements of the circuit 'varies with the subject, the relative balance of forces and specific historical contexts' (Philo *et al.* 2015: 448), and is a continually evolving site of ideological struggle. The circuit has been transformed materially and ideologically in recent years. The neo-liberal shift in power towards global finance has been supported by the progressive dilution of democratic controls on capital as corporations have increasingly moved into the political process (Monbiot 2000, Beder 2006). In what Lagna (2016) describes as 'the financialisation of the state', politicians have progressively moved away from making public debt-related decisions to behaving as co-actors in a marketplace. This shift is rooted in a belief shared by politicians, academics, bankers and regulators in the primacy of financial innovation, which 'naturally' and efficiently resolves any economic uncertainties, a belief bolstered by the long, if uneven, period of stability prior to the crash (Froud *et al.* 2012, Johal *et al.* 2012). A necessary outcome of this blurring of the public and the private is reduced clarity on democratic accountability. In this context, Wedel (2011) describes the emergence of a 'shadow elite', those working as government advisers, financial lobbyists, think tankers and business consultants, who draw on these discourses of 'naturalisation' which legitimise the interests of finance to directly influence policy (Miller and Dinan 2003, Froud *et al.* 2012). The shifting nature of political party finance in the UK, in which accountability to mass membership has given way to wealthy private investors often drawn from the world of finance, further serves to cement the nexus between the core executive and city elites. Miller defines this process as the 'short-circuit' of communication which *Closes* out the public entirely (Dinan and Miller 2008, 2012, Miller and Harkins 2010). As a general rule, the activities of these *Collective* groups are beyond the reach of the media and public debate, but public relations (PR) agencies for global finance feed directly into the production of media which publics *receive* in unprecedented numbers of ways.

However, the media is a site of *Contested* interests, and the movement of traffic is not simply one-way. Journalists operate within a system which is answerable to the pressures of ownership, editorial imposition and financial interests but, ultimately, the commercial imperatives of delivering audiences (Herman and Chomsky 1994, Philo *et al.* 2015). A further factor is the norms and ethics of journalism, such as adherence to balance and neutrality, and the need to challenge decision-making, although these are open to shifting content and interpretation (Doyle 2006, Guerrera 2009, Tambini 2010). There is a reliance upon a restricted range of official sources – of which politicians are the most significant – due to their authority status and direct access to decision-making (Lupien 2013, Wahl-Jorgensen *et al.* 2013). However, even journalists operating in the most constrained organisational structures can possess a need (and desire) to feature a wider range of views – which routinely lead to the inclusion of *Contested* and, hence, *Chaotic* accounts, often within the same news outlet. Audiences expect the powerful to be held to account by the media, and sometimes newspapers and TV respond accordingly. The banking crisis and arguments over tax evasion have focused public attention on corporate activity and the accumulation of corporate and private wealth in recent years. This can have the effect of undermining elements of corporate self-interest, notably in the mainstream media attacks on the tax evasion of global companies such as Google and Amazon, which gain populist mileage from harnessing public outrage.

Digital media in these instances can facilitate *Collective* ways of *Contesting* the logic of finance through globalising and interconnecting local campaigns as with the Occupy movement. They can also allow for opposition to global corporate PR in other ways. Propaganda can be discredited at a much faster pace by activists and experts operating in digital media than journalists working in the mainstream (Robinson 2010). Wikileaks, the global online organisation which has 'leaked' classified documents, was set up not only to release information which powerful groups sought to keep confidential, but also to eliminate PR spin. When the UK bank Northern Rock collapsed in 2008, the mainstream media were prevented by a judge's order from revealing the details, but Wikileaks released a confidential briefing which legal groups attempted and failed to block (Leigh and Franklin 2008). In this way, Wikileaks' releases showed real potential for the breakdown of governmental and corporate controls on the release and shape of information at the national and global levels.

However, business and political groups also resist such action through a *Collective* show of power; in the case of the US State Department leaks, companies such as Amazon and PayPal bowed to government pressure and blocked the organisation, making it more difficult for Wikileaks to sustain their online operations. Digital media can also aid PR in more direct ways by the simultaneous reinforcement of constructed messages across media in relation to, for example, damage limitation. The circuit model allows for the potential role public response, both online and offline, may play in shaping public debate – as politicians will, for example, consider in advance how what they release will be received and interpreted by media audiences and the likely range of responses. In this way, *Contesting* interests continually shift the balance of power. However, the evidence suggests that the 'short circuit' of decision-making is not routinely disrupted by audience (inter)activity. I will now discuss the way in which these processes operate in relation specifically to financial reporting and coverage of the crisis.

Financial journalism

Theoretically, financial journalism has traditionally been defined as having a watchdog function in terms of holding to account state or corporate power (Tambini 2010). However, financial reporting has undergone a significant transformation in recent years (Davis 2002, Clark *et al.* 2004, Schifferes 2011), which Davis (2002) connects with the changing financial system and the reallocation of power in the political and social spheres. He argues:

> corporate communication imperatives … have been more instrumental in shaping business news in the last two decades. City corporations, aided by the employment of proactive financial PR, have managed to 'capture' financial news production. (Davis 2002: 60)

Whilst corporations promoted the idea that financial PR grew in order to meet the information demands of investors and regulators as the sector expanded, in practice it became more and more proactive in generating a supply of information which *Conformed* with broader corporate aims (Miller and Dinan 2000, Davis 2002, Tambini 2010, Johal *et al.* 2012). This was made possible because, in contrast to other journalists, the suppliers of information, the main source of advertising (and the corporations paying for it) and consumers of financial reporting are drawn from the same global interest group (Featherstone 2009, Schechter 2009). Former reporters note that 'crossing the aisle' from journalism to join 'friends' in the financial sector is commonplace (Schechter 2009, Fahy *et al.* 2010).

But, as Froud *et al.* (2012) note, the stories which circulate must also carry credibility to facilitate a shift in political decision-making. The long period of economic stability evidenced the wider benefits of financial innovation and cemented the expert status of the financial experts who were most vocal in promoting it (Davis 2002, 2012). There was a sense that the facts spoke for themselves. This limited any resistance amongst the political classes and instead led to an increasing reliance on those experts to direct policy-makers and regulators. In this sense, the finance pages inform the politicians too. Politicians may be the primary definers of public debate and their commitment to prioritise an issue leads the media. However, in this case, the influence of financial elites on politicians, and their interconnectedness with them, offers them agenda-setting powers too.

The privately owned press, whilst responsive to political shifts, are too led ultimately by their own economic interests both at the macro- and micro-levels. For example, Schechter (2009) notes that media companies take billions in advertising revenue from lenders and credit card companies. But the bulk of the British media, as private enterprises with corporate owners, also tends to support 'free markets' and deregulation at the ideological level (Philo *et al.* 2015). The adherence to journalistic norms of balance, truth and impartiality may operate to *Contest* dominant ideologies, but where corporate priorities are in conflict with the public interest, the need to support the former is likely to shape reporting. There is then a confluence of stories and, in respect of the 'short-circuit', the material culture of financialisation can be seen to be effectively *Closed* to external influences.

The financialisation of news

Financial reporting, however, is no longer only a case of elites speaking to themselves. There has been not only a transformation from niche to mainstream, but also a broader shift in news values across journalism. The penetration of financial markets into increasing areas of public and private lives (Fine and Hall 2012), such as home ownership (Robertson, this collection), has been accompanied by a rising public interest in financial news (Davis 2002, Schifferes and Coulter 2012). The structural support for increased participation in the market coincided with a significant growth in advertising for financial products, including mortgages and other forms of credit – with total global spending worldwide tripling during the 1990s and fuelling consumer demand (Greenfield and Williams 2001, Clark et al. 2004). Personal finance generated high advertising rates, which in turn fuelled interest in financial products, paying for more coverage of companies and financial products and, therefore, leading to an increased demand for coverage of the financial markets and broader financial journalism in a self-perpetuating way. Such growing public interest extended the demands upon financial reporting across depth (understanding the financial system as a whole) and breadth (to include broader social and political implications).

In relation to the former, the expansion of audience reach and more mainstream coverage posed particular issues for financial journalists in that the financial system is highly complex, and there is the difficulty of communicating risk and uncertainty to a lay audience who are looking for simplified explanations (Clark et al. 2004, Guerrera 2009). In a 24-hour news cycle dominated by entertainment values (Barnett 2011), Doyle (2006) argues that the transition from finance to headlines exposed the sector's limitations, finding itself caught up 'between two stools', often in Contradiction: the need to provide both in-depth numerical coverage for professional groups and general coverage for lay audiences with low levels of knowledge and understanding. Doyle argues that, in meeting the demands of the latter, the drivers of financial stories tend to be large corporate names and dramas, in which blame may be placed on individuals or companies (Tambini 2010). These are also the kind of stories which operate to ensure journalists are ever more reliant on industry 'insiders', those least critical of the system.

But whilst Doyle argues 'breadth' is often marginalised in such financial reporting, conversely Mills (2015), in his account of the neo-liberal transformation of BBC news journalism, documents the way in which the reporting of broader social and political issues instead became bound up with the values of finance. He identifies a cultural shift away from presenting news from the perspective of organised labour to a reflection of the 'naturalising' role of markets in the political system and a growing acceptance of financial logics. An aspect of this is the metaphorical construction of the public as financial subjects, as a 'nation of shareholders' (Mills 2015) with 'personal responsibility' for public debt (Clark et al. 2004). In other words, there is not only an increase in reporting of finance, but also a move towards the financialisation of news itself which is seen in the shift towards interpreting and quantifying events, and defining the public in financialised terms.

The media and the financial crisis

As the financial crash hit in 2007–2008, with its roots in the collapse of the sub-prime mortgage market, a central question was why the media Collectively and systematically failed to warn the public (Lashmar 2008, Schechter 2009, Fahy et al. 2010, Tambini 2010, Berry 2012). Some of this relates to the ideological resilience of the infallible market which in their role as consumers, the public promoted through their engagement with the property market. But in fact a small number of economists, journalists and commentators had raised the potential risks and threats (Starkman 2009, Marron et al. 2010, Berry 2012, Philo 2012, Mercille 2013). The mainstream media did not provide them with an effective platform to voice their concerns (Berry 2012). Schechter's (2009: 26) claim that the majority of the media 'missed the run-up to the crisis, just as much as the press was uncritical of the run-up to the war in Iraq' alludes to the processes by which sources of information were systematically drawn from groups least likely to provide any critique of it (Lashmar 2008, Schechter 2009, Fahy *et al.* 2010, Tambini 2010, Berry 2012, Mercille 2013). In this case, there were direct vested interests in the form of the profits and the sizable bonuses being made from sub-prime mortgage lending supported by a genuine inability to consider market failure. Davis notes the 'capture' of financial news by those representing and contained within the system, and their intercon-nection with successive governments and journalists and the sharing of commercial imperatives as well as ideological positions, meant that criticisms were effectively silenced (Davis 2002, Berry 2012, Philo 2012). US financial journalist Schechter (2009) notes that he attempted to raise the alert of the impending crisis but was dismissed as an 'alarmist'. As Philo notes, the bankers and corporations as well as growing profits and house price rises were celebrated as long as the economy appeared to be booming (Philo 2012).

As the events unfolded, the British popular press reflected the anger of their readers (Philo 2012), as did the global media, with expressions such as 'greed', 'madness' or 'irrational exuberance' being commonplace (Philo 2012, Meissner 2013). The sensationalism in language and focus partly reflects not only the transformation of financial news to entertainment and the need to find personalities and drama on which to hang simplified stories (Manning 2013), but also a tendency to apportion blame (Philo 2012). As *The Sun* explains in this editorial:

> Many will ask if it is right that tax payers are forced to subsidise irresponsible borrowers and greedy banks. But what was the alternative? Neither America nor Britain could stand by and watch their economies disintegrate. (*The Sun*, 20th September 2008, quoted in Philo 2014: xiii)

In this way, the financial sector is reinforced as beneficial to the economy and blame is imposed on groups of individuals guilty of wrong-doing or errors rather than on systemic failures which, if addressed, might lead to more attention to radical transformations. As Berry (2012), who analysed coverage on the BBC's flagship news programme *Today* across two months in 2008, found, the range of experts consulted on the crash included representatives from the financial community, poli-ticians and lobbyists – all of whom were fundamentally supportive of the ideology of free markets and deregulation. Therefore, even as the crash took hold, commentators prioritised 'getting the credit markets going again' (quoted in Berry 2012: 260) and even continuing to invest in the property market (at 'great value') (Mercille 2013).

Media representations of solutions

Berry (2012) also examined coverage of potential solutions to the British banking crisis on the *Today* programme. In spite of the existence of a number of reputable economists raising a range of reforms including nationalisation of the banks, re-introduction of capital controls and restrictions on the banks' ability to create credit, these arguments were rarely found in his content analysis. When they were, they were often dismissed; for example, nationalisation was strongly argued against, with one BBC journalist describing it as 'meddling' in the banks. City voices continued to be promoted as (impartial) experts. As Berry notes:

> this means that City voices are given almost monopoly status to define the issues and how they might be resolved. The consequence of this is that far-reaching reforms are either completely absent or appear briefly only to be instantly downgraded. (Berry 2012: 15)

The longer-term consequences of the crisis have been the economic recession and increased unem-ployment as the government prioritised the need to tackle the fiscal deficit (Philo 2012, Stanley 2014). The British government, a coalition of Conservatives and Liberal Democrats, elected in 2010 to replace the New Labour government, presented a financial 'solution' by increasing general taxes such as value-added tax and cutting government spending in local services, education and welfare. In the context of expanded household and individual credit-fuelled expenditure, a widely referred to 'household metaphor' which paralleled state finances with those of the household effec-tively (if inaccurately) presented austerity as 'common sense as a well-managed household avoiding the accumulation of unnecessary unsecured debt' (Stanley 2014: 905). This was offered in direct opposition to the previous government onto whom both the media and the first Cameron Coalition Government effectively shifted blame for the financial crisis; a failure of politics rather than the market. As Pirie argues:

> the failure of the Labour Party to advance a clear analysis of the crisis played an important role in enabling the dominance of Conservative narratives of the crisis focused upon public spending. (Pirie 2012: 341)

The media constructed a false opposition between New Labour and coalition policy, which in fact was largely one of continuity in respect of the broader free market principles (Cobham *et al*. 2013). In this way, radical solutions were again excluded from public debate.

The circuit of communication, however, does not operate only to promote powerful interests and there is the paradoxical argument that the media were implicated in exacerbating the financial crash by being negatively predictive of the effects of the crisis and causing panic (Davies 2009, Parliament Publications 2009). As discussed previously, the shaping of media content is *Contested* ideologically, often *Chaotically* and subject to a range of influences including journalistic norms and audience interest. In the case of coverage of the financial crisis, Schechter (2009) highlights the example of *The Daily Telegraph*, nominally a free market and Conservative-supporting newspaper, which was most outspoken of all of the British press in its predictions about the financial problems looming. Journalists on the paper were denounced as alarmist when, as Schechter argues, they were often most accurate in predicting what was to come:

> What started as a kind of anglophile bashing of Wall Street and Americans for the lack of regulation turned into scrutiny of British practices in the Northern Rock affair and its aftermath. (Schechter 2009: 25)

Overall, the extent to which media are 'open' to alternatives and may feature many *Contesting* views is likely to vary in relation to a range of political, economic and institutional factors. However, the interdependency both materially and ideologically of financial experts, policy-makers and journalists means that the trend towards the 'preferred' stories and explanations as well as the *Closing* of alternatives is well supported.

Audience response to media coverage

The material culture of financialisation also integrates an analysis of the way in which the structures, processes and relations shape responses by subjects – and how these 'preferred' interpretations of the finance system are *Construed* in as much as they are accepted or *Contested* at the level of individual or *Collective* responses. Within the circuit of communication framework, the way in which audiences negotiate content, including acceptance and rejection of the message, is dependent upon a range of different factors. Audience members carry with them diverse cultural values, preferences and levels of interest, and research has shown that acceptance or rejection of media accounts can also depend on the use of processes of logic and reasoning (Philo 1990, 1996) as well as the generation of fear and panic (Philo 1996, Briant *et al*. 2011). A consistent finding across research, however, is that audiences draw on their own direct experience or alternative sources of knowledge to evaluate media messages (Philo 1990, Philo and Berry 2011, Briant *et al*. 2011, Happer *et al*. 2012, Philo and Happer 2013) – with the corollary that where these are absent, then the power of the media message increases, and the audience becomes more reliant upon it to make sense of explanations and events. In this context, we return to debates about the democratisation of information dissemination via digital and social media, this time more specifically to reporting of finance and coverage of the crash (Rosen 2012). As discussed, theoretically at least, such technologies may be a significant channel for the transmission of alternative sources of knowledge and competing perspectives. Drawing on these arguments, in this final section, I will first consider the extent to which audiences have the power to *Collectively Contest* or renegotiate the 'preferred explanations' of the root of economic problems and solutions.

As previously discussed, in the period preceding and during the crisis, increased interest in the economy and financial reporting was paralleled by increased audience exposure to information in the media on the subject (Davis 2002, Schifferes and Coulter 2012). In 2010, for example, two years after the crash, 75 per cent of British people said that they were following news about the state of the economy closely, with only 1 in 10 saying that they hardly ever checked the news – a significantly higher level of interest than before the crash, when nearly half only looked once a month (ICM quoted in Schifferes 2010). There is also evidence that audiences were accessing a wider range of media sources, including online sources in this period (Schifferes and Coulter 2012). There is a body of research that argues that the advent of online news, and the increasing use of social media, has led to a shift in the relationship between mainstream journalists and audiences which ultimately poses a threat to the 'authority' of the former (Robinson 2010, Siapera 2011, Rosen 2012). An element of this is the way in which audience response via blogs, social media or online comments sections can 'fact-check' or challenge the perspectives offered by reference to *Collective* knowledge and expertise (Jenkins 2006, Robinson 2010, Marchionni 2013). In theory, this potential may be enhanced by the widely reported low levels of public trust in representatives from the financial world after the crash (including the journalists who failed to predict it), in that audiences are likely to be seeking alternatives.

In spite of the fact that individuals and households increasingly entered financial markets in this period through, for example, home-owning and other forms of borrowing (Robertson 2017), the evidence suggests that the actual workings of financial markets are considerably more distant than other areas of media coverage (FSA 2006, Langley 2008, Fine and Hall 2012). Research by Philo and Happer (2013) shows that, in those areas in which clarity or further information is sought (often following TV headlines), and trust in the information environment is low, there is a tendency to digitally scan the range of coverage in order to gain a sense of consistency across different sources. The range of sites accessed, however, tends not to be independent blogs and alternative news sites. This process is largely designed to expose the differing agendas of reputable news outlets to allow accuracy of basic factual details and arguments to emerge. Particular weight is given to traditional and authoritative news sources online (Horrigan 2006, Siapera 2011, Philo and Happer 2013). Patterns of online news consumption during the crash bear this out (Schifferes and Coulter 2012) – they show an increase in traffic across recognisable news brands including the BBC and Yahoo, and the importance of mainstream bloggers, most significantly the BBC's Robert Peston. In this way, in the context of low trust in the information environment, audiences sought out respected brands such as the BBC to interpret events – which evidence shows gave a privileged platform to the same elite sources who failed to critically assess the system when it was heading towards the crisis (Berry 2012). The moves between the range of established news brands, all of which are dominated by the exclusive group of elite sources, result in audiences being subject to the reinforcement of the limited range of perspectives on the causes of, and potential responses to, the crash. The circuit allows for *Contestations* – such as those of the range of commentators who were at least invited onto the BBC in Berry's sample. However, access to, and knowledge of, the financial world is highly exclusive and ideologically coherent (Davis 2002). As such, the range of commentators who are in a position (both ideologically and structurally) to *Contest* dominant perspectives in an informed way are limited and their penetration into the mainstream media is also highly restricted.

Social media provides a further avenue for the promotion of alternatives. However, research has shown that Twitter is closely aligned with the mainstream media, with the latter shaping the agenda, to which corporate and political agencies have disproportionate access, rather than the other way around (Newman 2011). In the case of financial reporting and financialised news, the 'Collective intelligence' to sway the discussion towards alternative solutions and broader critiques of the system did not exist (Jenkins 2006). Most people do not know enough about finance to assess the arguments critically *Collectively* or individually. As such, general audiences were not routinely hearing alternative arguments promoted in any area of reporting and, in practice, social media can operate to reinforce and cement the message of mainstream media (which largely promote the free market).

A further aspect of the media's role in shaping audience understandings was the focusing of attention upon individuals and the sensationalist nature of their stories and away from the wider systematic failings. The importance of the Robert Peston blog, and his elevation to almost celebrity status, may offer insight into what at least some audiences sought from the coverage; the levels of entertainment and drama increasingly expected of finance reporting, indeed of all reporting (Clark *et al.* 2004, Doyle 2006). In contrast, audience reach for websites hosting Q&A's on the wider impacts and personal finance stories in relation to mortgages and pensions were sourced relatively rarely in the period (Schifferes and Coulter 2012). There was no evidence that the wider interest in coverage enhanced the public's understanding of the financial system, nor the ability to assess impacts and responses critically. A 2010 poll showed that people still felt ill-informed on the way in which, for example, the financial developments that they were reading about might impact on personal finances (ICM quoted in Schifferes 2010). The financialised metaphor of 'government as household' was effective in this respect – offering a powerful way of connecting arguments at the 'common sense' level with direct experiences of finance, but simultaneously shutting down any more complex explanations (Stanley 2014). In spite of intense media coverage, a YouGov poll found that the majority of the British public are incorrect about which is greater between the deficit and the public debt, with more than a third simply offering a 'don't know' (Jordan 2013). If anything, the coverage operated to maintain the general ignorance of finance, beyond the key players involved in the drama of the crash. All of the above illustrates how the financial media are both *Closed* and *Conforming* to an extraordinary degree despite both the significance for everyday life and the evidence of extreme dysfunction wrought by the (financial) crisis. This is itself contingent upon the *Context* of neo-liberalism, by which the benefits and efficiencies of free markets have remained the default, illusory position, as well as *Commodification*, which in the context of financialisation rendered the financial system unknowable (Langley 2008). Further, the parasitical *Construction* of financialisation on top of the productive system through speculation, such as with sub-prime mortgages, is deeply *Contradictory*. It is conducive to a *Chaotic* culture of knowing the financial system to be to blame but, ultimately, being drawn not only to leave it barely challenged but even subject to massive bail-out and other forms of support.

Audience response and social change

The evidence therefore is that, with the material culture of financialisation, audiences have limited access to the means to strongly *Contest* the 'preferred interpretations', and so respond in ways which may facilitate a change in direction in terms of societal outcomes. Whilst social changes at the level of policy do not require public support, they are facilitated by it and, equally significantly, by the containment of active opposition. This is primarily because governments need to maintain electoral support. In the period following the crash, general audiences were very reliant upon media representations which reinforced dominant messages about the causes and possible responses. The limiting of solutions to economic problems (Berry 2012), is, therefore, likely to impose limitations on what people consider possible in the absence of alternative perspectives on which to draw. That markets were fallible and therefore might be altered in a radical way was not promoted. In line with this, the government spending cuts promoted by financial experts (which politicians are increasingly reliant upon both financially and ideologically) were met with widespread public support across Europe (YouGov 2011).

This has been bolstered by the campaigning and results of the 2015 UK election which put into power a Conservative Government which proposed more 'austerity' rather than any moves to limit the activities of the financial sector. In this sense, we see the way the circuit of communication operates; alternatives to the current financial model are marginalised, broader explanations are absent, spending cuts are presented as an inevitable 'solution' to the economic crisis and this limits the potential for public understanding, let alone *Contestation*. Whilst the interplay of public opinion, policy implementation and social change is complex, the media play a powerful legitimising role.

Conclusion

The way in which financialised reporting at the global and national levels impacts upon social change across policy and individual action is highly complex and dynamic. The arguments presented here provide evidence for the material culture of financialisation as seen through the 10Cs, not least through their integration with the circuit of information supply which operates to promote and legitimise the system. A key element, therefore, in the way in which finance is *Construed* is the lack of available alternatives to the naturalised logic of the market which operate to limit any *Collective Contest* to it. Factors such as journalistic norms and ethics, the level of access that audiences have to alternative explanations and a lack of coherence between media, political and corporate objectives can, partially and temporarily, coincide to *Contest* promotion of hegemonic interests – as in the example of the run on Northern Rock in 2008. In this case, media representations were *Chaotic* in respect of the dominant and reinforced messages of mainstream media on the ongoing need to invest in housing (Berry 2012, Mercille 2013). Indeed, as growing sections of the population are structurally excluded from home-ownership, it is likely that *Contestations* to the dominant discourse of owner-occupier will be given further space in the media (Robertson, this volume). But currently there are stronger, chronic examples where political, corporate and journalistic objectives conform with one another in order to *Close* the avenues for resistance and its conversion into action.

The central point, though, is that the media are instrumental in sustaining the material culture of financialisation and that structural transformations in the circuit of communication, through the redistribution of power in the era of neo-liberalism, cement this further. That media and communications can and do make a difference is, therefore, a founding presumption. The financial crisis exposed the way in which this has been highly damaging at the level of society, in that the circuit of communication operated to marginalise the critical analysis required to take a different path in response to it. The interconnectedness of the corporate world, politicians and reporters promoted *Conformity* of ideology and practice, and in this sense, the media can be seen to play a decisive role in maintaining the system and limiting social change.

Acknowledgements

I would like to acknowledge the work of Greg Philo and David Miller on the circuits of communication model upon which this paper is theoretically founded. I would also like to thank Mike Berry who helpfully shared his unpublished work. A debt of gratitude is also owed to Ben Fine, Kate Bayliss and Mary Robertson for their invaluable advice and comments on various drafts.

Funding

The author received financial support from the UKERC and Glasgow City Council. Research for this paper was supported by the project Financialization, Economy, Society and Sustainable Development (FESSUD), which is funded by the European Union under the Seventh Framework Programme (contract number 266800).

References

Barnett, S. (2011), *The Rise and Fall of Television Journalism* (New York: Bloomsbury Academic).

Beder, S. (2006), *Suiting Themselves: How Corporations Drive the Global Agenda* (London: Earthscan).

Berry, M. (2012), 'The Today Programme and the Banking Crisis', *Journalism*, 1 (18), pp. 253–70.

Briant, E., Philo, G. and Watson, N. (2011), *Bad News for Disabled People: How the Newspapers Are Reporting Disability* (London: Inclusion).

Castells, M. (2010), *Communication Power* (Oxford: Oxford University Press).

Clark, G., Thrift, N. and Tickell, A. (2004), 'Performing Finance: The Industry, the Media and Its Image', *Review of International Political Economy*, 11 (2), pp. 289–310.

Cobham, D., Adam, C. and Mayhew, K. (2013), 'The Economic Record of the 1997–2010 Labour Government: An Assessment', *Oxford Review of Economic Policy*, 29 (1), pp. 1–24.

Curran, J. (2002), 'Media and the Making of British Society, c.1700–2000', *Media History*, 8 (2), pp. 135–54.

Davidson, N. (2015), 'The New Middle Class and the Changing Social Base of Neoliberalism', *Oxford Left Review*, 14, pp. 4–10.

Davies, N. (2009), *Flat Earth News* (London: Viking).

Davis, A. (2002), *Public Relations Democracy: Public Relations, Politics and the Mass Media in Britain* (Manchester: Manchester University Press).

Davis, A. (2012), 'Evidence to the Leveson Inquiry, Module 3'. Available from: http://www.levesoninquiry.org.uk/wp-content/uploads/2012/07/Submission-by-Professor-Aeron-Davis.pdf [accessed 20 August 2015].

Dinan, W. and Miller, D. (2008), 'Transparency in EU Decision Making, Holding Corporations to Account: Why the ETI Needs Mandatory Lobbying Disclosure', in *Corruption and Democracy: Political Finances – Conflicts of Interest – Lobbying – Justice* (Strasbourg: Council of Europe).

Dinan, W. and Miller, D. (2012), 'Sledgehammers, Nuts and Rotten Apples: Reassessing the Case for Lobbying Self-Regulation in the United Kingdom', *Interest Groups and Advocacy*, 1 (1), pp. 105–14.

Doyle, G. (2006), 'Financial News Journalism: A Post-Enron Analysis of Approaches Towards Economic and Financial News Production in the UK', *Journalism*, 7 (4), pp. 433–52.

Fahy, D., O'Brien, M. and Poti, V. (2010), 'From Boom to Bust: A Post-Celtic Tiger Analysis of the Norms, Values and Roles of Irish Financial Journalists', *Irish Communications Review*, 12, pp. 5–20. Available from: http://dit.ie/icr/media/diticr/documents/Fahy%20OBrien.pdf [accessed 15 July 2015].

Featherstone, L. (2009), 'Identity Crisis: The Wall Street Journal Steers Away from What Made It Great', *Columbia Journalism Review* (May–June), pp. 31–35. Available from: http://www.cjr.org/feature/identity_crisis.php [accessed 15 August 2015].

Financial Services Authority (FSA) (2006), 'Levels of Financial Capability in the UK: Results of a Baseline Survey', *Consumer Research: Report 47* (London: FSA).

Fine, B. (2010), 'Neo-Liberalism as Financialisation', in A. Saad-Filho and G. Yalman (eds), *Transitions to Neoliberalism in Middle-Income Countries: Policy Dilemmas, Economic Crises, Mass Resistance* (London: Routledge), pp. 11–23.

Fine, B. (2013), 'Towards a Material Culture of Financialisation', FESSUD: Working Paper Series No. 15. Available from: http://fessud.eu/working-papers/ [accessed 21 August 2015].

Fine, B. and Hall, D. (2012), 'Terrains of Neoliberalism: Constraints and Opportunities for Alternative Models of Service Delivery', in D. McDonald and G. Ruiters (eds), *Alternatives to Privatization: Public Options for Essential Services in the Global South* (London: Routledge), pp. 45–70.

Froud, J., *et al.* (2012), 'Stories and Interests in Finance: Agendas of Governance Before and After the Financial Crisis', *Governance* 25 (1), pp. 35–59.

Greenfield, C. and Williams, P. (2001), 'Finance Advertising and Media Rhetoric', *Southern Review*, 34 (4), pp. 44–66.

Guerrera, F. (2009), 'Why Generalists Were Not Equipped to Cover the Complexities of the Crisis', *Ethical Space: The International Journal of Communication Ethics*, 6 (3/4). Available from: http://www.communicationethics.net/journal/v6n3-4/v6n3-4_feat3.pdf [accessed 15 August 2015].

Happer, C. and Philo, G. (2013), 'The Role of the Media in the Construction of Public Belief and Social Change', *Journal of Social and Political Psychology*, 1 (1), pp. 321–336.

Happer, C., Philo, G. and Froggatt, A. (2012), 'Climate Change and Energy Security: Assessing the Impact of Information and Its Delivery on Attitudes and Behaviour', UKERC Project Final Report. Available from: http://www.ukerc.ac.uk/publications/climate-change-and-energy-security-assessing-the-impact-of-information-and-its-delivery-on-attitudes-and-behaviour.html [accessed 2 October 2016].

Herman, E. and Chomsky, N. (1994), *Manufacturing Consent: The Political Economy of the Mass Media* (London: Vintage Books).

Horrigan, J. (2006), 'Online News: For Many Home Broadband Users, the Internet Is a Primary News Source', Pew Internet and American Life Project. Available from: http://www.pewinternet.org/2006/03/22/online-news-for-many-home-broadband-users-the-internet-is-a-primary-news-source/ [accessed 21 December 2015].

Jenkins, H. (2006), *Convergence Culture: Where Old and New Media Collide* (New York: New York University Press).

Johal, S., Moran, M. and Williams, K. (2012), 'The Future Has Been Postponed: The Great Financial Crisis and British Politics', *British Politics*, 7 (1), pp. 69–81.

Jordan, W. (2013), 'Few Think the Deficit Shrank in 2012', YouGov. Available from: http://yougov.co.uk/news/2013/08/24/few-believe-budget-deficit-shrank-2012/ [accessed 21 August 2105].

Krippner, G.R. (2005), 'The Financialization of the American Economy', *Socio-Economic Review*, 3 (2), pp. 173–208.

Lagna, A. (2016), 'Derivatives and the Financialisation of the Italian State', *New Political Economy*, 21 (2), pp. 167–86.

Langley, P. (2008), *The Everyday Life of Global Finance* (Oxford: Oxford University Press).

Lashmar, P. (2008), 'Sub-prime – the Death of Financial Reporting or a Failure of Investigative Journalism?' *The End of Journalism? Technology, Education and Ethics Conference*, University of Bedfordshire, 17–18 October.

Leigh, D. and Franklin, J. (2008), 'Whistle While You Work'. The Guardian, 23 Feb.

Lupien, P. (2013), 'The Media in Venezuela and Bolivia Attacking the 'Bad Left' from Below', *Latin American Perspectives*, 40 (3), pp. 226–46.

Manning, P. (2013), 'Financial Journalism, News Sources and the Banking Crisis'. *Journalism*, 14 (2), pp.173–189.

Marchionni, D. (2013), 'Journalism-as-a-Conversation: A Concept Explication', *Communication Theory*, 23 (2), pp. 131–47.

Marron, M., *et al.* (2010), 'The Scorecard on Reporting of the Global Financial Crisis', *Journalism Studies*, 11 (2), pp. 270–83.

Meissner, M. (2013), 'Portraying the Global Financial Crisis: Myth, Aesthetics, and the City', *European Journal of Media Studies*, 1 (1), pp. 98–125.

Mercille, J. (2013), 'The Role of the Media in Sustaining Ireland's Housing Bubble', *New Political Economy*, 19 (2), pp. 282–301.

Miller, D. (2010), 'How Neoliberalism Got Where It Is: Elite Planning, Corporate Lobbying and the Release of the Free Market', in K. Birch and V. Mykhnenko (eds), *The Rise and Fall of Neoliberalism: The Collapse of an Economic Order* (London: Zed Books), pp. 23–41.

Miller, D. (2015), 'Neoliberalism, Politics and Institutional Corruption: Against the "Institutional Malaise" Hypothesis', in D. Whyte (ed.), *How Corrupt is Britain?* (London: Pluto Press), pp. 59–69.

Miller, D. and Dinan, W. (2000), 'The Rise of the PR Industry in Britain, 1979–98', *European Journal of Communication*, 15 (5), pp. 5–35.

Miller, D. and Dinan, W. (2003), 'Global Public Relations and Global Capitalism', in D. Demers (ed.), *Terrorism, Globalization and Mass Communication* (Spokane, WA: Marquette Books), pp. 193–214.

Miller, D. and Harkins, C. (2010), 'Corporate Strategy and Corporate Capture: Food and Alcohol Industry and Lobbying and Public Health, Themed Issue on Corporate Power: Agency, Communication, Influence and Social Policy', *Critical Social Policy*, 30 (4), pp. 564–89.

Mills, T. (2015) *The End of Social Democracy and the Rise of Neoliberalism at the BBC*, Thesis submitted at the University of Bath.

Monbiot, G. (2000), *Captive State: The Corporate Takeover of Britain* (London: Macmillan).

Mudge, S.L. (2008), 'What Is Neo-Liberalism?', *Socio-Economic Review*, 6 (4), pp. 703–31.

Newman, N. (2011), 'Mainstream Media and the Distribution of News in the Age of Social Discovery', Reuters Institute for the Study of Journalism. Available from: https://reutersinstitute.politics.ox.ac.uk/fileadmin/documents/Publications/Working_Papers/Mainstream_media_and_the_distribution_of_news_.pdf [accessed 21 December 2015].

Parliament Publications (2009), 'Banking Crisis: Reforming Corporate Governance and Pay in the City – Treasury Contents'. Available from: http://www.publications.parliament.uk/pa/cm200809/cmselect/cmtreasy/519/51911.htm [accessed 21 August 2015].

Philo, G. (1990), *Seeing and Believing* (London: Routledge).

Philo, G. (ed.) (1996), *Media and Mental Distress* (London: Longman).

Philo, G. (2012), 'The Media and the Banking Crisis', *Sociology Review*, 21 (3). Available from: http://magazines.philipallan.co.uk/Magazines/Sociology-Review.aspx [accessed 20 May 2013].

Philo, G. (2014), 'Foreword', in E. Devereux (ed.), *Understanding the Media* (London: Sage), pp. xii–xv.

Philo, G. and Berry, M. (2011), *More Bad News from Israel* (London: Pluto Press).

Philo, G. and Happer, C. (2013), *Communicating Climate Change and Energy Security: New Methods in Understanding Audiences* (New York: Routledge).

Philo, G., Miller, D. and Happer, C. (2015), 'Circuits of Communication and Structures of Power: The Sociology of the Mass Media', in M. Holborn (ed.), *Contemporary Sociology* (London: Polity Press), pp. 444–70.

Pirie, I. (2012), 'Representations of Economic Crisis in Contemporary Britain', *British Politics*, 7 (4), pp. 341–364.

Robertson, M. (2017), '(De)constructing the Financialised Culture of Owner-Occupation in the UK, with the Aid of the 10Cs', *New Political Economy*. doi:10.1080/13563467.2017.1259303.

Robinson, S. (2010), 'Traditionalists vs. Convergers: Textual Privilege, Boundary Work, and the Journalist–Audience Relationship in the Commenting Policies of Online News Sites', *Convergence: The International Journal of Research Into New Media Technologies*, 16 (1), pp. 125–43.

Rosen, J. (2012), 'The People Formerly Known as the Audience', in M. Mandiberg (ed.), *The Social Media Reader* (New York: New York University Press), pp. 13–16.

Schechter, D. (2009), 'Credit Crisis: How Did We Miss It?' *British Journalism Review*, 20 (1), pp. 19–26.

Schifferes, S. (2010), 'Trust-Meltdown for Business Journalism', *British Journalism Review*, 2 (1), pp. 3–7.

Schifferes, S. (2011), INAUGURAL LECTURE: 'The Future of Financial Journalism in the Age of Austerity', Department of Journalism, City University London. Available from: http://www.city.ac.uk/__data/assets/pdf_file/0016/151063/The-Future-of-Financial-Journalism-in-the-Age-of-Austerity.pdf [accessed 21 August 2015].

Schifferes, S. and Coulter, S. (2012), 'Downloading Disaster: BBC News Online Coverage of the Global Financial Crisis', *Journalism*, 14 (2), pp. 228–52.

Siapera, E. (2011), *Understanding New Media* (London: Sage).

Stanley, L. (2014), '"We're Reaping What We Sowed": Everyday Crisis Narratives and Acquiescence to the Age of Austerity', *New Political Economy*, 19 (6), pp. 895–917.

Starkman, D. (2009), 'Blindness: The Media and the Meltdown', *Columbia Journalism Review*, 48 (1), pp. 24–31.

Tambini, D. (2010), 'What Are Financial Journalists for?' *Journalism Studies*, 11 (2), pp. 158–74.

Vanugopal, R. (2015), 'Neoliberalism as Concept', *Economy and Society*, 44 (2), pp. 165–87.

Wahl-Jorgensen, K., *et al.* (2013), *Breadth of Opinion in BBC Output*, BBC Trust. Available from: http://www.bbc.co.uk/bbctrust/our_work/editorial_standards/impartiality/breadth_opinion.html [accessed 15 August 2015].

Wedel, J. (2011), *The Shadow Elite: How the World's New Powerbrokers Undermine Democracy, Government and the Free Market* (New York: Basic Books).

YouGov (2011), 'Strong Public Support for Benefit Cuts'. Available from: http://yougov.co.uk/news/2011/05/16/strong-public-support-benefit-cuts/ [accessed 21 August 2015].

From happiness to social provisioning: addressing well-being in times of crisis

Marco Boffo, Andrew Brown and David A. Spencer

ABSTRACT

The paper offers a critique of happiness research based on subjective well-being (SWB) data and proposes an alternative approach to the study of well-being drawing on the political economy tradition. The World Happiness Report (WHR) interpretation of the impact of the Global Financial Crisis on SWB data is used to illustrate the problems with happiness research and the merits of an alternative political economy approach to well-being. The development of such an approach takes inspiration from broader notions of social provisioning rooted in political economy, and its application is seen to yield a better understanding of the meaning of, and the changes in, SWB data than that found in the WHR.

Introduction

Indicators of subjective well-being (henceforth SWB) have gained prominence as measures of progress in society. Garnering support from what has been dubbed as the 'new science of happiness' – which encompasses happiness economics and positive psychology (Layard 2005) – these indicators are increasingly presented as a powerful remedy to the well-known failings of GDP per capita as a measure of human progress. SWB indicators, it is claimed, allow individuals to speak for themselves about their levels of happiness. Thus, rather than inferring individual and societal well-being from recorded levels of GDP per capita, analysts can ascertain individual and, by aggregation, societal well-being by measuring self-reported SWB. The use of SWB data has yielded interesting and headline-grabbing results: first and foremost, the apparent disconnect between rising happiness and GDP levels in advanced economies. This result, named the 'Easterlin paradox' after Easterlin (1974) who first uncovered it, has promoted the view that policy-makers should look beyond the targeting of increased growth and instead should prioritise the maximisation of happiness in society. In this way, the science of happiness resurrects the spirit and intent of Jeremy Bentham's utilitarianism (O'Neill 2006a, 2006b), with happiness seen as something that is both measureable and requiring maximisation (Layard 2005, Duncan 2010, Stewart 2014).

The study of well-being has been given added impetus and urgency by the Global Financial Crisis (GFC) and ensuing austerity (Stiglitz *et al.* 2010, Jany-Catrice and Méda 2013). According to happiness research, SWB data provide a direct measure of well-being through these major global developments. This view is one that this paper seeks to question. The paper argues that *Context matters* in the definition and measurement of well-being. It would be extraordinarily convenient if social, material, cultural as well as personal, local and contingent *Context* could be ignored, enabling well-being to be directly 'read off' from SWB surveys. However, drawing on a philosophy of objective well-being, the paper argues that well-being measurement is inseparable from the study of socially specific *Context*. In particular, the paper stresses that processes of 'financialisation' have been transforming systems of social provisioning over the past 30 years or so, and that these processes form a *Context* that cannot be ignored when measuring well-being. The paper goes on to argue for a novel 'political economy' framework for the interpretation of SWB data that is sensitive to the social *Context*.[1] For a political economy approach, SWB survey responses can vary systematically and *independently of actual well-being* in response to contextual developments such as the GFC. The political economy interpretation of SWB data affirms an opposite assessment of well-being during the GFC and austerity than the interpretation that is characteristic of happiness research.

The paper proceeds as follows. Firstly, two basic and opposing philosophical approaches to well-being definition and measurement are set out briefly – the subjective and objective approaches. The two approaches are shown to differ fundamentally in their respective assessments of well-being through the GFC and ensuing austerity. Secondly, the definition and measurement of well-being are placed into the socially specific *Context*, by considering the political economy of contemporary capitalistic provisioning, during the past 30 years of financialisation, the GFC and ensuing austerity. Thirdly, on the basis of this *Contextualisation*, a different and more satisfactory framework for the interpretation of SWB data than happiness research is offered, affirming that well-being declined through the GFC and austerity. This affirmation runs counter to the World Happiness Report (e.g. Helliwell *et al.* 2013), a key exemplar of happiness research in action. The crux of the argument is that, in the *Context* of such a seismic event as the GFC, respondents will tend to lower the benchmark norms against which they answer SWB questions, spuriously inflating measured SWB. The paper concludes that SWB survey responses are not absolute indicators of well-being *contra* happiness research. Rather they are made relative to a complex social *Context* and so can only be validly interpreted through a political economy approach.

Two philosophies of well-being

Approaches to well-being are diverse and span multiple disciplines. In order to offer a systematic and integrated approach, it is helpful to begin at the abstract level of philosophy. Two opposing philosophical approaches to the definition and measurement of well-being are commonly identified – subjective and objective – and will be described briefly below.

Subjective well-being

Happiness research, in line with utilitarian philosophy, sees well-being as a discrete and subjective property or state of individuals. Layard (2005), to take one example, sees positive well-being as concerned with 'feeling good' and negative well-being with 'feeling bad'. Maximising well-being, understood in this subjective sense, forms the basis of ethical judgement according to happiness research, in line with utilitarianism. Happiness research argues that Likert-scale survey measures of SWB, for example, asking respondents to rate their happiness on a scale of 1–7 (described in more detail in the section on the World Happiness Report (WHR) below), provide an intersubjectively comparable and additive measure of well-being. Therefore, during the recent period of the GFC and austerity, well-being can, for the subjective approach, be measured, in the same way as in any other *Context*, through implementing SWB surveys on nationally representative random samples. As will be discussed in the section on the WHR below, survey results show a slight increase in reported SWB during the GFC and ensuing period of austerity when averaging across all countries globally, though SWB declined in some of the hardest hit countries such as Greece.

Eudemonia and 'objective' well-being

The 'eudemonic' approach to well-being has a lineage dating back to Aristotle and can be presented as in direct opposition to the subjective approach (Haybron 2008, Dean 2010, Austin 2015). According to the eudemonic approach, human thought and action are not guided by a purely subjective and one-dimensional 'utility' maximisation principle or a 'pleasure/pain' nexus. Instead, humans are understood to be self-reflexive, social and practically active beings. Accordingly, well-being is not about the maximisation of a subjective construct called 'SWB' or 'utility'. Rather, and to put it in Sen's (e.g. 1999) terms, well-being is a matter of what people are able to be and do ('capabilities', which when actualised, become 'functionings'). People need, develop and have reason to value a range of beings and doings, and it is in the capability to attain or achieve such beings and doings that well-being lies. In this sense, well-being concerns multiple *objective needs* understood broadly and dynamically, to include the fundamental need for creative development and personal flourishing. Well-being is, therefore, to be measured in terms of what people are able to be and do – involving the ability not only to access basic physical needs, but also to develop and realise their goals and projects, pursuing good family relationships, good social relationships, fulfilling – free and creative – activity in work, education or other pursuits.

Application of the objective approach is more complex in principle than is the case for the subjective approach because there are no set limits on what dimensions to be included, how they are to be measured and how, if at all, they are to be combined into an index. However, for the case of the GFC and ensuing austerity, the problem of choosing and weighting multiple dimensions is mitigated. This is because the GFC and ensuing austerity have caused deterioration across a range of objective dimensions of well-being. For the objective approach, income itself remains a very important dimension because the huge reductions in income during the GFC represent major reductions in what people can be and do, owing to the loss in purchasing power. Moving beyond just the dimension of income, Stuckler and Basu (2013) chart the deleterious impact of the GFC and austerity on homelessness levels, unemployment rates, inequality (as correlated to ill-health), welfare provision and benefit levels, suicide rates and HIV infection levels. Or, to focus on a particular dimension such as work, it is well documented (such as Leschke and Watt 2014) that there is not merely increased unemployment but decline in several indicators of the quality of work – such as pay and deleterious contractual conditions (e.g. through part-time, short-term or zero-hours contracts) – due to the GFC. In practice, then, an objective well-being index will tend to decline when applied to countries hit by the GFC and ensuing austerity, under any reasonable choice and weighting of individual dimensions.

Comparing the two approaches to the philosophy and measurement of well-being reveals, then, empirical as well as philosophical disagreement. The SWB approach sees a slight increase in well-being over the GFC and ensuing austerity, whereas, for the eudemonic approach, there is a decline in well-being over the same period. How might this empirical difference be explained? It is difficult to extract a clear answer from the existing literature. Perhaps the most straightforward answer would be that SWB and objective well-being are entirely different things, though this would imply a sharp dualism between subjective and objective aspects of human existence. Another answer might be that either SWB data or objective well-being measures, or both, are invalid. For example, a proponent of the objective approach might argue that SWB data do not measure anything because the underlying SWB construct is a fiction of utilitarian philosophy. However, the advent of good quality, nationally representative SWB surveys makes wholesale dismissal of any meaning to SWB data difficult to uphold because the data reveal systematic patterns that could not be explained by chance – a point stressed by happiness research as affirming the validity of SWB data, and a point not lost on policy-makers, as SWB has had an increasing influence on policy (Layard 2005). It is argued below that the apparent dualism of objective and subjective aspects of well-being arises because happiness research fundamentally misinterprets SWB data. A 'political economy' framework for the interpretation of SWB data will be developed that is different from, and can lead to opposing conclusions about well-being than, the framework of happiness research for interpreting SWB data. The starting point for the interpretation is the importance of political economy in *Contextualising* the study of well-being.

The need for comprehension of concrete social context

Much of the well-being literature has remained at a very abstract level concerning the philosophy of well-being and its immediate applications for well-being measurement in multidimensional indexes. In the case of the philosophy of SWB then such abstraction from the socially specific *Context* is consistent, because the whole approach is premised on the idea that SWB is a discrete measurable property of individuals, without the need to incorporate a complex social *Context*. However, abstraction from the socially specific *Context* is not consistent in the case of eudemonic philosophy. This is because objective well-being, as defined in the eudemonic tradition, is *internally related to concrete social relations and activities*. One can only be a banker within a socially specific banking system, a worker within a specific system of work, a family member within a specific form of the institution of the family or an artist within a specific system of art and culture – in each case, *the nature and meaning of what one can be and do are socially specific*. Therefore, without further development, an abstract philosophy of objective well-being cannot in principle achieve an integrated comprehension or measurement of actual well-being. For example, in the case of the GFC and ensuing austerity, whilst it can be shown that objective well-being has fallen across multiple dimensions, it is more difficult to assess the overall *nature and level* of well-being and so of the *degree* and *significance* of its fall. Such assessment requires comprehension of the socially specific *Context*, bridging the gulf between abstract philosophy and concrete data. It will be argued below that such comprehension of context is facilitated by political economy.

Objective well-being, political economy and systems of provision

Social provisioning and well-being

The tradition of political economy is centrally concerned with social provisioning of the material prerequisites of well-being (Lawson 2003). Provisioning represents an invaluable starting point to *Contextualise* any analysis of well-being because provisioning is the *sine qua non* for the satisfaction of needs, not to be considered in the abstract but integrally with its nature, conditions, content and modalities. Focusing on provisioning as opposed to exchange implies shifting away from the abstract emphasis on equilibrium, scarcity and market allocation characteristic of mainstream neoclassical economics (Lee 2009) in favour of the due consideration of institutions, processes, culture and values (Boulding 1986, Dugger 1996); the qualitative differences between distinct commodities and services (Nelson 1996, Fine 2002) as well as broader issues of ethics, power and gender (Nelson 1996, van Staveren 2001, Power 2004). Therefore, the view of provisioning belonging to the tradition of political economy has the potential to *Contextualise*, deepen and enrich the vision of well-being associated with the idea of eudemonia.

Capitalistic provisioning

An integrated range of key insights on social provisioning is developed in political economy and heterodox economics (Brown *et al.* 2007). Firstly, consider insights that concern the basic character of the capitalist system. A core insight concerns the predominant drive or motive of the provisioning process. Under capitalism, money becomes an end in itself, in the form of profit (and interest and rent). Objective well-being, a qualitatively rich, multidimensional goal, is not the direct motive of capitalistic provisioning, but is subordinated to the motive of making ever larger sums of exchange value in the form of money. Here, then, is an initial and troubling political economic insight into the capitalistic provisioning process, one denied by mainstream economics. Further core insights concern the employment relation. The notion of social provisioning means that, *contra* mainstream economics, labour is not a mere instrumental necessity. Instead, people have a fundamental need for creative autonomy *in* and *through* labour (Levine and Rizvi 2005,

Spencer 2009). Yet, capitalistic provisioning through wage–labour implies a social class which relinquishes this fundamental need – the need for creative autonomy in labour – to the purpose of capitalistic profit-making. This form of provisioning also has implications for the distribution of the fruits of the fundamental capability of social labour to produce a surplus over and above subsistence needs (Duzenli 2015). In a capitalist society, this surplus is not distributed according to objective need, but unequally in the form of profit, interest and rent, reproducing the inequality necessary to sustain the wage–labour relation.

Further discussion of these issues of creative work and the distribution of surplus under capitalism, which address in detail Sen and Nussbaum's ambiguous views in this regard, can be found in Duzenli (2015), Spencer (2015) and Levine and Rizvi (2005). Other relevant discussions are contained in larger literatures regarding alienation, exploitation and 'commodity fetishism' (Brown *et al.* 2007). For the purposes of this paper, two points can be emphasised. Firstly, though there are fierce debates on the details, it is clear that in some way capitalistic provisioning threatens fundamental dimensions of objective well-being, whether in work or outside it. Therefore, assessment of the *nature and level* of well-being cannot ignore these abstract *Contextual* issues regarding the character of capitalism. Secondly, however, in order to comprehend the nature and level of well-being, it is necessary to introduce much more concrete aspects of *Context* in a way that retains, develops and augments the aforementioned insights. We argue below that the application of political economy to the explanation of the contemporary period of capitalism does just this.

From financialisation ...

The political economy tradition develops from a basic characterisation of capitalism to theories of capitalist accumulation and crisis. These include theories that are applicable throughout capitalism and theories of specific periods of capitalism, such as theories of the contemporary period of neo-liberalism, globalisation and financialisation. Whilst the purpose of this paper is not to go into detail on these theories, it is crucial to point out that they are essential for the comprehension and assessment of well-being because they put the GFC and ensuing austerity into a rich historical and systematic *Context*. Take the example of financialisation (Fine 2013b). Theories of financialisation reveal that there have been complex structural shifts in provisioning over the past 30 years, driven by the increasing power of finance and the increasing role of finance and financial instruments in more and more aspects of life, changing the nature of well-being in complex ways. Financialisation involves increased individualism and managerialism; increased external control of the work process; decreasing worker rights; increased personal debt and indebtedness; increased inequality; and an enhanced role for the profit motive and private finance (over and above the motive of social need) in provisioning.

The changes under the heading of financialisation could be argued to indicate a systematic reduction in well-being in advanced Western economies over a range of relevant dimensions over the past 30 years. However, assessment of well-being over such a long period is highly complex, and arguments that remain at the general level of financialisation cannot be conclusive because there is still a great deal more to the concrete *Context* of everyday life. In order to aid comprehension and measurement of well-being, as well as to rebut the criticism that political economy is too remote from everyday experience, it is necessary to develop a yet more concrete comprehension of *Context*, further developing and augmenting the more abstract insights regarding provisioning thus far achieved. For these purposes, the 'system of provision' (henceforth 'SoP')[2] approach, as developed within political economy, comes into its own.

... to 'systems of provision'

The SoP approach (Fine and Leopold 1993, Fine 2002, 2013a) is precisely designed to illuminate provisioning in concrete practice. Furthermore, it aids understanding of the formation and influence of norms on social practice, and of the material cultures attached to provisioning. Initially borne out of the study of private commodity consumption, the SoP approach augments and develops the insights of political economy described above by proposing that there exist specific and unique SoPs attached to particular kinds of good or service. For example, water, housing, food, clothing, consumer durables, utilities and so on, all involve very different (though nevertheless related) SoPs, bringing together production and consumption in very different ways, involving very different norms, and therefore requiring separate analyses. Each SoP is important to well-being in its own right because it involves provision of a particular kind of need, in a particular form and manner (such forms and modalities of provision themselves being important to well-being). Each SoP is also important to well-being as a concrete aspect and development of wider systemic processes such as financialisation. Building up comprehension of particular SoPs serves to develop and deepen more abstract theories such as those of financialisation.

An excellent example is that of the UK system of housing provision (for details, see Robertson 2014, 2017). The UK housing SoP includes integral roles for the state, for rent determination, for finance (fictitious capital such as securitised mortgages), for wage determination and for culture (e.g. pro- or anti-homeownership), amongst a range of relevant aspects. More abstract theories of each relevant aspect must be applied, developed, augmented and uniquely integrated to grasp the contemporary UK housing SoP as a unified whole. The housing SoP is important to well-being in its own right because it involves the provision of a particular kind of basic need, in a particular form and manner (which is changing over time, e.g. the shift from housing as home to housing as asset). Within the UK a chronic undersupply, stemming from processes of financialisation and exacerbated by the crisis and austerity measures (inclusive of large-scale sale of public housing), has denied many people satisfactory access to this basic need. The housing SoP is also important to well-being as part of the financialisation process and of the GFC. The role of securitised mortgages in triggering and transmitting the GFC illustrates clearly this wider significance. Developing a comprehension of the housing SoP is not only a matter of theorising the housing SoP *per se*, but also of further comprehending the wider system within which the housing SoP is an integral part. Similar remarks apply to the SoPs for water, utilities, food and so on. Comprehending different SoPs, therefore, illuminates the complex concrete *Context* for the beings and doings, the lived experience and the well-being of people and groups.

It is clear that the GFC and austerity occurred in the *Context* of systemic developments under the rubric of financialisation that exacerbated rather than mitigated the tendency of capitalistic provisioning to prioritise private profits and finance over social need, in a manner harmful to the creative flourishing of people and hence their well-being. In order to continue to build up a comprehensive picture of well-being in *Context*, beyond the level of different SoPs, the next logical level of study is that of the lived experiences of social individuals and groups, their variegated vulnerabilities and complex responses to their circumstances. A broad programme of mixed-methods research engaging this concrete level has been ongoing in the Financialisation, Economy, Society and Sustainable Development (FESSUD) project, of which this paper and other papers in this symposium are a part. The remainder of this paper will focus on just one issue at the concrete level of lived experience, namely that of the interpretation of SWB data. Firstly, the happiness research approach to measuring well-being via SWB data in the period of financialisation, GFC and austerity will be illustrated via the example of the WHR. Secondly, a political economy approach will be developed to offer a detailed alternative interpretation of the meaning of SWB survey responses and a corresponding critique of happiness research and the WHR.

The GFC and reported happiness: the example of the WHR

The WHR, initiated in 2012 (Helliwell *et al.* 2012), with a second report in 2013 (Helliwell *et al.* 2013) and a third in 2015 (Helliwell *et al.* 2015) is an exemplar of happiness research in action. It seeks to promote a broad set of measures of well-being that go beyond GDP. These include the use of SWB measures drawn from surveys that ask people to rate their life satisfaction and happiness levels. These questions fall into two main categories: (i) *affect questions*, for example, questions asking people how happy they felt the previous day; and (ii) *evaluative questions*, for example, questions asking people to rate their satisfaction with their life as a whole. Questions such as the above are included in surveys conducted in different countries, and there is scope for cross-country comparisons of responses and their movement over time. Other high-profile examples of happiness research in action include ONS (2016) and Durand (2015). Like the WHR, other such examples refer to the problems of GDP measurement (such as the omission of household labour – see Waring 2015) that they attempt to overcome in whole or in part through SWB data. In some cases (for example, ONS 2016), SWB data are considered in isolation, in others (such as Durand 2015) SWB data are presented as part of a 'dashboard' of well-being measures, both subjective and objective. In all cases, the same basic misinterpretation of SWB data as found in the WHR, and revealed below, is made. Thus, the critique of the WHR that follows is illustrative of a general critique of the happiness research interpretation of SWB data.

The WHR, in Helliwell *et al.* (2013) and Helliwell *et al.* (2015), analyses the impact of the GFC on SWB. We saw above that a political economy approach will conclude that the GFC and austerity have caused a decline in well-being as measured across a range of objective dimensions. By contrast, despite the seismic socio-economic and political events of recent years, reported levels of SWB have not in general declined but have shown signs of improvement. To quote from the WHR: 'Despite the obvious detrimental happiness impacts of the 2007–08 financial crisis, the world has become a slightly happier and more generous place over the past five years' (Helliwell *et al.* 2013: 4). Although there is recognised variation in the impact of the GFC on SWB (see below), the overall conclusion is that, at the global level, happiness levels have not declined and have even slightly increased in the wake of the GFC.

A more detailed analysis, using data from the Gallup World Poll, reveals that some countries have fared worse than others. The Gallup World Poll uses the Cantril ladder whereby respondents are asked to evaluate the quality of their lives against a scale, 'with the best possible life for them as a 10 and the worst possible life as a zero' (Helliwell *et al.* 2013: 9). In the WHR, the average Cantril ladder scores are compared between 2005–07 and 2010–12 for a large number of countries. The experience across Western European countries appears as particularly diverse. Of the 17 Western European countries considered, 'six ... had significant increases, while seven countries had significant decreases, the largest of which were in four countries badly hit by the Eurozone financial crisis – Portugal, Italy, Spain and Greece' (Helliwell *et al.* 2013: 14). In the latter countries, the 'average fall in life evaluations, of two-thirds of a point on the 10-point scale, is roughly equal to moving 20 places in the international rankings ... or equivalent to that of a doubling or halving of per capita GDP' (Helliwell *et al.* 2013: 15). Further, the recorded fall in life evaluations in these countries is explained not only by declines in income and rises in unemployment, but also by an impairment of the social and institutional fabric of the countries concerned. Hence:

> the biggest hit, in terms of the implied drop in life evaluations, was in respondents' perceived freedom to make key life choices. In each country the crisis tended to limit opportunities for individuals, both through cutbacks in available services and loss of expected opportunities. In the three of the four countries there were also increases in perceived corruption in business and government. Social support and generosity also each fell in three of the four countries. (Helliwell *et al.* 2013: 15)

In short, according to the WHR, it is a combination of social and economic factors that explains the decline in SWB in the most crisis-hit countries of Western Europe, whereas for other Western European countries, such as the UK, well-being remained constant and in others it improved significantly. This conclusion is supported by affect measures of happiness, although the impact of social factors appears stronger for these measures than evaluative ones:

> The patterns of affect change are consistent in relative size with those for life evaluations. Positive affect fell, and negative affect grew in Greece and Spain, by proportions as great as life evaluations. For Italy the affect picture

was mixed, while for Portugal there were no significant changes. ... For Greece, but not the other countries, the affect changes are comparatively larger than for life evaluations, as reflected by the greater number of places lost in the international rankings. (Helliwell *et al.* 2013: 17)

The erosion in trust is seen as an especially important factor in explaining the 'exceptionally large well-being losses in Greece' (Helliwell *et al.* 2013: 17).

Reinterpreting SWB data

The SWB data, as interpreted in the WHR, are in isolated instances consonant with a political economy approach, for example SWB data fall for some of the countries hardest hit by the GFC and austerity, particularly Greece. However, taken overall, the SWB data, as interpreted in the WHR, contradict the political economy view developed above. Reported SWB has increased or remained stable in many countries, inclusive of countries hard hit by the GFC and austerity such as the UK, leading globally to a slight rise in reported SWB. How can so many countries experience the worst downturn in a lifetime, and ensuing austerity, with significant decline in objective dimensions of well-being, and yet continue to report high, stable or even rising SWB? It is argued below that this paradox can be resolved by reinterpreting the SWB data through a political economy perspective on how individuals respond to SWB social surveys. The process of responding to SWB surveys centrally involves the *norms and expectations* of survey respondents, which are dependent on *Context*, as recent philosophical and political economy approaches have illuminated in some detail.

The importance of context: philosophical insights regarding norms and expectations

An important philosophical insight consonant with political economy is that there is a *social and ethical dimension* to the norms and expectations held by survey respondents. As Haybron (2007a, 2007b) stresses, the act of self-evaluation of life satisfaction or of expressing some degree of happiness with one's life entails ethical judgement. Under some cultures (for example, a range of religious doctrines), it may be considered a moral obligation to report high well-being – and an ethical failing to report low well-being. More mundanely, it may be simply a matter of pride or self-esteem not to report low levels of satisfaction or happiness with life, regardless of the actual level of well-being achieved by people. For other cultures, there may be no such obligation or indeed an obligation to be modest in reporting well-being. This is not just an individual matter; rather, it also concerns sociocultural systems. The level of reported SWB will, therefore, differ systematically across countries reflecting different cultural norms prevalent in each individual country, independently of the respective actual well-being levels. An example is East Asia's well-documented 'modesty bias', whereby respondents consistently report lower well-being scores (see Gough 2015). It is, therefore, *invalid* to interpret the *level* or the *cross-country difference* of reported SWB in surveys as reflecting actual well-being *contra* the WHR.

A further insight is that norms and expectations regarding well-being have a *practical and reflexive dimension* – in keeping with the core philosophical idea of the self-reflexive and practically active individual. In so far as practical day-to-day activity is concerned, it would make no sense to evaluate one's own well-being against a benchmark that is not practically attainable. A rich empirical literature on SWB data in respect to work well-being serves to illustrate and substantiate this philosophical insight, examining in detail how survey responses of those with low well-being are inflated through the practical orientation of respondents (Brown *et al.* 2012). Walters (2005), for example, finds that survey responses regarding well-being at work were made relative to the benchmark of *feasible available alternatives* – in this case, alternative available jobs. For the low paid, this was a very low benchmark of comparison giving rise to high reported well-being at work. Responses to the same questions when made through in-depth interview may, however, reveal a very different picture. In-depth interviews invite interviewees to step back from the day-to-day practical orientation, allowing them to expand and reflect upon their survey responses. Specifically, this allows for the consideration that day-to-day feasible alternatives may be very limited in relation to those enjoyed by members of other social groups. Thus, when asked to reflect more deeply on well-being in in-depth interviews, Walters (2005) found low-paid women were all too aware that they had limited opportunities relative to others. As Walters puts it, in in-depth interviews, it becomes clear that the true satisfaction of low-paid people is not being expressed by SWB data; rather, what she terms 'satisficing' or making the best of a bad situation is being exhibited.

The importance of context: towards a general framework

The level of abstraction of the SoP approach is sufficiently close to the level of concrete individual experience and activity that it can offer insights into the relationship between the actual beings and doings of people that are constitutive of their well-being, on the one hand, and their norms and expectations, on the other. Though internally related, the relationship between well-being (beings and doings) and norms and expectations is not straightforward. Rather, for the SoP approach, the relationship is likely to be *complex* and *Contradictory*. This is why, as argued above, different *Contexts* can elicit different responses to SWB questions (the example given above was the difference between the *Context* of a survey and that of an in-depth interview). In fact, through ongoing application of the SoP approach, a whole series of insights regarding the relationship between culture and material practice has been developed, yielding a general framework for addressing material culture. According to this framework, material culture is subject to what have been termed the '10Cs': culture is *Constructed, Construed, Conforming, Commodified, Contextual, Contradictory, Closed, Contested, Collective* and *Chaotic* (see, respectively, Fine 2013a, 2013b, and Introduction to this Special Issue). Whilst not the place to detail each one of these aspects, there are two key points for the argument of this paper: firstly, the 10Cs, in conjunction with the arguments developed above, affirm the possibility of systematic movements of norms and expectations that mask the level and movement of actual well-being from SWB data; secondly, they sensitise the researcher to the many complexities of the norms and expectations held by any one individual or group, and help in the identification of the systemic significance of such local and specific norms.

'SWB' as a subjective assessment of objective well-being

Well-being, life satisfaction and happiness are, according to the above argument and evidence, well understood by survey and interview respondents. Thus, the standard criticism of objective approaches that they are 'paternalist' – asserting what is best for people regardless of the latter's stated views – is demonstrably incorrect. Where happiness researchers err is in failing to recognise the *Contextual* complexity and nuance behind the views expressed by survey respondents. Here the suggestions of O'Neill (2006a, 2006b) and Austin (2015) can be drawn upon. They argue (as part of an argument for what they call a 'scope' fallacy in happiness research) that survey respondents take due consideration of their *objective* well-being – their ability to pursue their goals and projects in terms of family, friends, relations, work, health and other valued dimensions. Respondents make a subjective assessment of their degree of capability across these objective dimensions. SWB data, then, provide a *subjective* assessment of *objective* well-being, made relative to benchmark norms and expectations that can change according to *Context*. This suggests a framework of interpretation according to which reported happiness or life satisfaction can be seen as dependent on *two* broad sets of factors as follows:

    Reported well-being in SWB surveys depends *positively* on (1) respondents' **actual well-being** and *negatively* on (2) respondents' norms and expectations.

This framework, unlike the happiness research interpretation, does not equate *reported* well-being changes with *actual* changes in well-being. The key point is that respondents' answers to affect and evaluative questions concerning SWB do not provide an absolute assessment of their well-being, but rather they are made relative to the benchmark norm or expectation against which they assess their well-being (Brown *et al*. 2012). Within this framework, one can only interpret movements in SWB data as directly reflecting changes in well-being if one can assume that norms and expectations are constant or if one can assume that norms and expectations are moving in the same direction as SWB data (in which case the observed SWB movements are being partially but not fully offset by counterbalancing movements in norms and expectations). This point bears on the evaluation of the results of the WHR. The GFC has reduced the quality of people's lives on a range of dimensions, as argued by a political economy approach, but it is also likely to have caused people to lower their norms and expectations about life, inflating their reports of SWB and so offsetting the effect of falling well-being on SWB data. This may then explain the paradoxical result of slightly rising reported SWB in the *Context* of the GFC and austerity. This result, crucially, can be suggested to mask a reduction in the quality of peoples' lives during the years of GFC, illustrating the invalidity of SWB data as a direct measure of well-being.

The political economy framework appears simple, but its depth and nuance are illustrated by the irony that happiness research recognises, and indeed emphasises, the presence of 'adaptation effects'. These effects appear in explanations of the Easterlin paradox – mentioned above – and the notion of the 'hedonic treadmill' (Brickman and Campbell 1971) according to which people display the tendency to return rapidly to relatively stable happiness levels, despite major positive or negative events, shocks or life changes. Yet, a glaring absence in the happiness literature is the obvious consequence of these findings: that SWB data do not necessarily reflect changes in well-being when the norms against which respondents assess well-being are also changing (Stewart 2014). The refusal to recognise that happiness indicators are a relative, not an absolute, measure of well-being has meant that happiness research has drawn conclusions about the direction of progress in well-being from SWB data that entirely overlook the possibility that the systematic lowering of norms and expectations, in adapting to the GFC and austerity, might conceal the negative effects of the GFC and austerity on well-being. This mistake is perfectly illustrated by the counterintuitive conclusion of the WHR that global well-being has, on average, been slightly increasing since the onset of the GFC.

Given this alternative political economy framework for interpretation, then SWB data *are* potentially of interest, but *not* because they measure actual well-being. Rather, they are sometimes suggestive of important social developments when put in their proper *Context*. For example, what really stands out in the SWB data presented and wrongly interpreted by the WHR are the marked declines in reported SWB in Greece relative to other countries and relative to the past. The contrast can be made to, say, the UK, with stable and high SWB data, despite deep recession and austerity. Our key argument is encapsulated in the interpretation of this contrast. The contrast does not mean that the level and nature of well-being has remained the same in the UK; to the contrary, the period of crisis and austerity has reduced well-being on multiple objective dimensions. The influence of changing norms and expectations on survey responses may instead have masked this fall in well-being from SWB data. By contrast, the marked decline of SWB measures in Greece suggests that the deterioration in actual well-being owing to the GFC and austerity is so great that many people in Greece have not been able to adjust their norms and expectations to enable stable day-to-day activity to carry on 'as normal'. The SWB data, therefore, may suggest threat to stability and order in Greece. Of course, this interpretation presupposes a host of more concrete considerations, not least those relating to the social and political environment of Greece. The crucial point is that to make sense of SWB data, there is a need for critical scrutiny of the broader concrete *Context*. The importance of *Context* thus lies at the heart of the suggested political economy framework for the interpretation of SWB data.

Conclusion

The paper has drawn on diverse literatures in philosophy, economics and social and political science in order to systematise a political economy approach that can offer insight into the definition and measurement of well-being. It has been argued that the measurement of the nature and level of well-being cannot be *Context*-free, but must incorporate the socially specific *Context* constituted by the basic character of the capitalist system, and its tendency to privilege profit over need, by systemic processes such as financialisation and, at a concrete level, by multiple SoPs. A feature of the paper has been the incorporation of the SoP approach which has proved helpful both in reinterpreting and making sense of SWB data and in forming and promoting critical insights on the concrete effects of financialisation, the GFC and austerity on well-being.

The paper has argued that one prominent modern example of research on well-being – the example of happiness research happiness research – is flawed in the sense that it asks us to take at face value the results of SWB data. In practice, it leads to confusion when SWB data remain unaffected by, or even show signs of improvement in the *Context* of, severe and long-lasting negative shocks to the economy such as the GFC and ensuing austerity. The paper has introduced and developed an alternative approach to the interpretation of SWB data that (1) recognises the separable influence of norms and expectations on SWB data, and thus avoids the mistake of inferring rises in well-being when economic conditions are getting much worse; (2) defines the well-being of people in terms of the objective beings and doings that they are capable of achieving and that meet their needs, understood broadly to include the need for creative development and personal flourishing.

The reader expecting insights into a 'science of well-being' that is entirely separable from political economy will be left disappointed by the paper. For well-being is not some discrete property, 'utility' or some such, lurking in the heads of atomistic individuals, immune to social *Context*. No such property exists. There are just people, their beings and doings constitutive of well-being, to be comprehended in an integrated way and in the proper social *Context*, which cannot be done without political economy. Accordingly, the broader goal of the paper has been to promote the importance of political economy for well-being research and *vice versa*.

Notes

1. The core idea of this alternative framework for the interpretation of SWB data was first suggested (to the knowledge of the authors) by O'Neill (2006a, 2006b) and later by Austin (2015). The idea was previously developed for the interpretation of work well-being by Green (e.g. 2006) followed by others such as Brown *et al.* (2007), and the framework developed in this paper generalises and adapts this previous framework in order to address the case of SWB in general.
2. From now onwards, we will refer to the systems of provision approach as the SoP approach, to any specific system of provision as an SoP and to more than one system of provision as SoPs.

Disclosure statement

No potential conflict of interest was reported by the authors.

Funding

Research for this paper was supported by the project Financialization, Economy, Society and Sustainable Development (FESSUD), which is funded by the European Union under Seventh Framework Programme [contract number 266800].

References

Austin, A. (2015), 'On Well-Being and Public Policy: Are We Capable of Questioning the Hegemony of Happiness?', *Social Indicators Research*, 127 (1), pp. 123–38.

Boulding, K. (1986), 'What Went Wrong with Economics', *American Economist*, 30 (1), pp. 5–12.

Brickman, P. and Campbell, D. (1971), 'Hedonic Relativism and Planning the Good Society', in M.H. Apley (ed.), *Adaptation-Level Theory: A Symposium* (New York: Academic Press), pp. 287–302.

Brown, A., Charlwood, A., Forde, C. and Spencer, D. A. (2007), 'Job Quality and the Economics of New Labour: A Critical Appraisal Using Subjective Survey Data', *Cambridge Journal of Economics*, 31 (6), pp. 941–71.

Brown, A., Charlwood, A. and Spencer, D. A. (2012), 'Not All That It Might Seem: Why Job Satisfaction Is Worth Studying Despite It Being a Poor Summary Measure of Job Quality', *Work, Employment and Society*, 26 (6), pp. 1007–18.

Dean, H. (2010), *Understanding Human Need* (Bristol: The Policy Press), pp. 31–42.

Dugger, W.M. (1996), 'Redefining Economics: From Market Allocation to Social Provisioning', in C.J. Whalen (ed.), *Political Economy for the 21st Century. Contemporary Views on the Trend of Economics* (Armonk, NY: M.E. Sharpe), pp. 31–42.

Duncan, G. (2010), 'Should Happiness-Maximization Be the Goal of Government?', *Journal of Happiness Studies*, 11 (2), pp. 163–78.

Durand, M. (2015), 'The OECD Better Life Initiative: How's Life? And the Measurement of Well-Being', *Review of Income and Wealth*, 61 (1), pp. 4–17.

Düzenli, F.E. (2015), 'Surplus-Producing Labour as a Capability: A Marxian Contribution to Amartya Sen's Revival of Classical Political Economy', *Cambridge Journal of Economics*, first published online 25 June. doi:10.1093/cje/bev041

Easterlin, R.A. (1974), 'Does Economic Growth Improve the Human Lot?', in P.A. David and M.W. Reder (eds), *Nations and Households in Economic Growth: Essays in Honour of Moses Abramovitz* (New York: Academic Press), pp. 89–125.

Fine, B. (2002), *The World of Consumption: The Material and Cultural Revisited* (London: Routledge).

Fine, B. (2013a), 'Economics: Unfit for Purpose', *Review of Social Economy*, 71 (3), pp. 373–89.

Fine, B. (2013b), *Towards a Material Culture of Financialisation*, FESSUD Working Paper Series No. 15.

Fine, B. and Leopold, E. (1993), *The World of Consumption* (London: Routledge).

Gough, I. (2015), 'Climate Change and Sustainable Welfare: The Centrality of Human Needs', *Cambridge Journal of Economics*, 39 (5), pp. 1191–214.

Green, F. (2006), *Demanding Work. The Paradox of Job Quality in the Affluent Society* (Princeton: Princeton University Press).

Haybron, D.M. (2007a), 'Life Satisfaction, Ethical Reflection, and the Science of Happiness', *Journal of Happiness Studies*, 8 (1), pp. 99–138.

Haybron, D.M. (2007b), 'Do We Know How Happy We Are? On Some Limits of Affective Introspection and Recall', *NOÛS*, 41 (3), pp. 394–428.

Haybron, D.M. (2008), 'Happiness, the Self and Human Flourishing', *Utilitas*, 20 (1), pp. 21–49.

Helliwell, J.F., Layard, R. and Sachs, J. (eds.) (2012), *World Happiness Report* (New York: Earth Institute).

Helliwell, J.F., Layard, R. and Sachs, J. (eds.) (2013), *World Happiness Report 2013* (New York: UN Sustainable Development Solutions Network).

Helliwell, J.F., Layard, R. and Sachs, J. (eds.) (2015), *World Happiness Report 2015* (New York: Sustainable Development Solutions Network).

Jany-Catrice, F. and Méda, D. (2013), 'Well-Being and the Wealth of Nations: How Are They to Be Defined?', *Review of Political Economy*, 25 (3), pp. 444–60.

Lawson, T. (2003), *Reorienting Economics* (London: Routledge).

Layard, R. (2005), *Happiness. Lessons from a New Science* (London: Penguin).

Lee, F. (2009), *A History of Heterodox Economics. Challenging the Mainstream in the Twentieth Century* (London: Routledge).

Leschke, J. and Watt, A. (2014), 'Challenges in Constructing a Multi-dimensional European Job Quality Index', *Social Indicators Research*, 118 (1), pp. 1–31.

Levine, D. and Rizvi, A. (2005), *Poverty, Work and Freedom: Political Economy and the Moral Order* (Cambridge: Cambridge University Press).

Nelson, J. (1996), *Feminism, Objectivity and Economics* (London: Routledge).

Office for National Statistics [ONS] (2016), 'Personal Well-Being in the UK: 2015 to 2016', *Statistical Bulletin*.

O'Neill, J. (2006a), 'Citizenship, Wellbeing and Sustainability: Epicurus or Aristotle?', *Analyse and Kritik*, 28 (2), pp. 158–72.

O'Neill, J. (2006b), 'Happiness: Lessons for a New Science', *New Political Economy*, 11 (3), pp. 447–50.

Power, M. (2004), 'Social Provisioning as a Starting Point for Feminist Economics', *Feminist Economics*, 10 (3), pp. 3–19.

Robertson, M. (2014), *Case Study: Finance and Housing Provision in Britain*, FESSUD Working Paper Series, No. 51.

Robertson, M. (2017), '(De)constructing the Financialised Culture of Owner-Occupation in the UK, with the Aid of the 10Cs', *New Political Economy*. doi:10.1080/13563467.2017.1259303

Sen, A. (1999), *Development as Freedom* (Oxford: Oxford University Press).

Spencer, D. A. (2009), *The Political Economy of Work* (London: Routledge).

Spencer, D. A. (2015), 'Developing an Understanding of Meaningful Work in Economics: The Case for a Heterodox Economics of Work', *Cambridge Journal of Economics*, 39 (3), pp. 675–88.

van Staveren, I. (2001), *The Values of Economics. An Aristotelian Perspective* (London: Routledge).

Stewart, F. (2014), 'Against Happiness: A Critical Appraisal of the Use of Measures of Happiness for Evaluating Progress in Development', *Journal of Human Development and Capabilities*, 15 (4), pp. 293–307.

Stiglitz, J.E., Sen, A. and Fitoussi, J.-P. (2010), *Mismeasuring Our Lives: Why GDP Doesn't Add Up* (New York: The New Press).

Stuckler, D. and Basu, S. (2013), *The Body Economic: Why Austerity Kills* (New York: Basic Books).

Walters, S. (2005), 'Making the Best of a Bad Job? Female Part-Timers' Orientations and Attitudes to Work', *Gender, Work and Organization*, 12 (3), pp. 193–216.

Waring, M. (2015), *Counting for Nothing: What Men Value and What Women Are Worth* (Toronto: University of Toronto Press).

Index

Note:
Page numbers in *italics* refer to figures
Page numbers in **bold** refer to tables
Page numbers followed by 'n' refer to notes

For Product Safety Concerns and Information please contact our EU
representative GPSR@taylorandfrancis.com
Taylor & Francis Verlag GmbH, Kaufingerstraße 24, 80331 München, Germany